To Beirut and Back:
An American in the Middle East

By
Abe F. March

PublishAmerica
Baltimore

© 2006 by Abe F. March.
All rights reserved. No part of this book may be reproduced, stored in a retrieval system or transmitted in any form or by any means without the prior written permission of the publishers, except by a reviewer who may quote brief passages in a review to be printed in a newspaper, magazine or journal.

First printing

At the specific preference of the author, PublishAmerica allowed this work to remain exactly as the author intended, verbatim, without editorial input.

ISBN: 1-4241-3853-1
PUBLISHED BY PUBLISHAMERICA, LLLP
www.publishamerica.com
Baltimore

Printed in the United States of America

Dedicated

To my family for their love, understanding and endurance.

Contents

Introduction 9

Part One

Chapter 1 Entreprenurial Beginning 13
Chapter 2 Canada 29
Chapter 3 Greece 38
Chapter 4 West Germany 59
Chapter 5 Setting New Goals 66
Chapter 6 To Beirut, Lebanon 68
Chapter 7 Christmas in the Cedars of Lebanon 82
Chapter 8 A Change in Attitude 91
Chapter 9 Middle East Business Mentality 99
Chapter 10 Business Struggles 107
Chapter 11 Iranian Connection 129
Chapter 12 Violence Escalates 134
Chapter 13 Warring Factions 142
Chapter 14 Abduction/Detention 152
Chapter 15 The Foreign Exodus 163
Chapter 16 End of the Line 171
Chapter 17 The Last Days 175

Part Two

Chapter 1 Starting Over 189
Chapter 2 Dammam, Saudi Arabia 198
Chapter 3 Riyadh, Saudi Arabia 209
Chapter 4 Abu Dhabi—United Arab Emirates 216
Chapter 5 Big Projects—Kuwait 225
Chapter 6 Palestinian Raid—Amman, Jordan 230
Chapter 7 First American Back 240
Chapter 8 Aftermath of War 254
Postscript: 2006—Germany 264
End Notes 265

"Then a woman said,
Speak to us of Joy and Sorrow.
And he answered:
Your joy is your sorrow unmasked.
And the selfsame well from which
your laughter rises was oftentimes
filled with your tears."

"When you are sorrowful,
look again in your heart,
and you shall see that in truth
you are weeping for that
which has been your delight."

Kahlil Gibran, *The Prophet*

Introduction

The will to risk is as fundamental to success as in the fight for a just cause.

The events in the Middle East continue to have a profound effect upon us all. In 1973 I visited Beirut, Lebanon, for the first time. For the previous five years, ever since leaving the job security of IBM, I had worked for an international cosmetic company as an independent distributor and later as an executive for that company in Canada, Greece and West Germany. It was during my post in Greece that I first visited Beirut, the Lebanese capital. Its strategic location serving the Middle East marketplace made a lasting impression on me. With numerous international banks represented in Lebanon and the availability of secret accounts, Beirut was known as the Switzerland of the Middle East.

The congeniality of the Lebanese people and their eagerness to entertain new ideas or business concepts was exhilarating, and after my second visit to Beirut, I resolved that one day I would go there to conduct business.

A year later I was ready to embark on a new venture. The death of the founder of the company, for whom I worked, placed the company in chaos; it began to slide into financial difficulties and eventually wound up in bankruptcy. I was now free to make my own way and made the decision to open a business in Lebanon. I secured the funding by liquidating all personal assets. Either this venture would succeed or I would be financially ruined.

In preparation, I traveled to the State Department in Washington, D.C. to obtain the certification I would need to prove the validity of my

USA Corporation. I then negotiated an exclusive agreement with a Canadian cosmetic company, placed an order for product and arranged for its immediate shipment to Beirut. Full of optimism and the vitality of youth, I departed for Beirut in January 1974. The events that occurred during the next several years: the oil embargo, the tension between Israel and her Arab neighbors and the outbreak of civil war in Lebanon, affected my attitude toward the participants in the Middle East struggle.

When the twenty-seventh cease-fire in the Lebanese civil war failed to hold; the prospects for salvaging my business became hopeless and the safety of my family was in jeopardy, I was compelled to leave Lebanon.

I returned to Beirut one year later and witnessed the civil war's devastation. A British journalist portrayed my presence in Lebanon with a headline article, "The First American Back," describing the optimism of this entrepreneur looking to recover past losses by early bird tactics.

This book's story bears witness to the risks of the entrepreneur in a foreign land with the hazards of unpredictable events. It also provides a look at the customs and life of the Arabs, their mentality and their business practices.

To Beirut and Back is a true account of that experience. Although this episode is in the past, we still remember the excitement of the risks we took together with the joy and sorrow of our triumphs and disaster.

NOTE: The dialogue contained in this book is based on the author's recollection and from notes over an extended period of time. Although exact quotes cannot be considered accurate, it portrays conversational content as remembered and expressed. In addition, names of some of the characters in this book have been changed to protect their privacy.

Part One

Chapter 1
Entreprenurial Beginning
Summer 1969—1971

"Hello, this is Abe March. Dr. Becker suggested I call you about making extra money."

"Fine, when can I see you," said Dan Peters.

"What's this all about," I asked.

"I made $143,000 my first year in this business. I've just spent over $40,000 on a business presentation and I'm not going to blow it on a ten-cent phone call. If you're serious about making money, you can see me in my office. I have an opening tomorrow at 2:00 PM. Will you be there?"

I told him I would and got directions. I didn't know anyone who made that kind of money and soon began to worry if it was something illegal or mafia connected!

Later that day, my wife, Gisela, asked me if I had made the phone call. I said I had, but didn't think I would keep the appointment.

"But what's it all about?" she asked. I said I didn't know. Perhaps, I thought, I'd check it out just to see what it is. It may be legitimate and I couldn't afford to miss out on a way to earn money.

I had become restless with my career. It was the summer of 1969. I was thirty years old. After six years with an IBM subsidiary, I knew I had leveled-off in my position as operations analyst and that further promotions would be few and far between, especially without an advanced degree. I was in a rut. My daily commute to New York City, catching the 6:00 AM train and returning home around 7:00 PM, left little time for anything other than eating, watching some TV and then starting the daily process all over again.

I had started with IBM in Chicago, and having excelled in my job, I was promoted and transferred to Washington D.C. Then another promotion and a transfer to Boston, Massachusetts, as manager of administration. My promotion and transfer to New York as an operations analyst made me consider my future since my career path seemed to have reached a dead end. I didn't know anyone who was rich and worked for someone else, and a life of mediocrity would not satisfy me.

Having moved several times and dealt with the problems of finding a home, I thought of an idea to automate the search process of house hunting. Although "Multiple List Services" existed, I felt that a central computer service could be instituted whereby a person seeking a home would be able to find what he wanted by completing a simple form, indicating the regional area of choice, the size of the house and the purchase price range. The computer could do a search and list all homes on the market that fit the requirements. I was so caught-up with this notion that I quit my job so I'd have the time to put my idea into motion. I visited many realtors in Westchester County, N.Y., putting forth my business concept. It was well received, except for the existing multiple listing service bureau that felt my idea threatened their existence. Only after incorporating a company and working to develop the program, did I realize the high cost of the computer required to do the processing. At that time, computer rental of $40,000 per month would be required. Without sufficient operating capital and not knowing how to attract investors without forfeiting my idea, I was not able to continue. I was out of a job and the bills were still coming in. Gisela was pregnant, and her position as a programmer with IBM would end when the baby came leaving us with no income.

I had just finished reading a book by the late Robert Kennedy, entitled, "To Seek a Newer World," and something I read stuck with me. It said that no one ever succeeds without having failed. I therefore looked upon my business setback, not as a defeat, but as a step forward. Having told my co-workers how I was going to become successful when I left IBM, I couldn't bear the thought of returning to the company, so in desperation, I took a job as a common laborer for a local construction company. The pay was far less than I had earned before and it didn't cover my bills. I had a wife, a son and a daughter to support, a house to finance and another baby due any day. I feared losing the possessions I had worked so hard to accumulate and didn't know what to do.

I had just completed a business correspondence course with Alexander Hamilton Institute and they wanted to present me with my diploma in the presence of my employer. I couldn't imagine receiving the presentation of this certificate in a drainage ditch, so I told them to mail it. Instead, a Dr. Becker from the institute made an appointment to see me at my house. On the morning of his visit I took off from work and dressed in a suit to make a good impression. After the simple presentation, Dr. Becker asked me if I would be interested in making some extra money. I said yes immediately. When I asked what it was about, he wouldn't tell me, but gave me a telephone number to call Dan Peters who would explain everything. When Dr. Becker left my house, I had placed the call.

* * * * *

It was a hot August morning. I had to take another day off from work to keep my appointment with Dan Peters in Larchmont, N.Y. I arrived ahead of time and walked around the horseshoe-shaped building complex. The office was located on the lower level with no sign on the door. When I knocked, the door was opened immediately by a tall, impeccably dressed man.

"Hi, I'm Dan Peters. You must be Abe March. Come in. As you can see, I'm in the cosmetic business."

The shelves were lined with cosmetic products and the aroma was pleasant, but I knew nothing about cosmetics and felt it was a sissy business.

"I'm sorry, Mr. Peters but I don't know anything about cosmetics and I don't want to waste your time. It's not for me," I said.

"You say you don't know anything about cosmetics. Most people don't. Why not have a seat and let me tell you about it. What have you got to lose?"

I was hot and the office was air-conditioned. I decided to sit and cool off, perhaps get the gist of what it was about, before I left.

Mr. Peters then began to relate a most fascinating story. He told me about the huge profits in cosmetics and that many people were making large sums of money. He used hypothetical examples to illustrate how the money could be earned. One could start at the bottom and work their way to the top, but it was also possible to start at a much higher position where one could build an organization of other independent distributors and also earn a percentage of their production. As he talked, I began to realize that every woman uses cosmetics and why it was a multi-billion dollar industry, practically recession proof. The potential for making big money got to me and my attitude towards cosmetics changed. Mr. Peters showed me copies of his checks supporting his claim of high earnings and proving that the program worked. I couldn't imagine starting at the bottom but rather at the higher position. For this position, however, there was an investment of $2250 for which I would receive $5000 in product at retail value. This was the required initial inventory supposedly needed to supply my organization.

I was infatuated with the marketing scheme and when I left Mr. Peter's office my head was spinning. I wouldn't commit to joining the company and told him that I wanted to think it over and discuss it with my wife. The truth was, I didn't know where I would get the $2250, but I definitely wanted to join.

I raced home anxious to tell Gisela about it. She was now on maternity leave with the baby due within the next two weeks. She was waiting for me as I walked in the door and asked, "What is it?"

I tried to explain the system of marketing but only succeeded in confusing her. I couldn't explain it the way it was presented to me but I was convinced about the merits of the program and wanted to do it. When I finished my explanation, I asked, "What do you think?"

Gisela stared at me, and holding both hands on her large tummy said, "Don't expect me to sell cosmetics! I can't sell! Besides, where do you expect to get the money?"

"I haven't figured that out yet," I said, "But I'll find a way."

I had never been in sales before and had even failed an aptitude test for sales while at IBM. Due to my excitement, I gave no thought to the fact that this was sales. I thought everyone I would tell about the program would also want to join.

The following morning I went to the bank to apply for a business loan and presented the business to the banker. I was turned down. I went to another bank and tried for a personal loan. Without steady employment, they also turned me down. I was irritated. I have excellent credit, I reasoned, equity in my home, how can they turn me down for a loan? They just don't understand. I must have this loan. This is my opportunity to make it big.

I returned to the first bank determined not to leave until I had the money. I presented a different case to the banker.

"Look," I said. "Let's forget about the business for a moment. What kind of loans do you give here?"

"We give personal loans for any worthwhile purpose such as home improvement loans, loans to buy a new car or furniture and even for people wanting to take a vacation."

I thought for a moment. I wanted an unsecured loan and didn't want to tie-up my home. I also didn't want the banker to know that my present income didn't cover my bills. A different approach was necessary.

"When you make a loan, what is your primary concern?" I asked.

"Repayment, of course," replied the banker.

"If I can prove to you that I have the equity and that I have an excellent credit rating, does it matter what I use the money for?"

"Well, yes and no. We do need a purpose for the money which goes on the application but of course what you do with the money is not my personal concern."

"Well", I said. "I want to improve my house and what I intend to do with the money will definitely do that."

The banker smiled and pulled out an application from his desk drawer. I filled it out. The banker promised to call me that same afternoon after a credit check.

The loan was approved and I joined the distributorship program the next day. Mr. Peters was my sponsor in the program and directed me to bring people to him and he would present the business opportunity on my behalf. I was instructed not to explain the program or the business to anyone since people may have preconceived ideas about it as I had. "Simply get them to me," said Mr. Peters. I complied explicitly with these instructions. I was so excited that most everyone I talked with wanted to discover what it was that had me so turned-on.

Things began happening for me immediately. Most of the people I brought to Mr. Peters joined the program and I earned commissions based on the volume of inventory they were required to purchase to join. Each morning Mr. Peters would call me like clockwork. I expected the call and knew he would ask me how many people I would be bringing to his presentation. I worked diligently and was always prepared to bring someone. With my immediate results, I was even more convincing with new prospects. My success meant that I was now eligible to advance to the top organizational position but it required an investment of an additional $2500. I would also be required to attend a one-week training course at a cost of $250. Mr. Peters told me it was imperative that I attend the upcoming class. I was apprehensive about attending this class since it appeared that Gisela was due to deliver the baby any day. I promised I would attend the class if either Gisela had the baby or if it appeared there would be some delay.

The class was to begin on Sunday, August 16, 1969. Caroline was born on Saturday, August 15th at 6:00 AM. Gisela had a difficult time and required several blood transfusions but the doctors had been prepared. I had witnessed the birth of a beautiful baby girl who, but for an error in birth control, would not have been.

I was now perplexed. I felt it my duty to be with my wife. Gisela knew how much this new business meant to me and encouraged me to attend the class. She had always been like that. She would sacrifice her own wishes to help in furthering my career.

The training class opened my mind to a new world. I was taught the importance of attitude and how it affected what I did and those around me; how my life was directed positively or negatively based on my thoughts and attitudes. I was taught about setting goals. Without a goal, my life had no meaning; that I would be drifting like a ship without a rudder. I was told that with a goal, I could direct my life and with persistence, I could achieve any worthwhile goal I set for myself. The key was knowing what one wanted. I was taught that as a ship can only reach one port at a time, I could only expect to reach one goal at a time; to concentrate my energies on one specific goal, wanting it strongly enough, to achieve it. I was taught the psychology of selling, what made people act the way they do, what made them buy. I learned how to close the sale and so many other new things that my head was swimming. I was required to learn a scripted sales presentation, which was the single requirement in passing the course. I studied diligently, walking the hotel corridors each night, memorizing the script. The process of repetition sold and resold the program to me. I could hardly wait for the training to end so I could put the things I learned into action.

I called Gisela several times a day during class breaks but only went to the hospital once to visit her. The long training sessions coupled with the distance from the city of New York to the hospital in Mt. Kisco, N.Y., did not allow sufficient time to visit her. I did leave the class to bring Gisela, and our new baby Caroline, home from the hospital. Gisela was very understanding and although I half-heartedly offered to drop out of the class to be with her, she would not hear of it.

My excitement about the program continued after the training was finished and I wanted to share this wonderful program with everyone. I made the decision to leave NY and move to my home area in Pennsylvania where I could open a new territory and introduce the program to many of my friends. When I announced this plan to Mr. Peters, I was astonished at his reaction. "You can't leave! You don't understand the program!" He said.

"What do you mean?" I asked. "I completed the training and I have already a good number of people in my organization."

"That doesn't mean anything," he said. "I have been giving the presentations on your behalf and you have yet to give a single presentation on your own. Understanding something and re-explaining or presenting it, are two different things. I want you to get a tape recorder, buy one if you don't have one, and be in my office on Saturday morning. I'll give you my presentation and I want you to learn it. Only when I'm satisfied that you know it, can you leave."

The following evening I had people attending Mr. Peter's presentation along with several other distributors. There were twelve guests waiting for Mr. Peters to begin. He stood up from his desk and said, "Tonight Mr. March will be giving the presentation. He will soon be leaving us to go to Pennsylvania and build an organization there." Mr. Peters got up from his desk and left the room.

My face was flushed and I didn't know what to do. There was no way out. I had never given a presentation in front of anyone before, let alone a group of people. I was a shy person. In school, I never raised my hand for fear it would draw attention to me. I would have had difficulty leading a group in silent prayer. In my job as an operations analyst, I had worked alone.

I got up from my chair with weak knees and seated myself behind Mr. Peter's desk. Slowly and with much thought, I began the presentation making every effort to repeat the things Mr. Peters said when he presented the business. When I finished, I turned to the lady nearest to me and asked the question Mr. Peters always asked when closing the first segment of the presentation.

"Based on what I've shown you thus far, would you pay $11.99 for this kit?"

The lady, whose arms were folded tightly in front of her, shook her head no. My face reddened even more now. I was perspiring. No one had ever said no to Mr. Peters.

"Perhaps you misunderstood," I said. "I'm talking about all the things that are in this kit. Don't you think they're worth $11.99?"

Just as the lady began shaking her head again, Mr. Peters, who had been listening outside the door, walked into the room.

"How's it going?" He inquired. I said, "I asked the lady if she would pay $11.99 for the kit and she said no."

Mr. Peters excused me and took his seat behind the desk. He then began to cover the same points I had, but he did it with excitement and enthusiasm. When he finished, he turned to the same lady and asked, "Now wouldn't you pay $11.99 for all this?"

The lady said, "Why of course!"

When the meeting was over, Mr. Peters said, "Just make sure you're here on Saturday. You'll understand then what you didn't do right tonight."

Saturday morning I was in Larchmont at his office with my tape recorder. After recording the presentation, Mr. Peters explained what he did and why. By selling hard the retail end of the business, the prospective distributor would see that most everyone would buy the product, thus it made sense to be in a higher wholesale position with a larger buying discount where one could make the big bucks. He explained that although my presentation flowed logically, it lacked excitement and enthusiasm. Mr. Peters turned to me and said, "You see now what was missing in your presentation? It wasn't so much the words you used, as it was your lack of conviction. You've got to get this presentation down pat so it flows without thinking of the words. Then you can generate the excitement in your voice when you deliver it."

I played the tape constantly while driving my car. By the time I completed my move to Pennsylvania, I was beginning to sound like Dan Peters and I knew I would be successful. Therefore, instead of holding out for a higher price on my house, I sold it at the first offer. Since time was money, I felt that I could earn much more money with the time spent in the business.

In Pennsylvania, I rented a house rather than buy something I could afford at that time. I knew it wouldn't be long before I could afford something better. Using one of the bedrooms in my rented house as my office, I began recruiting distributors. Before long, the living room was full of people for my weekly training sessions, so I decided to rent an office.

Gisela had become excited about the business, had taken cosmetic training, and now functioned as my trainer. While the men heard the business presentation, Gisela gave their wives a facial. After each presentation, I would invite the men to ask their wives how they liked the product. It closed the sale!

The office I rented was filled to capacity at each presentation. I followed the recruiting techniques of my sponsor and instructed each person I recruited to bring their prospects to me and I would sign them into the business on their behalf.

It was time to set personal goals. Through the process of elimination, I decided on my one goal. I always wanted to own a farm, but it had only been a hope that someday it might happen. Now I had a vehicle to achieve it.

One day, while driving on a country road, off to my right I noticed a beautiful farm situated on the side of a hill overlooking a river. I stopped my car and took in the view. A white board fence surrounded the pasture where horses grazed. The stone farmhouse was nestled among giant maple trees and a red barn stood on the opposite side of a long circular driveway. If only something like this were for sale—but it would probably cost too much, I mused. I stopped my daydreaming and drove away not giving another thought to it. I didn't realize the mental impression that farm had left with me. Daily I would read the newspapers looking for "farms for sale." Nothing seemed to sound right. Then one evening as I was reading the paper, the description of a farm caught my attention. It sounded perfect. I immediately called the real estate office. The lady agent said it had just been listed. She was showing it later that night but if I wanted to see it now, she could come at once.

Within the hour, I was in the agent's car. I had no idea where we were going and was engaged in answering a lot of questions. The road seemed familiar and then I spied the farm in the distance as the one I had fantasized about.

"Where are we going?" I asked.

"It's not much farther," she replied, then slowed the car and turned into the lane leading to the farmhouse.

"What are we doing here?" I asked, since there was no 'for sale' sign on the property.

"This is the place," she said.

I was speechless. I couldn't believe it. Before we reached the house I knew I must have it. I didn't know the price and was afraid to ask.

As we walked through each room, I held my breath. I didn't want to see anything I wouldn't like. I would then breath a sigh of relief and continue to the next room. Then into the basement, the garage and out to the barn. I was no longer looking but thinking how I might be able to handle the purchase.

"Well, what do you think? Do you like it?" The agent asked.

"How much is it?" I inquired, not wanting to hear the answer.

She told me the price and in the same breath said that I was the first person she had shown the farm to; that another party would meet her that same evening and if I wanted it, I would have to place a deposit, otherwise it might be gone.

I didn't know what to do. I needed time to think. I wanted Gisela to see it before I made a final decision although I knew that if I wanted it, she would consent.

"Look," I said. "I do like it but before I can make a decision of this magnitude, I want my wife to see it."

"That's understandable. Why don't I write up a binder agreement, subject to your wife's approval?"

"All right, I'll do it! How much do you require as a deposit?"

"You can give me $2500 for the binder agreement. If your wife approves, I'll then prepare a formal sales agreement and you can then give the balance. Ten percent down is normal."

I knew I could handle that without a problem, but I would need a mortgage and that there would be additional funds required. I will worry about that when the time comes, I thought. I hardly heard a word the lady was saying on my way home. I was engrossed in my thoughts about securing the farm and could hardly wait to tell Gisela about it.

Gisela listened carefully while I described the farm to her. I was so excited, I couldn't sit. I paced back and forth giving her all the details. The next day, I arranged for her to see the farm.

Talking excitedly as we went, I led the way through the house and barn. Gisela followed along, saying nothing.

"What do you think?" I asked. "Isn't it great?"

"If that's what you want, it's okay with me." She was not about to say anything to dampen my spirits. But I had been with her long enough to read between the lines. The fact is she didn't like it at all. She didn't like the smell of the barn, she didn't like the house and all she could see was the work that would be required. As a small child, Gisela had worked on a farm and vowed that her children would not have to work as she had, but she said nothing.

The following morning I went to the small rural bank where I had my checking and savings account. I was given a mortgage application form to complete. In the space marked employer, I wrote, "self-employed." Under income, I wrote, "$6,000 per month average."

I called the bank the next morning to see if my mortgage was approved. I was asked to stop by the bank as they had some questions about my application. The young Vice President told me my credit checked out fine, but there were some questions that needed clarification.

"You indicate you are self-employed. What kind of business is it and how long have you been self-employed?"

I explained that I was in the cosmetic business. As a distributor, I could hire sales ladies and other sub-distributors to sell the products. I had already built a sizeable organization and was receiving overrides on their sales including my own production. I tried to make him understand that every woman uses cosmetics and that most everyone who was given a chance to try it, would buy it. I talked about the large sums of money that was possible while the banker listened in silence. The banker then said, "I'm sorry, Mr. March. Without a two-year financial statement on the business, we cannot approve your application."

I was angry. Here, some clerk with a fancy title, who at that time probably earned in a year what I could potentially earn in a month, was turning me down.

"I suppose if I had a steady job earning $150 a week, you would be more inclined to give me the mortgage," I said.

The banker's eyes lit up and he said, "Yes, we look for a history of steady employment."

I looked at the banker and with a calm voice said, "If the bank I give my business to cannot serve me, I am dealing with the wrong bank!"

I stood, and raising my voice said, "I wish to withdraw in cash the money I have on deposit with you, and I would like it now!"

"But Mr. March, you must understand our guidelines and policies. I'm sorry…"

"Please get my money for me," I demanded, and handed my savings passbook to him.

"Mr. March, we require advance notice for a sum this size and then we prepare a check."

There were other customers within hearing distance, so I spoke for all to hear, saying, "It's only $12,000! I gave you my money in cash and that's how I want it. If this bank cannot serve me when I need it, then I must do business with a bank that will!"

"Please Mr. March, we can work this out. Please be seated, I'll see what I can do."

The banker went into his manager's office. After conversing with his boss, he went behind the cashier's cage to get the money.

"I'm sorry we didn't have enough large bills on hand. We had to include smaller ones - but it's all here."

I counted the money, then with both pockets bulging, left the bank. I immediately drove to the main branch of a larger bank in the city. I asked to see the manager and was invited into his office.

"How may I help you?"

"Do you give mortgage loans at this bank?" I asked.

"Yes, we do for our customers. Are you a customer?"

"What do you consider a customer?" I asked.

"Do you have an account with us? Savings, checking or other?"

I took the cash out of my pockets and placed it on his desk."Would you open an account for me?" I asked.

"Yes, of course," said the manager. He immediately summoned his secretary who counted the money then left to prepare the necessary forms.

"I need a mortgage for a farm." I went on to explain the details showing him the farm's appraised value.

"How much do you plan to place as a down payment?"

"One third," I replied.

"In that case, I'll approve it. If you're willing to place down one third, I see no problem in approving it."

"You're a businessman," I said. "I will like doing business here."

I secured approval for my mortgage but had created a big problem for myself. I didn't have the money required to place one third down. I would need at least another $18,000 and I needed it within the next six weeks before the closing date; otherwise, I would forfeit the money I had already placed on the property. In my excitement to get the farm, I did not condition my sales agreement on obtaining a mortgage or on terms that I could afford. Either I got the money I needed, or I would lose my down payment and the farm. During the next six weeks, I worked all day and late into the night trying to recruit every person I met. I worked with a purpose and was persistent. Every person that joined the business was required to purchase a sizeable amount of cosmetic products, for which I received commission. My sales volume was increasing dramatically. Finally, two days prior to the settlement date, I acquired the balance of the money I needed. I not only achieved my goal, but in the process, I achieved sales awards for my outstanding performance. I won a new Thunderbird automobile and was inducted into the company's Round Table Club and my success continued. I showed my farm and my new car to prospective recruits as evidence of the program's success.

I loved the farm. I purchased farm equipment, some livestock and had a mare heavy with foal. Instead of buying the curtains Gisela needed for the house, I purchased a breeding bull instead. Gisela went along with what I wanted. She seldom went to the barn and when she did, she covered her nose to block out the smell. I busied myself planting oats and corn. It's almost like the TV program, "Green Acres," I mused, including my foreign, farm-shy wife who spoke with an accent! Except that my farm in no way resembled the rundown version depicted on the popular TV series. I was so determined to make it a success, I even taught my eight-year-old son Duane how to drive a tractor. Needless to say, he was thrilled; my wife was not.

I worked the farm from early morning until noon, would have lunch, then go to my office. I was busy. Each moment at the office was filled with activity.

One morning as I was on my farm tractor, Gisela brought me a glass of iced tea. She also carried the company newsletter, which had just arrived in the mail.

"I want you to read this," she said, pointing to the column entitled, 'Sales Leaders.'

I read the article and learned that I was one of the top ten distributors in the entire country and in the same league as my sponsor, Dan Peters.

Gisela said, "What do you think you could do if you got off that silly tractor and worked at this business full time?"

I thought for a moment, and then said, "Perhaps you're right." I let the tractor standing where it was, went into the house, showered, then went to my office. Each day thereafter, instead of working on the farm in the morning, enjoying the fresh air and the physical exercise, I joined others drinking coffee and talking. After all, I had much more time now and there was no need to hurry. I functioned in a more relaxed manner. My excitement and enthusiasm or sense of urgency was no longer the same. Consequently, my sales began to slide. The adage, "a busy person gets things done," was no longer part of my psyche. Having obtained my goal, I lacked motivation. Once I realized the cause of my complacency, I no longer sat around gossiping but occupied myself again with the farm and gave full attention to my business when there was something to do, and sought another challenge.

Together with two other partners, I purchased an office-building complex, which could be used as a training facility and office space rental. By collecting dues from members desiring to use the facility, the mortgage and overhead expenses were covered. Sales increased dramatically.

My sales performance brought me to the attention of the corporate executives. Mr. Peters was to become the President of the Canadian company and had selected me as his replacement in Larchmont, N.Y. I accepted this honor.

Soon after Mr. Peters arrived in Canada, he telephoned asking me to join him, "but first," he said, "I want you to achieve the "President's $50,000 Club. Can you do it?"

"Of course," I replied. "When do you want me to come?"

"When will you achieve the President's Club?" He asked.

"By the first of July," I replied.

"Good. I'll expect you here then. I'm telling everyone here that you will be joining me and that you will be coming as a 'President's Club' winner."

After I hung up the phone, I realized the seriousness of the commitment I had made. It was already May the 26th, so I had a little more than one month to do it. I had no way out. Either I achieved the Club or I would lose face and credibility. To achieve the Presidents Club, $50,000 in sales was required within one calendar month, so I needed to start at once. My back against the wall.

Halfway through June, it didn't appear I would make it. I began to think of good reasons I could use to justify my failure. After all, I was still in communication with my own training center making sure it was being managed properly. I had this new center in Larchmont to run in addition to my own personal recruitment and sales activity. I needed to visit my family and handle whatever problems Gisela faced on the farm. Surely they will understand, I thought.

Then I remembered my commitment. The month wasn't over yet and I was already trying to justify failure. No, I decided, I will give it my best. I won't quit! Somehow I'll do it and if I should fail, it will not be because I gave up.

It came down to the wire. It was the last day of the month and all orders to qualify had to be postmarked before midnight. I needed one more sale to generate the remaining $5,000. I had just one more prospect to see that evening. He will join, I thought. He will have no choice.

Three and one half hours of selling, and I had the application and check in my hand. I then drove to the main Post Office in New York City to get the envelope postmarked since all other branches were already closed. On my way back to my room in Larchmont, my sense of relief was transcended with the feeling of victory. I had done it! I thought of my negative self-defeating thoughts of two weeks earlier. I vowed then and there never to give up on any project. If the desire was strong enough, there was always a chance for victory, if one persisted.

Chapter 2
Canada
Summer 1971—Fall 1972

To many Americans, Canada is a cold country north of the border. Except for the Border States, Canadian news broadcasts are rarely heard in the U.S.A. In Canada, however, American TV programming can be found throughout the country. And, since news by its very nature is bad, Canadians have the luxury of being critical without themselves being criticized.

I knew little about Canada when I arrived there on July 5th, 1971. I had no preconceived ideas. After finding a place to live, I went back to Pennsylvania, rented my farm, traded my old Mercedes for a new one, and returned to Canada with my family. My children entered school in Don Mills, a suburb of Toronto. Christine entered the third grade and Duane the fourth. Our youngest child, Caroline, was not of school age.

I began my work with much expectation but soon became disillusioned with the attitude of the people in the Toronto area. I found them to be cold and distant and felt their resentment toward me as an American. It was the time when President Nixon placed a surcharge on Canadian goods entering the U.S. market and anti-American sentiments were openly displayed. Cars with U.S. license plates were refused service at many gasoline stations. My nine-year-old son, Duane, was attacked by other school children. It was difficult for him to understand the taunts from his schoolmates: "American go home," and that his bloody nose and black eye was due to the fact that he was an American kid. We learned later that Christine had been skipping school and hiding in a ravine during the day because, she said, her classmates and teacher hated her.

News broadcasters were beating the drums promoting nationalism and certain news reporters were asking for the removal of American goods from their store shelves.

I was confused and bewildered. I had never been exposed to anti-American sentiment and believed America to be right in whatever it did at home or abroad; that its interest in other countries was for the benefit of that country. I was to learn a lot about the world—and about America—in the coming years.

Everywhere I looked, I saw American goods. If American foodstuffs were taken from the stores, there would be little left to eat. I didn't know why Nixon placed the surcharge on goods but came to realize how politics caused resentment and hatred among peoples of the world. Citizens of a country, whose government is unpopular, often become the objects of attack or abuse.

The early 70's saw a new wave of rivalry within Canada. English speaking Canadians were suspicious of French-Canadians after President Charles DeGaulle of France made his infamous speech in Quebec proclaiming, "Long live free Quebec." This statement led to separateness within the country. Despite this confusion, our company's business in Quebec was doing well. The people of Quebec were especially warm by comparison to the Province of Ontario. They sought opportunity and were easy to motivate.

Although I had proven myself as a salesman in the states, I was now expected to prove myself in Canada. I once more functioned as an independent distributor, was not on a salary and my expenses were my own. Mr. Peters told me privately that he wanted me as his Vice President of Sales but due to the strong pro Canadian feelings, I would have to do something exceptional so he could justify the promotion. He wanted to implement his style and methods of conducting business that had earned him success in the USA, and he had no one but me who understood his methods. In a short while I was given the title of Regional Vice President but without compensation for that position. I still blindly followed and supported Mr. Peters while spending my own money to support myself.

In Ontario, I found the people to be more skeptical than in the U.S. Many people I talked with felt they could earn more money doing nothing than to work for it. Social programs made it too easy to be complacent. The middle and upper class workers paid a severe penalty in the form of high taxes to support welfare recipients. My training was designed to motivate and inspire the desire for achievement; to provide instruction on setting goals and then offer a vehicle for its attainment. I had proven this concept in my own life and knew what I taught could be accomplished.

Mr. Peters asked me to go to Ottawa and "pump-up" the training center in that city. As it was to be a temporary assignment, I left my family in Don Mills and rented a room in Ottawa. I conducted seminars and held meetings on a continuous basis for the distributors and for prospective new recruits. My inspiration had increased the productivity in Ottawa and two months later, I was called back to Toronto with a new assignment.

"I want you to go to Calgary, Alberta," said Mr. Peters. "There is little activity there and they don't seem to understand the program. You do. If you can go out there and create a President's Club Winner out of someone, I'll bring you back as the Vice President of Sales. Can you do it?"

"Look," I said. "I've done whatever you asked since I've been here, at my own expense. Because I'm helping others, my income doesn't even cover my expenses. My bank balance is getting thin and the tenants on my farm are behind on their rent. I would like to go to Calgary but I simply cannot afford it."

"You're right," said Mr. Peters," and I appreciate what you've done. If you agree to go to Calgary, I'll pay your expenses to get there and also give you $1,000 per month. I know it's not much but it's the best I can do at the moment."

I considered what he said. Once again I was being asked to prove myself, but the crumbs offered as compensation was a slap in the face. I'll do it just one more time, I thought, and then if he doesn't deliver on his promise, I'll leave Canada. I remembered what he told me about the opportunity in Canada when he invited me to join him. "The company is in trouble, and if I can pull it out, it will make those who were part of it, heroes. There is nothing to lose and everything to gain. It can't get any worse."

He asked for my help and I obliged.

"O.k.," I said. "I'll go."

"Before you go, I'd like you to do something else first. Bob Cummings will be touring Canada as our Director of Public Relations and I'd like you to escort him here in Ontario and Quebec. Can I count on you," he asked.

"Of course," I replied.

Gisela and I met with Bob and his wife Gigi for dinner at The Inn-On-The-Park Hotel. Bob suggested that we dine in his room so he wouldn't be bothered by autograph seekers. We got acquainted and for the next ten days, I escorted Bob to various TV appearances and to company sponsored events. Although Bob was aging, many people still remembered him from his comedy TV Series, "Love That Bob." I told Bob about Duane's encounter with his schoolmates and asked him if he would autograph a picture for Duane. He was delighted to do so and wrote," To Duane, your daddy's best friend," and he signed it, "Uncle Bob Cummings." Duane proudly showed his autographed picture to his schoolmates and at once became somewhat of a celebrity. Christine received an autograph from Bob's wife, Gigi, dressed in a Kimono. Thinking that she may improve her situation, Christine showed the autographed picture to her teacher, who kept it. When Christine asked for it back several days later, the teacher told her that she had lost it.

Mr. Cumming's final TV appearance was in Ottawa. We left Montreal in plenty of time but I was having difficulties locating the TV station. It was a live TV show and we had to be on time. As Airtime approached, Bob's irritation became vocal. He always wanted to be at the station ahead of time and utilize the station's make-up artists, but time was running out. As I drove over bumps in the street, he began to apply his own make-up in the back seat of the limousine and his irritation grew louder. He was not angry at me but at the full schedule that had been thrust upon him. He was exasperated when we finally pulled up in front of the studio just three minutes before Airtime. We rushed into the studio leaving the car illegally parked with its lights flashing. Bob was ushered behind the curtain just as they made his introduction. He closed his eyes for a few moments and was at once on camera. He was calm and without the slightest trace of anxiety, a true professional.

* * * * *

It was the end of May 1972 when I arrived in Calgary. I immediately took charge of the office and called a meeting of the sales leaders.

"Gentlemen, I'm here for one reason only and that is to help you increase your production, which means putting more money in your pockets. One of you will achieve the President's Club during the month of June. I don't know who it will be yet, but I'm going to commit my energies to working with that individual or individuals who are serious about their future and in making a lot of money. You know my background. I achieved the President's Club and know what it takes to do it. It's going to require a commitment on your part with a lot of persistent hard work. Unless you are deadly serious, don't bother to try. You must want it! For that person or persons who commit today to achieve the Club, I will commit myself to working for you this month. I will do the interviews; all you need do is get the people to me. Forget that I'm a Regional Vice President. As of this moment, I'm demoting myself. I'm a salesman/instructor just like you. Who of you feels he has what it takes to make the President's Club?"

I waited. Mr. Emerson raised his hand and almost simultaneously, Mr. Snell raised his hand.

"Thank you gentlemen for responding. I want no more hands. For those of you who have to think about it, you're obviously not sure it's important enough. I would like Mr. Emerson and Mr. Snell to remain. For the rest of you, this meeting is adjourned."

When the others departed, I said, "I don't know which of you has the greatest desire and is willing to do whatever it takes to accomplish this worthwhile goal. It is not only a high honor but it signifies the character and ability of the individual. It also means that upward mobility is likely. Tomorrow at 10:00 AM, I will conduct my first interview. Which of you will have someone for me to see?"

Mr. Emerson said, "I will!" Mr. Snell said, "I'll take the next appointment."

The next days and weeks were filled with activity. I found the people in Calgary to be friendly and receptive. Either it was because there were many Americans living in Calgary working with the oil companies, or it was simply the friendliness of the westerner. Regardless, I felt at ease and was made to feel welcome. Both Emerson and Snell were competing fiercely and their results were showing, with Emerson leading.

I took Mr. Snell aside and said, "If Mr. Emerson continues working the way he is, he's going to make the Club. You have as much or more potential than Emerson. With your background, contacts and experience, you should be the one achieving this Club. There's still time remaining. Do you think you can beat Emerson?"

Without hesitation, Mr. Snell replied, "You just wait. Like you say, the month's not over yet. Don't count me out. If anyone's going to make the Club, I am!"

It was the last day of June. Mr. Emerson had acquired the necessary sales volume the day before and was celebrating his achievement. Mr. Snell was one sale short to qualify, but he had an appointment scheduled for that evening at his home. He asked if I would come out to his ranch so we could both work on the prospect, "even if it takes all night," Snell had remarked. The prospect was a friend of Snell's and knew how important this sale was. After the prospect had all his questions answered, I knew he would join but was delaying his decision just to give Mr. Snell a hard time. He waited until 11:45 PM before he signed the papers and wrote his check. I verified the transaction as the Regional Vice President.

I was just as excited as Emerson and Snell. They had achieved what most had thought was the impossible. I too had achieved the goal I had set for myself when I came to Calgary. Not only did I create one President's Club winner, but one more for good measure.

I called Mr. Peters with the news. He expressed his surprise and sincere congratulations. Now, I thought, he will invite me back to Toronto and I'll receive the promotion.

Before I could ask when I should return to Toronto, he said, "Bob Cummings is scheduled to be in Calgary around the middle of July. It would be good if you could look after him. He will be a good sales aid for the people there and should generate a lot of interest in the business. Would you look after it?"

I agreed. Mr. Cummings' arrival did create excitement. The world famous Calgary Stampede (Rodeo) was beginning and Mr. Snell arranged for Bob Cummings and me to attend. Due to Bob's celebrity status, we were seated in a special section of the Grand Stand. Sitting to my right was Bob Cummings and to my left, Chief Dan George who starred in many western roles. Both were introduced before the large Rodeo crowd. Later that night, Bob and I were made Honorary Calgarians at a special ceremony with the traditional "Yahoo" upon presentation of a certificate and white cowboy hat.

I completed my assignment with Mr. Cummings and called Toronto for Mr. Peters. I was told that he was in California at the home office. Several days later, I received a call from the Toronto office.

"This is Bob Delana. I'm your new boss. Mr. Peters has been given a new position in California and I have replaced him as President of the Canadian company. As soon as I get settled here, I want to meet you. Mr. Peters has spoken very highly of you."

I was shocked. I thanked Mr. Delana for the call and asked if there was a number to reach Mr. Peters in California. I recorded the number and placed my call. I was informed that Mr. Peters was not available to take any calls so I left a message.

I had just finished a meeting in Red Deer, Alberta, when I received a call from Mr. Peters.

"Abe, I apologize for not getting to you sooner. Things have been happening fast and this is the first opportunity I've had to call. I understand from Bob Delana that he's already called you."

"Yes he has, and I was quite shocked. What's going on?" I asked.

"Bob feels very strongly about selecting his own man as V.P. I recommended you for the job but we'll just have to give it some time, Abe."

"Dan, I'm sitting out here in the middle of nowhere. I came to Canada to work with you. I did the job you asked. At this point, I don't know if I want to be here, and secondly, I don't feel I need to prove anything to a new man. I'm leaving Red Deer tonight and returning to Calgary. I'll decide what I'll do when I get there."

"Abe, I know I've made promises to you which I'm unable to keep now. Let me see what I can do. Don't leave Calgary until you hear from me."

I returned to Calgary that same night and discussed the situation with Gisela. She agreed with my position on the matter. In July she had driven across Canada with the children to join me and it was great having the family together. We had visited the Canadian Rockies at Banff, had a picnic at Lake Louise and enjoyed visiting the Calgary Zoo and Heritage Park. The children were now instructed to get their belongings together for the long drive back east.

Dan Peters called the following day and said he needed more time. I told him I was leaving Calgary and heading back to Toronto and that he could let me know what the situation was when I arrived.

The following afternoon, we were on our way taking the southern route through the northern U.S. I said goodbye to my many new friends that morning. For all they knew, I was being recalled to the home office.

The long journey gave me much time to think and reflect. What if I had stayed where I was in Pennsylvania instead of coming to Canada? I'd be much better off financially. In fact, if I had stayed with IBM where I had security, I'd be better off. What will I do now? If the company doesn't come through with the promotion, must I revert back to being a distributor again?

Having placed my future in the hands of the company, I felt abandoned. I felt like the ship without a rudder, helplessly drifting. I thought of businesses that I could start together with Gisela. We talked about franchises; we racked our brains but came up with nothing appealing.

Four days later, we arrived at our apartment in Don Mills, Ontario. I immediately called the Toronto office to see if there was a message from Mr. Peters. There was none, but I was told that Bob Delana wished to meet with me.

When I arrived at the office, Mr. Delana was in the middle of a training session with all the sales leaders in the east and asked me to sit in. Mr. Delana told the class that he had some important announcements to make. At this, I became hopeful.

After a short coffee break, Mr. Delana stood up and said, "I'm pleased to announce the appointment of our new Vice President of Sales. The man I've chosen, I believe will do an outstanding job. Please congratulate Mr. Claude Gravel."

My face flushed while many in the room turned to look at me. They had assumed I would be the next V.P. of Sales. Then they all turned to Mr. Gravel who took the floor to accept his promotion. I heard very little of what he had to say while buried in my own thoughts.

After Mr. Gravel returned to his seat, Mr. Delana stood up and said, "That's not all. I'm pleased to announce the promotion of another worthy individual. He has done an outstanding job and is most deserving of his new post. I've just been informed that Mr. Abe March is to be the Vice President of Sales in Greece."

I wasn't sure I heard right. Greece? Where's that, I thought with amusement. Then I was receiving the congratulations of everyone. Mr. Delana was smiling, fully aware of the shock it had given me.

"Dan Peters told me to make the announcement but I'm afraid I have no more details than that," said Mr. Delana. "Dan will be calling you with more information."

I understood the significance of Claude Gravel's appointment for the Canadian company

Being from Quebec and being Canadian, it would better solidify the position of the company. I called Gisela and announced, "We're going to Greece!"

Chapter 3
Greece
Fall 1972—Summer 1973

The company was starting a new operation in Greece and George Spiro was appointed the managing director. Mr. Spiro was born in Greece, immigrated to the States ten years earlier and was now a U.S. citizen and a distributor for the company. Recognizing the opportunity for advancement, George succeeded in raising funds to establish the Greek subsidiary. Since George did not have the experience in training, a strong person for V.P. of Sales was needed and I was chosen.

Mr. Spiro was already in Greece and was anxious to commence operations. He called me the day after my promotion was announced. He expressed his delight at my appointment and was anxious for me to join him.

"What I want to know is, how fast you can get here?" said George.

"No one has given me any details yet," I said. "There are things I must clear-up here first. I must make arrangements to move out of Canada and take care of some affairs in Pennsylvania before I can travel. How soon do you need me?"

"I need you just as fast as you can get here. I'm putting together a class to kick things off. Just tell me the earliest you can come and I'll set it up. Call Tom Mitchell in California. He's the head of the international division and will make your travel arrangements and answer all your questions. I'll call you tomorrow at 9:00 AM, your time, for the date of your arrival."

I called Mr. Mitchell.

"I'm most impressed with your record and I think you're the right man for the job," he said. "I'd like to see you here in California before you leave but George has been pressing me to get started and he wants you in Greece as soon as possible."

"I'm anxious to go", I said. "I've been given no details whatsoever. Can you fill me in?"

"Certainly. You'll be paid out of California in U.S. dollars. You will receive a base salary of $2500 per month plus expenses. As incentive, you will receive five percent of the company's net profits, calculated quarterly. Is that acceptable?"

"Sounds fair to me," I said. "What about my transportation to Greece? Will my family be able to go?"

"Yes, of course. I would suggest however, that you go there first and get the feel of the situation and perhaps locate living quarters before bringing your family. We will cover all your moving and travel expenses. Contact Mr. Cohen in my office here. He will handle those details. I understand you have some things to clear up first, but when do you think you can leave?"

"Can I have a week to ten days," I asked.

"That's reasonable. What date then should I arrange for your travel?"

I decided on a date commencing nine days later and immediately began making preparations. Mr. Spiro called the next morning and I informed him of my scheduled date and time of arrival. Two days later, the moving company picked-up my household effects and I left Canada with my family for Pennsylvania.

I was forced to evict the tenants on my farm who were behind three months rent and had made a mess of things. Nothing outside had been cared for and the house inside was a filthy mess. In the short period of time available, I sought new tenants and solved other problems associated with my office training center. I found temporary living quarters for my family until they could join me in Greece.

Gisela gathered brochures on Greece and talked excitedly with the children about their upcoming new adventure. She was fully capable of handling remaining details and I was able to depart for Greece on schedule.

Arriving before noon in Greece, I took a taxi to the Hilton Hotel as instructed. There was a message waiting for me to call the office immediately upon my arrival. I was tired and wanted to rest and freshen-up first, but I placed the call.

"This is Abe March".

"Just a moment sir, Mr. Spiro wishes to speak with you."

"Hi Abe. Welcome to Greece. How fast can you get to the office?"

"Whoa! I just arrived. I haven't unpacked yet and I need a shower and shave. Besides, this jet lag has me rather fuzzy."

"I have a class sitting here waiting for you. As soon as you get here, you go on. This is our first class. I'm sending a car for you."

"O.K. I'll be there as soon as I get cleaned up."

My excitement overcame my fatigue. My thoughts turned immediately to the outline of instruction I had prepared for the class.

When I entered the office, the chatter of voices emanating from the large classroom further stimulated my senses. George Spiro shook my hand and led me into his office where we conferred briefly over a cup of coffee. For the first class, George had selected people he knew personally and others who also understood English.

"At least most of them know some English," he said. "There are thirty-two students in the room waiting for you. Just let me know when you're ready and I'll make the introduction," said George in his thick Greek accent.

I organized my thoughts and then said, "I guess I'm as ready as I'm ever going to be. Let's do it."

As George and I entered the room, the people all stood and applauded. George went to the front of the room and gave the introduction in Greek. I wished I knew what was being said but decided it didn't matter. They would get to know me soon enough. Amidst applause, I took my place at the podium.

"Good afternoon. I'm thrilled to be here. This is my first time in Greece and from what I've seen so far; I'm going to like it here. You have been especially chosen to attend our first seminar. Some of you will have the opportunity to become part of this company in a responsible position. All of you today are starting out on an equal basis.

You have the same opportunity. The results from your efforts will be the deciding factor. You have the ground floor opportunity to be part of something great. Great things are going to happen in Greece. Some of you will be earning more money than you have ever dreamed of. We are going to talk about this opportunity during the next several days. What one must do to realize the rich rewards is what this seminar is all about."

"First, I'd like to give you background information on the company and the industry. I want you to take notes. We will then talk about the product and the marketing plan. We will show you exactly where you fit in and what you must do."

I began slowly and methodically to provide the details. The students took notes and conversed among themselves. Some understood everything while others needed translation. The pace was slow but the excitement showed on their faces.

It took all afternoon to give the basic introductory details. The next day, Sunday, I would continue. I went to bed early and awoke at 3:00 AM. With the jet lag, it would still require more time to adjust to the time difference. By the time class was ready to begin, I was already feeling sluggish. However, the enthusiasm of the students revitalized my energy to overcome my fatigue.

I began talking about attitude, the importance of attitude in dealing with others and how it reflects on oneself. I explained that one's attitude was as important, if not more important, than one's aptitude. The sparkle in their eyes told me that they had never heard such things before. I talked about goals, how to set goals and how they could be achieved with our marketing program. I allowed them to dream and discuss their goals, which increased their excitement. I told humorous stories to make a point. The audience laughed and at serious moments, tears could be seen in their eyes. It was an emotional and exciting five days.

Although the product inventory had not yet arrived, there were samples of the product for the students to see. For the final day of class, I asked the students to bring their spouse for the graduation ceremony. They came and the room was packed. All students graduated, and when receiving their diploma, voiced their commitments to building their distributor organizations and expressed their eagerness to begin work.

The following week, a second class was scheduled and the students intended to fill it with prospects they wanted to introduce to the program. There was a fee of $250 per student and they all paid cash.

George was exuberant in his praise of me and expressed his feeling that the program would catch on rapidly. I wanted to be appraised of the situation regarding the company. People were asking me questions, which I was unable to answer. Primarily, when was the product coming? However, George was evasive about the exact date of the products arrival.

"Abe, you let me worry about the product and the management of the company. Your job is to recruit and train. You concentrate on the sales and I'll handle the rest."

"That's fine," I said. "But when do you think the product will arrive. You know if we recruit people and take their money for product we don't have, it could create a problem for us."

"Don't worry about them. I can talk with them. I'm Greek and they'll listen to me. Just don't worry about that, O.K.? We should be getting some product in a week or two. It's coming out of Italy and they promised it within two weeks."

I was apprehensive. I didn't like the idea of getting started without having all the tools to work with and felt that this operation had started somewhat prematurely, especially without products. But, I told myself; it's not my problem. George certainly must know what he's doing or they wouldn't have appointed him to run the company. Every person who attended my training, joined the program as a Master distributor and paid the equivalent of $2,250 in cash. The cost for the class was an additional $250, which they had all paid. The next class already had 65 students scheduled.

By telephone, I arranged with Gisela to select those goods she wanted shipped and to arrange for the remainder of the furniture to be stored. I also asked her to arrange for the purchase of a new Mercedes to be picked-up at the factory in Germany. When the arrangements were finalized, she was to call me and I would meet her in Germany and drive with her and the family to Greece.

The second training class was a complete success. The following day, the day before Christmas 1972, I flew to Frankfurt to meet my family. Gisela and the children had arrived in Germany several days earlier and were staying with her parents. On the day after Christmas we left for Greece.

It was a pleasant trip through southern Germany and into Austria, though it was cold and the snow made driving over the Alps hazardous. As we passed through ski villages, we dreamed of one day spending a Christmas holiday there with the family. It seemed so romantic. I could even visualize the family sitting around a large fireplace at the ski village, sipping warm drinks after a day on the slopes.

Leaving Klagenfurt, Austria, we crossed into Yugoslavia and things changed dramatically. We passed by Ljubljana then continued to Zagreb. The farther into Yugoslavia we went, the more drab and dreary it became. The roads were heavily traveled by trucks and were rough and full of potholes. Our original plan was to go as far as possible, then stop for the night. We brought sandwiches with us but the children wanted something to drink, so I stopped at a roadside cafe. I ordered three cokes and three bananas to go and paid what they asked. When I got into the car and computed the exchange rate, I discovered they had charged me an outrageous sum.

"I suppose they don't expect to see us again," I said to Gisela. "They're right. I don't think it's wise to stay here overnight. Let's try to drive straight through."

"All right, but as soon as you get tired, pull over and I'll drive for awhile," said Gisela.

We passed Belgrade and it was getting dark. An hour later, I pulled off the road and Gisela took the wheel so I could sleep.

I was awakened when the car came to a sudden stop. Vehicles were bumper to bumper on the right lane and we were stopped in the middle lane. A police officer stood in front of our car with his hand raised. He motioned for us to pull off the road. Abruptly awakened, I was confused and didn't know what was happening. Gisela wasn't sure what the officer wanted her to do and she began moving forward. The officer stepped in front of the car and she stopped just short of hitting the officer.

"What does he want me to do?" Gisela shouted.

"I think he wants you to pull off the road. What are you doing in this middle lane anyway?"

"I just followed the other cars and he waved them all past but stopped me. I don't know why."

The officer came to the car window and asked to see our passports.

Gisela said, "What do you want, I don't understand," hoping the officer would wave us on. Then he spoke in German, which she understood but again said in English, "What do you want? Do you speak English?" The officer then repeated, "Pass."

I handed the officer my passport. The officer looked at it and placed it in his pocket, once again motioning for us to pull off the road. He halted traffic so Gisela could pull to the side. I got out of the car and waited. The officer continued directing traffic for a while and then came toward me. He indicated that he wanted the passports of everyone, which I presented. He also placed these passports into his pocket and indicated for me to remain where I was. The officer then got into his VW police car with another officer, and they drove away.

I didn't know what to do. We couldn't leave the country without our passports. I surmised they had stopped us because of our big Mercedes, cognizant that we were foreigners in transit by our oval international license plates. I was thankful that Gisela hadn't bumped into the officer or we might be sitting in jail.

Forty minutes later, the police car returned. The officer came over to me and said, "Fifty dinars."

"For what?" I asked. The officer repeated his request.

"Give him the money and let's get out of here," said Gisela.

I handed the officer the fifty dinars, not really caring how much money that was. The officer then reached into his pocket, pulled out the passports and handed them to me. He then went back to his car.

"I guess it's all right for us to leave," I said. "I'll drive!"

I started the car and pulled onto the highway. Through my rearview mirror, I noticed that the police car was following me. I suspected that they wanted to catch me doing something else so they could collect more money.

The fog was extremely thick and I followed the taillights of the truck in front of me. Occasionally, the fog separated, leaving an opening with clear visibility. The police car was still following and I decided to try and lose it the next time there was a break in the fog and I could see to pass.

Before long an opening appeared, so I passed the truck and raced to the next patch of fog where I was forced to a crawl. The illumination of lights ahead indicated a service plaza and as I passed it, a police car pulled out from the plaza and began following me.

After the next several breaks in the fog, I had increased the distance separating me from the police car and could no longer see them. I continued driving in this manner for the next hour and then eased up on my speed and tried to relax. The glare on the wet windshield from oncoming cars was causing a severe strain on my eyes. The hour was late and I had difficulty keeping my eyes open. I asked Gisela to talk to me but soon that didn't help. I opened the window, turned the radio on loud, that too failed.

"Pinch me, do anything, hit me," I said.

Gisela smiled and said, "Now's my chance."

She watched me carefully from the corner of her eye and would slap and pinch me when my eyes closed. This continued until we reached the border of Greece.

From the Yugoslavian border, it was only a short distance to Thessaloniki, the largest city in northern Greece. I learned to call it Salonica like everyone else and was looking forward to the next training session that was to be held at the Macedonian Palace Hotel in Salonica, where I was now headed. It was nearly 3:00 AM when we checked into the Macedonian Palace to spend the night.

The next day we traveled south toward Athens. We enjoyed the drive, stopping occasionally to take in the view and stretch our legs. Everyone was excited about being in Greece and couldn't wait to get settled.

We stayed at the Athens Hilton hotel. Each day, Gisela would be driven around Athens and the suburbs looking for a house to rent. When she had narrowed the possibilities, I went with her. We were both delighted with the villa we found in Ekali, a village on the road north from the city. This would be our home. Ekali is a rich suburb of Athens and the villa we rented had recently been vacated by Mr. Pappas, the oil magnate servicing the U.S. Sixth Fleet. The owner of the villa, Madame Kaluti, a widow of means, was delighted when we rented the villa. She enjoyed the children and loved Gisela. Madame Kaluti had inherited the villa along with other properties upon the death of her husband with a stipulation in his will that the inheritance was hers provided she never remarried. Although she had a boy friend in Italy whom she visited often, she remained unmarried.

Madame Kaluti provided us with a gardener and loaned her maid to Gisela three times a week. The maid, Mrs. Perma, formerly the maid to King Constantine before he was ousted from power, was now in the employ of Madame Kaluti. Gisela began her first Greek lessons in order to communicate with Mrs. Perma who spoke no English.

In 1973 Greece, the birthplace of democracy, had been under the rule of a military "junta" led by Colonel Papadopoulos ever since a coup by army colonels in 1967 had overthrown the democracy established after King Constantine had been exiled. It was the first time I had ever lived in a country not governed democratically and it felt uncomfortable. Greeks, who normally speak so passionately about politics, had become reticent in public. The secret police could be anywhere and portraits of Papadopoulos could be seen everywhere one went. I had never been one to involve myself in political discussions and determined to live and let live, since there was nothing I could do in any case.

The Greek currency was stable and pegged to the US dollar, however the movement of currency in and out of Greece was restricted. Barter became a useful method for international business.

The villa in Ekali was magnificent and we quickly settled into a pleasant routine. As soon as the weather allowed, I insisted on taking breakfast on the house's expansive veranda. The mornings were invariably warn and sunny. The villa was screened from its neighbors by trees and the view from the veranda was marvelous.

My wife soon learned to communicate with Mrs. Perma by means of sign language and phrases in English or Greek. She was a cheerful addition to our household and her children played with ours. Her family was not wealthy, yet she, like Madame Kaluti, were supporters of the exiled King Constantine. One day in the spring, Mrs. Perma arrived at the house with red eyes. When my wife asked her why she was cried, she reported that the colonels had asked the Greek parliament to decide on whether to restore Constantine as constitutional monarch. The parliament resolved to ban the King from Greece and refused a restoration.

With the family settled in our new home and the children in school, I continued to conduct training seminars, alternating between Athens and Salonica. The classes were held in hotels to accommodate the growing body of students. The respect and admiration of the students flourished. Arriving in Salonica for one of my training sessions, I was met at the airport by several hundred people waving and applauding and then presented with flowers as I entered the terminal. It was their way of expressing appreciation and bestowing honor.

I was elated with the progress and focused my full attention to my duties. We needed someone as trainer for cosmetics and Gisela was appointed as the Director of Training. She taught the women the art of cosmetic and skin care application and I taught the men the business end. Using samples, Gisela demonstrated the products giving a facial and applying makeup to one of the students while the others watched. Skin care products were still not available.

I worked without rest or relaxation. George wanted to achieve a one million dollar month in sales and applied more pressure. Two interpreters were needed to keep up with me.

In January 1973 I flew to Heraklion, Crete, for an overnight visit to conduct a meeting and initiate activity there. There was no time to investigate the island and see the historical sites but I did have a bit of a fright when an earth tremor interrupted my sleep. I was told that this was a common occurrence on Crete.

I was exhausted. Upon my return to Athens, I asked George if it were possible to reschedule the class and move it ahead one week. George was alarmed and told me it was imperative that the class be conducted as scheduled in Salonica and I reluctantly consented.

I flew to Salonica and checked into the Macedonian Palace Hotel the night before the class. Although I felt weak and feverish, I tried to take my mind off my miseries. I was taught that illness is a state of mind, and that strong people with a positive mental attitude don't get sick. I had been told that the reason there was no cure for a common cold was that colds were mentally inflicted. One could get rid of a cold by willing it away. I tried my best to concentrate on other things but I still felt miserable.

The next morning it was difficult to get out of bed. I had a temperature of 103 degrees and felt like I was burning up. My throat was sore and my head ached. "I can't conduct a class feeling like this," I exclaimed to myself. "I've simply got to cancel." I called George in Athens.

"George, this is Abe. I'm really feeling bad. I'm weak and burning with fever. I'm going to cancel the class. I don't know how I can teach them anything in this condition."

"Abe, come on! You'll feel better once you get started. You know how important this class is! I can't see any other choice. The people have paid their money and most have taken off work to be there. Somehow, you've got to do it!"

"I'll try George," I said.

With extreme difficulty, I began the class. I pumped myself full of aspirin and other medication, which affected my ability to concentrate. I spoke from rote memory, repeating lines I had learned and followed my outline. When there was a break in the class, I drank tea and took more medication. Over and above my physical inadequacy, I felt miserable that I was not able to perform at my best. The people deserve better, I thought.

I somehow survived the first day and felt slightly better when I arose the next morning. As I was preparing to get ready for class, the telephone rang.

"Hello…"

"Hello, hello, who is this?"

"Schnuck…" I heard the sobs and knew it was Gisela.

"What is it? What's the matter? Speak to me!"

"My mother died. Please come home. I need you."

Gisela sobbed and I tried to comfort her. I didn't know what to do. My duty to my job, to my family, trying to please everyone, what could I do?

Gisela's mother had been planning to come from Germany to Greece for a visit. Gisela's parents didn't have a telephone in their home and Gisela had coordinated the planning of the trip with a neighbor. Gisela was to call that morning and talk with her mother and give her the flight schedule. When Gisela called, the neighbor said, "I'm so sorry, Gisela. It was so sudden. How did you know?"

"Know what?" Asked Gisela.

"Oh! You don't know? Your mother died this morning."

Gisela was in a state of shock and I was unaware of these details. My duty to my job had always come first. I must finish the class.

"I'll come as soon as I can," I said. "I know how you must feel."

"No, you don't know. I don't know what I'll do without her. She can't be gone. No, it can't be true." Gisela continued to sob.

"Sweetheart, I'll come just as soon as I can. I can't leave now. I'm in the middle of a class."

I hung up the phone full of guilt feelings and anxious for the class to end. (I would only later realize that blind devotion to a job was not only often inappropriate and unfair to my family, but often went unrewarded.)

We traveled to Germany for the funeral. Gisela was still finding it difficult to accept the fact that her mother was gone. Her mother had also been her best friend.

* * * * *

After six months into our operation we had achieved our first one million dollar sales month but still had no product. I met with George on numerous occasions and each time George told me the product was on its way. Now it was learned that before the skin care products could be imported, the Greek government must first approve the formulas. Other make-up items and fragrances did not require approval and could be imported.

I was worried and angry. This is gross incompetence, I thought. It was improper to start this business without checking these things out. This should all have been taken care of in advance.

The formulas were promptly secured and translated, then submitted for approval. At that same time, a small shipment of make-up items and fragrances were actually shipped and were enroute. Unknown to the company, one of the distributors had lost patience and went to the Attorney General complaining that the company was taking money for product but had no product to sell. Word reached George that an investigation was underway and for the first time, George finally showed concern. It was about time! Greek law is much more swift and severe than in the U.S. and operates under the French proviso that one is deemed guilty until proven innocent. As it happened, the product arrived just two hours before the police arrived. When they saw actual product on the premises, they departed. Because of the investigation however, the office responsible for formula approvals delayed any approval action until such time as the investigation was completed. The distributors were no longer willing to accept excuses and were becoming more restless.

I too was becoming concerned and critical of the company. I had not been paid in U.S. dollars as promised but in Greek drachmas. It was not possible to exchange drachmas for dollars and take them out of the country. Therefore I was unable to pay the mortgage on my farm and was forced to put it up for sale. I had always been a man to honor my own verbal commitments. I was learning that others did not always share my attitude.

Paul Korletes, my top producer and my right hand man, approached me. "Mr. March," he said. "The people here don't trust Mr. Spiro anymore. They like and respect you. They have come to me one by one and we held a secret meeting the other night. They have unanimously agreed that you should become the President of the company and have George thrown out."

"Stop right there Paul!" I said. "I'm going to forget we had this conversation. I don't ever want to hear this again. It is my job to support Mr. Spiro and I will have no part in any coup to have him thrown out. Is that clear?"

"But Mr. March. The people won't listen to him anymore. They are serious. They may actually do him physical harm. They think he has lied to them and ripped them off. All these excuses about the product coming we discovered, have all been lies. I have friends working at the transportation authorities and elsewhere. All lies. Something must be done."

I realized that this situation had become critical and I silently agreed with him, but I would not be part of their coup. This seemed to be the Greek method of solving problems and how the current regime there had got into power. They must realize that this is an American company and that any decisions of replacement must come from California.

"I will talk with Mr. Spiro about the emotional level of the people but I will not tell him of this conversation. Perhaps he will do something to change the attitude of the people."

"It's gone too far. They won't listen to him," said Paul. "If you want, I'll write a letter to California and let them know what's going on."

"No, don't do that. I'll take some action. Leave it to me."

Paul reluctantly agreed. I knew I had to do something. I immediately sat with George expressing my concern about the legalities of the situation without product. I also made it clear that the people were losing faith in the company. "All the success we've had is about to reverse itself," I said. "The people don't want to introduce anyone else into the business unless they are assured that these new people will get their products, and that they will first get their own products."

"Who told you these things?" asked George. "You just tell me who told you this and I'll take care of them."

"George, I'm afraid that wouldn't help. I've been getting fragments of information. People have been telling me that this is what the others are thinking. I feel the situation is serious."

"You don't understand the Greeks. They're bluffing. Don't you worry about them. Let me handle it."

He just wouldn't get it. I knew that further talk was useless. I decided to place a call to Mr. Mitchell in California.

"Mr. Mitchell," I began. "This is a very difficult phone call for me to make."

"Hello Abe. I don't understand. You're doing a splendid job. Everyone's talking about the Greek operation."

"I'm afraid you don't understand. It's true we have made outstanding progress and this has been accomplished with virtually no product." I went on to explain the close call with the police and that we still did not have the skin care products, which was the majority of our product line.

"The people are getting very restless. I have been approached by some people who wish to take matters into their own hands."

"What do you mean?" asked Mr. Mitchell.

"Simply, that they are upset with management. They feel they have been lied to and the credibility is gone. I strongly suggest you send someone here to look into the situation. I feel it's imperative that it happen quickly before it becomes too late."

"Thanks for calling Abe. I'll send Hank Devito over there right away. Give me your home phone number so Hank can call you."

I complied and waited. The following day I received a call from Hank telling me that he was arriving two days hence. He instructed me not to inform George, that this was to be a surprise visit.

Unknown to me, George had called a general meeting for the distributors of Athens on the same date as Hank's arrival. George told me, "I called a meeting to stop this nonsense. When I get through with them, they'll forget about the product. It's not important anyway. They're making money recruiting. Who cares about the product?" Unbelievable!

It was now obvious to me why we had delays in getting the product and I was glad Hank was coming. Unless this situation was resolved, I could no longer serve as the Vice President of Sales under George. It could only lead to legal action and I didn't want to have any part of that.

George told me that I didn't need to be present at the meeting. He would be talking in Greek and I wouldn't understand what was being said, anyway. I was happy about this since I was picking up Hank at the airport just prior to the meeting and I wouldn't have to explain my absence.

I took Hank directly to my home. I informed Hank about the conversation I had with Paul. I went on to say, "I want you to understand that I have fully supported George. Although I've disseminated information to the people based on what I was told, the people don't know that."

The conversation was interrupted by the telephone. Gisela handed the phone to me.

"Mr. March. This is Paul. We're here at the office meeting and things have gotten out of hand. The people won't let George leave the room. They are insisting on talking with you. They refuse to listen to him. What do you suggest we do?"

"Just a moment Paul. We may be in luck. The company has sent someone here and he's sitting with me right now. Just hold on a moment."

I explained the situation to Hank. "What do you suggest?" I asked.

"See if they will let George go if they are promised that someone will be there from the home office tomorrow. We can set up a meeting and I'll talk with them," said Hank.

"Paul, tell the people that someone from the home office in California will be there tomorrow. They will be able to talk with him. Tell them the Vice President of the international division will listen to their gripes. See if they'll let George go. In any event, let me know what happens."

"That should do it. Thanks Mr. March," said Paul.

It wasn't too long before the telephone rang again. This time it was George.

"What's going on Abe? Who's coming from California?"

"Hold on George. I'll put Hank Devito on the phone". I handed the phone to Hank.

"Hello George. I made a surprise visit to see you. When I couldn't reach you, I called Abe and he picked me up at the airport. I understand there are some problems. What's going on?"

I waited as Hank listened to George. "Why don't we talk about this tomorrow. I'll be at your office first thing in the morning. We can talk about it then. I'll see you tomorrow," said Hank.

"I suppose I arrived just in time. I'm going to talk with George privately tomorrow and try to sort this thing out. I also want to talk with Tom Mitchell tonight. Take me to the hotel so I can get some rest."

I complied. Tomorrow would be an interesting day, I thought. At least some action would be taken to resolve this mess.

The meeting between George and Hank took place while I waited in my office. I tried to keep my mind on work but my thoughts were elsewhere. I sensed that the end was drawing near for George and myself. What a wasted opportunity! Quick-buck thinking had ruined a chance to build something profitable and lasting. Sadness turned my thoughts to the wonderful things that had happened in such a short period of time. The hospitality of the Greek people, their warmth and friendliness toward my family and me. I remembered the trip to Florida where we had taken more than thirty people with us who had never been out of Greece before. To go to America had been the greatest thrill of their life. I smiled to myself as I remembered the excitement and anticipation of the trip that I had shared with them.

Boarding Olympic Airlines, Gisela and I were seated in the First Class section, courtesy of the travel agency for the large booking of passengers. Then to our surprise, Christina Onassis boarded the plane and sat in front of us. Christina had another woman with her, obviously her attendant and an older man with dark glasses who Christina referred to as Mr. 'G'. Gisela whispered to me, "That's Christina Onassis, one of the richest women in the world. Do you think we can talk with her?" I told her that when we got airborne we would introduce ourselves and say hello. But that didn't occur. After waiting for a half hour, Christina said to Mr. 'G', "This is typical of Olympic. Let's take another airline." They left the plane and I found it amusing that it was her father who owned the airline and it would someday belong to her, as sole heir, since the death of her brother.

I thought about our family life in Greece and the near tragedy with our ten-year-old daughter Christine. She was rushed to the hospital

TO BEIRUT AND BACK

because of severe swelling of the tracheotomy, fighting to breathe. It was a close call. The swelling was attributed to a severe allergic reaction. Christine was so pleased by the kindness and concern of everyone. She said, "I thought I was a goner".

My thoughts took me to Beirut, Lebanon and the group of Greeks we had taken there for a training class. I remembered staying behind with Gisela when the others had departed. What a beautiful city with beaches and mountains nearby. I thought about the severe sunburn I got at the beach and the remedial treatment by our maid when I returned home. A bathtub full of tea had drawn out the pain of the burn. I also recalled the incident when we arrived in Athens from Beirut and were on our way from the Airport to the office by Taxi. There were student demonstrations against the ruling "junta" and for "dimokratia" and the Police were out in force. We stopped in front of our office building and stepped out. A couple policemen were screaming at the driver and telling him to keep moving. He tried to tell them that our luggage was in the trunk and wanted to get it for us. They wouldn't let him get out of the car but yelled at him and hit him over the head through the open window. They told him to get going. While this was happening, Gisela was banging with her fist on the trunk to let them know our suitcases were in there, to no avail. The Taxi left with our luggage inside. We went into the office, and then to the US Embassy to report it. The next day we were instructed to go to the Airport to retrieve our luggage. The Airport personnel wanted a description of what was in the luggage before it was opened. We were finally able to retrieve our luggage and go home.

My thoughts were interrupted when Hank knocked on my office door.

"Abe, are you busy?"

"No, come on in. How's it going?"

"This situation is a real mess. If we had known about the problem with the product, we could have helped. I'm setting up a meeting for tonight with the distributors. I only hope I can calm them down. I'll be making my own recommendations to Tom Mitchell about this situation and I'd like you to come back to California with me to help sort things out. Can you free yourself to leave?"

"Have you discussed this with George?"

"Yes, I told him you were needed. He has his own work cut out for him. His first priority is getting those formulas approved and getting the product here before all hell breaks loose. All else is unimportant."

The following day, Hank had a change of plans.

"Tom Mitchell feels I should remain here for awhile but he would like to see you at once. I've already made your travel arrangements. You'll pick up your tickets at the TWA ticket counter at the airport. You're scheduled to leave at 9:05 AM."

Three days later, I was sitting in Tom Mitchell's office.

"Abe, I know this may be uncomfortable for you, but I must know the details about the situation in Greece."

I carefully and methodically recounted what I knew. There was much that I only assumed since most conversations with visitors to the office had been in Greek. Although I only knew what I was told, my observations were important to Mr. Mitchell.

When I concluded, Mr. Mitchell said, "Abe my instructions were not followed. I wanted all administrative details completed before operations commenced. George assured me that he had everything under control and that he was ready to commence business. Under the circumstances, I have no choice but to remove him as managing director. It appears his own safety is in jeopardy if he remains. Hank's pretty high on you. He tells me the people admire and respect you. I'd like to appoint you as managing director if you feel you can do the job."

"Mr. Mitchell. You don't know how much I appreciate the offer. Yes, I'm confident I could do the job, but I'm not the man to become the next managing director. It would be temporary at best. I've supported George in everything that was said and done. My own credibility may not be important now but I'm sure it will later. I believe the best move is a clean sweep that will have no reference with the past. If I were to be named their managing director, the people may feel that they have been successful in getting rid of George through me, something like a coup. Regardless of how they feel about me now, it won't be long before they'll attempt to undermine me also. They want me to be their President and that's the reason why I should not be. It must not be shown that they have that kind of power. If you want to promote me, send me to Lebanon. I'll start an operation for you there."

"We won't discuss Lebanon, just yet. I do respect your opinion Abe, and I feel you are the most qualified for the job. But I also believe you're right. From what you've told me, it requires a new man. I'll have to find someone else fast, though. I will expect you to remain there until you can be replaced. I'll also look for a new assignment for you."

"What about Lebanon," I asked.

"I don't know enough about that part of the world and we have grown so rapidly that I'd like to strengthen our existing operations before opening any new ones. That doesn't mean I won't consider it at a future date. Get me more details about the country, the market, population, etc., so I have a better idea about it."

I departed for Greece the following day. Upon my arrival, Hank briefed me on the situation and I discovered that George was already enroute to California to meet with Mr. Mitchell and be relieved of his post.

A new managing director was selected and I was asked to go to West Germany on a temporary basis to lend a hand with a floundering operation there.

I began making preparations to leave Greece. My primary concern was in getting my money out of the country and I also needed an exit visa for my car. I went to the appropriate government office to obtain the visa and was told I must pay taxes on my car for the time I was in Greece. I argued the point. The Greek consulate in Germany had told me I could take the car into Greece using the oval international plates for one year without paying any tax. However, my arguments were ignored. I was told that things have now changed. New government regulations, the clerk claimed, now required payment. The clerk also asked for other documents.

After several visits to the government offices, I continued to get the run-around. Finally, I consulted with a friend within the company who offered his help. I was annoyed when I was advised to pay the clerk some money under the table to get the necessary stamps on the documents. Finding no other way, I accompanied my friend to the government office. My friend spoke to the clerk and they reached an agreement. I was to walk down the hallway with 600 drachmas (about twenty dollars) in the palm of my hand and the clerk would walk alongside me and take the money. This was done. When I went to see the clerk again moments later, the stamps were placed on my documents and I was permitted to take my car out of Greece.

If they can change their regulations or become devious in dealing with me, I thought, I'll do the same. I'll take my money out any way I can. The company could not help, so I took matters into my own hands. Drachmas were hidden in the lining of my wife's vanity case, in clothing packed in suitcases and in the bottom of shoes. Gisela took the children in the car loaded with suitcases, drove to Patras (on Greece's western coast), passed through customs without incident and boarded a ferry for Genoa, Italy. They then took a leisurely drive through Italy, Switzerland and into Germany while I remained a few days longer in Greece before flying to Germany.

Greece left a lasting impression on our family. My wife and children (and, all too seldom, myself) spent summer days basking on the acropolis, learning the charms of sesame cakes, evenings in Piraeus, octopus tentacles and calamari, the blue Aegean Sea and the ruined remains witness to the birthplace of democracy and our western heritage. Duane grew so fascinated with Greece's past glory that he would one day earn a doctorate in Ancient History. It was a learning experience for me as well. Learning and adjusting to a different mentality would benefit me in the future.

Chapter 4
West Germany
Summer 1973

    The business in Dusseldorf, West Germany, was a separate division of the company promoting oil-additive products. Its marketing program was similar, so getting to know the product line was only a technicality.

    I was to be the V.P. of Sales and a new managing director (President) was coming from Italy. There had been three successive managing directors and V.P. of Sales in this company during its first year of operation. Numerous reasons were given why the company had not progressed but the net result was a dismal record of performance. My temporary assignment was to assist the new managing director until he got the operation on a positive footing.

    I arrived in advance of the newly appointed M.D. to sort things out. Two weeks later came the shocking news that the owner and founder of our conglomerate company had been killed in an airplane accident. It was his leadership that built the company and it was his philosophy of personal achievement that was the driving force behind its success. I had met the founder and spent a weekend on his yacht as a reward for winning the President's Club. I admired and respected him greatly. Without his leadership, I felt the company would never be the same.

    I was called to Rome, Italy for a meeting with Mr. Mitchell. A general distributors meeting was in process at a major hotel and many distributors from other European countries were present. As I watched the proceedings, I was pressed from behind. I turned and recognized Peter Stavros from Greece. On one occasion while performing my duties in Greece, I had been harsh with him, when he insisted on his wife becoming a cosmetic trainer, but she was not qualified for this position. He had sent a threatening message to me and I had simply ignored it refusing to be intimidated. Now he stood behind me and when I turned toward him, he showed me a large knife he had concealed in his trousers. He said, "the people of Greece have been ripped-off and someone is going to pay." I didn't answer him and turned away. I felt his threat was not directed at me but possibly at the leadership, Mr. Mitchell, and I couldn't ignore this possibility. I discretely walked away and sought Mr. Mitchell's assistant. I expressed my concern about a possible threat to Mr. Mitchell. Within the hour, two large muscular men were hired to protect him and I had identified Mr. Stavros for them. They kept a watchful eye on Stavros and were ready to take action if needed. Fortunately, there was no attempt to harm anyone but apparently just another effort to intimidate. In my meeting with Mr. Mitchell, I was informed of new changes and that the transfer of the managing director to West Germany was not to take place since he was needed elsewhere. Mr. Mitchell asked me to assume the post of managing director. He offered me $6,000 per month as salary, $10,000 for school expenses for the children, a five percent residual on the net profits, plus a house and car.

"I know the company is in financial trouble. I want you to examine the books and let me know how much is needed to turn things around. As soon as you tell me, I'll arrange to have the money transferred to you," said Mr. Mitchell.

I returned to Dusseldorf and examined the books. I soon discovered that the company was over $200,000 in debt. The rent for the office was past due and there were insufficient funds to pay the office staff. I requested $50,000. With this, I felt I could make partial payments to the creditors while I created my own cash flow by pumping up sales.

I learned that the previous management teams had all made promises to the people, which were not kept, and the people were now extremely skeptical. Déjà vu.

Upon informing Mr. Mitchell of my financial requirements, he said he would send me $35,000 within the next 24 hours. I immediately called a meeting of the distributors in the area.

Sixty-three distributors filed into the meeting room. When they were seated, I went to the front of the room and began the meeting.

"I want to thank you all for coming. As you know by now, I have been appointed as the new managing director. The death of the founder of this company is causing many changes. Change is the one thing most people resist, yet it is the one thing we can count on. To grow, to progress, means change. I understand there have been several leaders here before me and I also understand they have made many promises to you, left unfulfilled. I did not invite you here tonight to tell you what I'm going to do and to make promises. I will promise you only one thing, and that is, I will make no promises I cannot keep."

"Most of you now have a 'wait and see' attitude. With that attitude, nothing will happen. That, you can count on! I cannot do or accomplish anything without your cooperation and help. I can't do it alone. I need your help. If you are willing to work, I'll work with you. If you're not, why don't we just save each other a lot of time and close the doors now. I don't want that and I'm sure you don't either. You all joined this program to earn money. A wait and see attitude, or doing nothing, will produce nothing. Action is required. What has happened in the past we cannot change. Just as it's impossible to unfry an egg, it's impossible to change the past. We can start today to make things happen."

"How many here tonight will work with me? Can I see your hands?"

I waited. One by one, hands were raised. Then they started pounding their fists on the tables in front of them—the German sign of approval. I was elated. When the noise had stopped, I said, "I want to thank you for your support. I know we can turn this company around and make it successful. The company's success is a reflection of your own. We must work together. I want to meet each of you and will set appointments with you privately, starting tonight. Who may I speak with first?"

Over the next week, I met with each distributor. At the same time, I contacted the creditors and told them that they would be receiving a partial payment shortly. Those who gave me a hard time, I simply told them that they had no choice. If they chose not to wait, they could put the company into bankruptcy and get nothing. They agreed to wait.

Twenty-four hours passed and the money had not been transferred. Mr. Mitchell promised that the money would be there within the next twenty-four hours. It didn't arrive. I was then given excuses that due to the death of the founder; it was administrative problems that were holding things up. I believed what I was told and continued to make progress with the recruitment of new distributors and reactivating old ones. Things were happening and I was excited. However, my concern over the financial indebtedness of the company weighted heavily on my mind. I discovered that in Germany, when a company goes into the red, it must be reported to the authorities. If this isn't done, the managing director could become personally liable for the debt. Upon learning this, I delayed placing my name as managing director on the books or having my name registered as such with the authorities.

One month had passed and there was still no money transferred. I had created cash flow sufficient to cover the administrative salaries and the most pressing creditors but was unable to pay myself. I was optimistic that if the money would arrive and take off some of the pressure, I could have the company out of debt within a short period of time.

I continued to press for the money and twice more, the promises went unfulfilled. I then received a call from California. The international accountant was to make a fact-finding trip to see me to determine what the financial situation was. I told the accountant over the telephone that it was imperative that he arrive soon, otherwise there may be no company for him to visit; that the money was needed and that if it was not forthcoming, I recommended that the operation be shut down.

A few days later, the accountant arrived. Upon reviewing the situation, he agreed with my assessment. He left saying that he would recommend that the monies be sent forthwith.

It was several weeks before I received a phone call. The accountant advised me that Mrs. Patton, the founder's wife who became owner upon her husband's death, didn't want to put good money after bad and that any company that was not in the black was to be phased-out. He asked me to begin the phase-out and that a meeting was being set up in London with the European management and I was to attend.

This news was disappointing. My efforts were producing results but it was too little, too late. I thought of the distributors and how this would affect them. There was some inventory on the premises, so I began giving it to those distributors who had product credit with the company. The landlord discovered that product was being taken out of the office and promptly prohibited anymore from leaving the premises until the rent was paid. Of all the creditors, the landlord was the only one who had been unreasonable. He believed the mother company to be rich and that it could pay. I therefore held frequent meetings with each distributor. They would leave with a small amount of product concealed on their person when leaving the premises.

Prepaid air tickets were waiting at the airport for my trip to London. On my arrival, I checked into the hotel arranged for by the London office. The meeting was convened and I was questioned on how my phase-out had progressed, and they were all pleased. Mr. Mitchell chaired the meeting and informed me of the phase-out of a number of foreign operations. He told me, that at the moment there was no opening for me at another post but that I was first in line when an opening did occur. I was distraught over the news and the dilemma this placed me in. I felt Mr. Mitchell was sincere but distrusted his ability to make good on any promises since he had not been able to arrange the transfer of the money. "What do you suggest I do?" I asked. "What about the money that's owed to me?"

"How much do we owe you?"

"According to my calculations, it is exactly $12,000 in salary plus an additional amount for expenses."

"Give me the total figure and I'll have the office in Italy send the money to you. Where do you wish it sent?"

I was certain I wouldn't see the money for a long time, if ever, should I leave London without it.

"Mr. Mitchell", I said. "I've done everything you have asked. I have exhausted my own funds and I cannot even leave Germany without the money. I must have the money now!"

"Let me check with the office here in London and see if they can handle it," said Mr. Mitchell.

"Fine. Tell them I'm not checking out of this hotel until I get the money."

I returned to my room full of anxiety, wondering what to do next. In a little while, I received a call from the accountant at the London office. He called to verify the exact amount I requested. He said he would be at the hotel within the hour to pay me.

I made my air reservations and began to pack. One hour before flight time, there was a knock on my door. The accountant entered the room rather perturbed and gave me a statement to read. It said that the amount stated herein is all the monies due to me and that I would have no future recourse for any other claims against the company.

I signed the papers and the accountant counted out the equivalent of $13,500 in British pounds. After I had received and recounted the money, the accountant said, "By the way, you're only allowed to take 2,000 pounds out of the country - but that's your fuckin' problem."

I had less than an hour to catch my plane and my bags were already in the lobby, so I grabbed a pillowcase from the bed and stuffed the money inside. I went immediately to the lobby, checked out, and hailed a cab. The cab driver wanted the luggage to go into the trunk but I insisted it go with me in the back seat.

Enroute to the airport, I placed pound notes in small envelopes, some in my briefcase, some in my inside coat pocket and the larger remaining portion I stuffed under clothing in my suitcase.

When I arrived at the airport, I raced to the ticket counter but the counter was already closed and I was told to go directly to the gate. I was perspiring heavily. I knew I would be checked by airport security and that the risk of discovery was very real.

As I approached the security station, I exclaimed, "Please hurry, I'm about to miss my plane. Can someone please take my luggage to the plane?"

Security asked me to open my briefcase and made a cursory glance for weapons and immediately passed me through to the gate.

As I sat on the plane, I wondered if my luggage got on board. If for some reason it missed the plane, I would have to identify it by the description of its contents in the presence of customs and security personnel. I thought about the Greek operation and how fortunate I was that I did the right thing and left the country when I did. I learned that the law had come down on the company and the managing director had to be smuggled out of the country to avoid prosecution. I recalled the words of Napoleon Hill, "With every adversity, there is the seed of an equivalent or even greater benefit." With my new adversity, I wondered what the future had in store and what that benefit might be.

Upon arriving in Dusseldorf, Germany, I waited by the conveyor belt for my luggage. Everyone had picked-up their bags, and as I was about to leave the baggage claim area and report my loss, I noticed a lone piece of luggage at the far end of the conveyor belt begin to move my way. It was mine.

A few days later I departed Germany for the U.S.A. with my family. Shortly thereafter, the company filed for bankruptcy.

Chapter 5
Setting New Goals
Summer 1973—Spring 1974

The farm was gone, but I was the sole owner of the office building and training center complex in Pennsylvania, which now stood empty. I bought an inexpensive home and contemplated my future. The lure of the Middle East, especially Lebanon, preyed on my mind constantly. My entrepreneurial instincts were ripe for a new venture.

George Spiro called. He wanted to discuss a business proposition and was coming to see me. When George arrived, I learned of his plan to start a new business promoting costume jewelry and sell distributorships. He wanted me to be his partner and function as his Vice President. The memories of Greece were still fresh on my mind and at this point, I didn't want to get involved with him again. I politely refused, expressing my desire to do my own thing.

I went to my office daily. I rented out some of my office space and spent much time contemplating my future. I reminisced about the past, about what might have been, if only…. I knew I had to do something to create a new future. The lure of earning large sums of money consumed my thoughts. The adventure in foreign lands was also a factor. I could not imagine achieving my goals locally nor could I decide on a product or business that would satisfy me. Finally, I reached a decision. I would go to Lebanon. Gisela was delighted with the news and was supportive of my wishes.

I prepared the necessary documents to have my corporation, which owned the office building, serve as my company, and traveled to the

State Department in Washington, D.C. for the certifications I would need in my foreign business.

Using the office building as collateral, I secured a loan. I traveled to a cosmetic company in Toronto, Canada, negotiated an exclusive agreement on their entire line of cosmetic and toiletry products for the Middle East market, and placed an immediate order. I was always mindful of the problems that occurred in Greece and didn't want to go to Lebanon without product.

In order to maximize my capital, I liquidated all my possessions. My house and car were sold privately and my furniture was sold at public auction. I couldn't sell the office building since it was secured by my loan. I established contact with Edgard Zehil, the only person I knew in Beirut. I got permission to use his mailing address and then directed that the product be shipped. Not until the products were in the hands of the shipper did I make preparations to leave for Lebanon.

* * * * *

The pursuit of success was a driving force. Having earned a substantial amount of money in the past, having realized my dream of owning a farm, my future hopes dashed with the demise of my previous employer, made me more determined to make it on my own.

The training I had received and taught evolved around the success principles taught by numerous authors. My success bible was "Think and Grow Rich," by Napoleon Hill. Setting a goal, making a commitment, burning one's bridges. These principles had worked for me. I was willing to risk everything to make it happen again but in a bigger way. The greater the risks, the greater the rewards, was my firm belief. Go as far as you can see, and when you get there, you can see farther. This was the attitude I had about going to Lebanon. There were so many unknowns but I felt I could sort things out as I went, rather than playing it safe. My impulsive nature, getting fired-up, had produced results for me in the past. Although this excitement often ignored basic logic or caution, my persistence and determination usually overcame the obstacles.

Chapter 6
To Beirut, Lebanon
Spring—Fall 1974

    The feeling of adventure and intrigue about Beirut and other parts of the Middle East was exciting, but the fear of the unknown was a constant companion. I was alone.
    I secured a room at the Holiday Inn, the newest and most modern hotel in Beirut. It's convenient location made it a center for business with a view of the mountains and the sea. From the huge chandelier hanging in the lobby to the marble floors and spacious sitting areas, the decor of the hotel combined western and middle-eastern tastes.
    During my first week in Beirut, I did not wander far from the hotel. I tried to learn as much as I could about my surroundings and the people. From the balcony of my hotel room, I would gaze at the mountains and daydream while on other occasions simply watch the people as they made their way through the streets. I was fascinated by the traffic jams and the apparent disregard for any rules of driving—if indeed they existed. The unrelenting sound of car horns exemplified the driving habits. Seeking an advantage over other vehicles, cars inched their way through intersections. I had yet to discover the car horn's usefulness except to alert other drivers that the horn worked. Most drivers did not observe traffic signals and the only rule seemed to be, "Drive offensively."
    When I began driving in Beirut, I learned to be aggressive in order to make progress, yet remained extremely cautious. Right foot on the gas, left foot hovering over the brake pedal, both hands on the steering wheel with the thumbs arched over the horn. No time to look into the

rearview mirror. Eyes straight ahead, always alert and wary of what the driver in front might do. I learned that the assertive driving attitudes of the Lebanese were in sharp contrast to their behavior once they got out of a car. The Lebanese took life quite leisurely, as if time were limitless. If it were inconvenient to accomplish a task today, it could wait until tomorrow.

Naive to the Lebanese mentality or their basic customs, I met with frustration in my initial business dealings but learned quickly. One thing I needed to revise was my attitude towards punctuality. In North America and in Germany, I knew punctuality as not only a much admired virtue, but also as a matter of course in the business world. In Greece and in the Middle East it was not so. During my first weeks in business people made appointments to see me only to arrive invariably at least an hour late. I soon learned, however, that almost no one showed up on time for anything. It appeared to me that an eleven o'clock appointment, for example, probably meant that a person began thinking about going to his appointment at that time or that the appointment would be kept within the stated hour. It was I who needed to adjust. Although learning through trial and error was costly, those lessons were well learned.

I remember with amusement the very first Arabic phrase I learned. "Kief Halek" (How are you?), which they generally pronounce "Key fuck." At first I thought there was a lot of profanity and that American vulgarity had reached the Lebanese. To my chagrin, I learned otherwise. Customs that initially appeared suspect to me were common practice. I would be invited into a store to see their wares and thought it unusual to be offered coffee or tea. I assumed that if I accepted, I would be obligated to buy. I discovered that this hospitality was a typical Lebanese custom.

During my second week in Beirut, I interrupted my morning reverie from the balcony of my room and made my way to the elevator. I was shaken by what sounded like an explosion. The elevator doors and windows rattled and the floor vibrated. Before I could move, two more successive explosive sounds reverberated.

I raced back to my room and onto the balcony. Sirens were wailing and people were running from the streets looking skyward. At first I thought something within the hotel had exploded, but then realized that the people were looking at the sky and not at the hotel. Since I could see nothing to account for the explosion, I went down to the hotel lobby and asked the receptionist what had happened.

"It was Israeli planes breaking the sound barrier. Nothing to worry about."

"They must have been very low," I said. "How do you know they were Israeli planes?"

The receptionist shrugged his shoulders and said, "It happens all the time."

"What are all those sirens?" I asked.

"They're air raid sirens. People are supposed to go to air raid shelters but they don't anymore."

I walked outside. People were in the streets doing business as usual. I thought the guy at the reception desk must have been wrong. Those planes could be their own and they were just blaming it on the Israelis—but then why the sirens?

The following morning I read with interest the account in Beirut's English newspaper, which ran to this effect:

"Israeli war planes have again invaded our air space. Their disregard for the sovereignty of Lebanon continues. Protests against these intrusions continue to be made to the UN General Assembly with no result. Israel continues to deny these violations. No protest to this latest incident is planned, according to a statement issued by the Defense Ministry."

I felt embarrassed and wondered whether acts like these could affect me and my business especially with America's strong support for Israel. If the Israelis did do it, I thought, they must have been provoked and were simply showing their strength as a warning.

I became an avid reader of the local newspaper to learn about regional events and was offended at the charges laid against Israel. I felt the newspaper was biased and that if I was to learn the truth, I would have to read The London Times or other western papers.

I continued with the task of registering my company and located temporary living quarters for my family. I then sent word for Gisela to bring the family and join me in Beirut. Together we would find a more permanent place to live. In the meanwhile, I obtained a residence permit without difficulty.

Note: While in Greece and prior to our trip to Lebanon, I went to the US Embassy in Athens to have my name changed on my passport, from Abraham Firestone March to Abe F. March. I felt that with a name like Abraham it might be assumed that I was an Israeli. I wanted to avoid any cause for suspicion that would interfere with our visit. Now that I was in Lebanon, my passport with this name was useful.

My family arrived with excitement and the spirit of adventure. Gisela was eager to see and experience the fascinating things that she had read about the Middle East.

These surroundings were ideal for my twelve-year-old son, Duane, with his academic excellence and his interest in history. These surroundings made his craving for adventure a stage for learning. He was able make a quick adjustment to this new world and put old friends behind. Duane spent that first summer exploring the city's western half on foot and often walked several kilometers from our apartment to visit me at my office; often with his little sister in tow.

By contrast, our eleven-year-old daughter, Christine, was more easy-going. She was content to be in one place and liked making friends. It was difficult for her to leave familiar surroundings and adjust to change. However, her sense of adventure would grow as she matured and she would fall in love with the Middle East.

Our youngest daughter, Caroline, was nearly five years old. She could care less about where she was so long as she was with her family. She adjusted readily but nevertheless, her young age often made life difficult for her brother and sister.

The family responded well to their new life in Beirut. After a first few months in a small apartment near the sea, we moved into lodgings temporarily vacated by the Atwood family. Mr. Atwood worked at the University and was taking a sabattical. It was a spacious fourth floor apartment located on the Rue de Mexique. The residence was in an old building and had a Mediterranean charm with which the family fell in love: tiled floors, oriental carpets, irregular rooms set on different levels and a spacious balcony which overlooked the street and where we often ate, entertained or just sat. Although the building had no elevator, the climb up the stairs soon became routine. We placed containers in the kitchen always ready to collect drinking water that trickled through a special faucet for a short time each day. Bathing water came from barrel containers on the roof and flowed under its own pressure. These containers needed longer periods for refill and the water was used sparingly.

Each day, after the children left for school, Gisela would take Caroline and do her daily grocery shopping. Beggars held out their hands chanting unintelligible gibberish, repeating "Allah, Allah, Allah," as she passed them. As time went by, she became less charitable and more critical of the beggars. On one occasion she observed a man coming toward her leading a small boy who had his eyes closed and his hand outstretched, begging. She ignored them and continued on her way to the market. Upon her return home, she noticed the same man and boy on the other side of the street with their roles reversed. This time the boy was leading the man who had his eyes closed and his hand outstretched. Her amusement turned to bewilderment when she noticed passers-by looking strangely at her. Looking down, she saw Caroline with her eyes closed, holding out her hand also.

* * * * *

I quickly settled into a routine. Arising early each morning, I would exercise, make my breakfast and sit alone with my thoughts as I planned my day. I preferred to make my own breakfast and have some quiet time alone with coffee and a cigarette.

Being frugal with my finances, I would make my way to the office in a service taxi. The service taxi traveled along designated routes, much like a bus, and picked-up as many passengers that would fit inside. For thirty-five piastres (about fifteen cents), it would take me within a few blocks of my office. I disliked traveling this way yet tolerated the rank body odor and learned to ignore the stares of the other passengers who thought it strange for a foreign businessman to use a service taxi. A westerner, especially an American, was presumed to be rich. They attempted to emulate the westerner in appearance in what they thought to be 'American style.' Most of their impressions were formed from motion pictures depicting Americans driving big cars and being big spenders. Although Lebanon had its super rich, a large gap existed between those who actually were rich and those who professed to be. Having a car was a status symbol and made one rich in the eyes of the poor.

I would use a regular taxi on occasion but disliked haggling over price so early in the morning. It was easy to summon a taxi. I needed only to raise my hand and the rush was on to compete for the fare, which was expected to be higher than from locals. I finally learned to ask the fare beforehand or to hand the exact amount to the driver when leaving the taxi. Numerous complaints from western foreigners about being ripped-off had caused a new taxi company to have meters installed in their cabs.

Lebanon had once long been a protecrate of France and its second language French. All official documents were, besides Arabic, also written in French and the western street names were also in that language, hence "rue" instead of "street". Anyone with any pretence of culture and education had to be able to speak French. Exception was, however, made for British and Americans, as English was also a language much admired and increasingly learned. I was amazed at how many apparently humble Lebanese could speak at least a little English. It must have been a result of the business instinct for which the Lebanese were famed throughout the Middle East. After all, if you want to do business with (wealthy!) Americans or British, it's best to speak their language.

I acquired office space in a new building located near the "souk" area, or open market. This is an area mainly used by the Moslems to conduct business. A newly constructed highway, Rue Fouad Chehab, now ran from the downtown shopping area of Hamra district to the "souk" area with a turn-off that exited at my office building. The area adjacent to the office was Ashrafeyeh, a predominantly Christian neighborhood.

I hired Edgard Zehil as my managing director. Edgard was my first connection in Beirut. I had met him on my first visit to Beirut in 1973, while working in Greece. Edgard had arranged the conference meeting for our Greek company. We had taken 35 people with us to Beirut for a special training conference as a reward for special sales persons. When the conference was finished and ready to return to Greece, it appeared that George Spiro did not have sufficient funds to pay the hotel bill. The hotel manager would not let us check out without full payment. To solve the problem, I agreed to remain behind with my wife until George could wire the funds from Greece to pay the balance.

During this stay in Beirut, Gisela and I had the pleasure of seeing more of the city and Edgard had been our guide. I was also to get my first impression of the Lebanese. I had brought with me sixty thousand Greek drachmas ($2,000) that I wanted to have exchanged in dollars. I placed the money on the bed while I was dressing and asked my wife to put it in her purse. We were in a hurry for our morning meeting and both left the room unaware that the money was still lying on the bed. When I returned to my room at lunchtime, a man was standing by my door. When I opened the door, he followed me inside, pointing to the money on the bed. He said he had found it there when he was cleaning the room and waited for me to return so it wouldn't be missing. I was most grateful to him yet surprised that the money had not been stolen.

Although there are many honest people, there are also many thieves. Beirut was a haven for thieves. Many could be instantly recognized or suspected as being thieves by the absence of an ear, an arm or a foot. This was the punishment accorded thieves by Moslem law. The number of offenses often determined the number of body parts missing. Being so marked, they left their own country and found refuge in Lebanon.

Either my "office boy", Amin, or I was the first to arrive at the office each morning. Amin was one of three Lebanese nationals I hired to comply with government regulations. He was paid the minimum wage amounting to 250 Lebanese pounds per month—approximately $100.

Amin was, however, no boy. He was fifty-nine years of age but looked much older. The lines on his face and deep-set eyes accentuated his beak-like nose. He could not stand completely erect and walked in a stooped position. The heavy-boned features on his scrawny frame revealed a hard life. Amin had worked as a debt laborer, paying the debts left by his father, and this had taken virtually a lifetime to settle. He could not speak any English but I found him to be completely honest and a faithful employee.

Each day, Amin stationed himself outside the office door where he could observe all who entered and what they departed with. Although Amin was expected to tidy the office, his efforts left a trail of disorder. Other than his 'watch-dog' activity, Amin ran errands and picked-up the mail as his primary function.

The first time my son, Duane, came to my office, Amin bowed, placed his hand over his heart in salute, then kissed him on the head. Being my eldest and only son, Duane received the high esteem that a son was accorded. In Arab tradition, he would be the one who would one day become head of the family. Sons are highly valued and accorded special respect. I still remember my son's surprised reaction when Amin kissed him and then his proud smile when he realized what that gesture meant. Needless to say, he never let his sisters, who had been present on that occasion, hear the end of it.

Several months after starting my business, I discharged Edgard Zehil as my managing director. He had been useful in implementing the business and in fulfilling the legal requirements but failed in his performance. Edgard felt his role did not include work to generate business. He was so enthralled with his title that he spent most of his time at the tennis courts. He accepted the dismissal in good spirits having gained prestige in working as a managing director for a western company.

On the day Edgard departed, I asked him to write down a series of English words and phrases for refreshments with their Arabic equivalents. In his absence, I would now have to order my own refreshments and I needed a method to communicate with Amin until I found a replacement.

A refreshment concession, located on the first floor of the office building, supplied all its occupants and they were expected to use it. It was customary to offer refreshments to guests entering the office. A direct telephone line existed to the concessionaire stand much like hotel room service. Since they did not speak English, Amin himself fetched the refreshments. Within an hour of Edgard's departure, I summoned Amin into my office.

"Amin, please bring me a cup of coffee," I said, pointing to the word in Arabic. Amin bowed and departed. He returned with a glass of water. I accepted the water deciding it was my own mistake and that Amin had erroneously read 'water' instead of 'coffee.' I waited a reasonable length of time and again summoned Amin. Carefully, I pointed to the word 'coffee' and repeated, "Coffee, Amin. Coffee!"

Amin bowed and departed as before. A few minutes later Amin returned with another glass of water. Not to be defeated, I drew a picture of a cup with steam rising from the top. "Coffee, coffee!" I said, pointing to the drawing.

Amin left and this time returned with the long-awaited coffee. Later that same day I summoned Amin requesting a bottle of 7-UP and pointed to the correct Arabic word for 7-UP.

Amin bowed, departed and returned with a cup of coffee.

"No, no, not coffee!" I shouted. "7-UP!"

Amin looked bewildered. At that moment, my attorney, Claude Chaiban, walked into the office.

"Claude, you're just the man I need to solve a problem."

I explained the morning's difficulties in communicating with Amin and asked him to look at the list of words to see if there was an error.

Claude studied the list and said, "It's correct. I don't understand why you had this problem. Let me talk with Amin."

Claude spoke with Amin making reference to the refreshment list. Finally, he dismissed Amin and said, "Mr. March, I'm afraid Amin can't read or write."

At this, both Claude and I broke out laughing. "You'll have to learn Arabic if you work here. Not everyone speaks English nor does everyone read and write," explained Claude.

With Claude's help and by phonetically writing the Arabic words, I learned the few simple words required to obtain refreshments, but a different problem soon arose.

The refreshment concession had recently changed hands with Ali Khalil as its new owner. New tenants were filling the office building, and Ali could be seen running up and down the elevator and stairwell with the aroma of coffee trailing behind him. Ali spoke a little English, and in order to use it, he would personally deliver any refreshments I requested.

"Good morning, sir. At your service, sir," he would say as he entered my office. For a time, I continued to order regular coffee from Ali but did not enjoy it. Although I drank Turkish coffee when it was offered and had even acquired a taste for it, it was no substitute for a cup of American-style coffee.

The pot of American coffee I brought to the office was now brewing in the next room. Ali's eyes roamed about in search of the source of the coffee aroma, which met him as he served refreshments to my guests. Ali suspected something was wrong since I no longer ordered coffee from him.

Early one morning, Ali walked into my office with a big smile. There, perched on his tray, was an American-type coffee mug.

"Good morning, Mr. March. Americanish coffee, special for you. At your service, sir."

I eyed the cup as Ali placed it on my desk. The coffee was milky white. Although I used milk, I used very little and never any sugar. The milk they used was already sweetened even though I emphatically requested, no sugar!

I reluctantly picked up the cup as Ali stood by awaiting approval. I sipped the coffee. It was terrible. It tasted sweet and had an odd burnt flavor. I did not wish to offend Ali nor did I wish to encourage him. I now had my own coffee pot and no longer wished to order from him.

"You now make American coffee?" I asked.

"Ali's eyes lit up and he said, "Yes, I buy new coffee machine—just for you. I now have American coffee. You like, yes?"

"It's fine. How much is it?" I asked.

"No, no, Mr. March. I no charge you for this cup. This special for you. I go now. You want more coffee, you call me."

I continued to make my own coffee but I would frequently order a cup from Ali, which I did not drink. I learned to accept graciously what was offered in order to be hospitable but felt that what I did behind closed doors was my own business. Refusal to accept what was offered could be considered a personal rejection and being accepted was paramount to operating a successful business.

Whenever I had difficulty conveying a point of view or communicating my thoughts, I was often confronted with the expression, "You don't understand the Arab mentality." I wanted to know about this so-called mentality but no one could explain it. Realizing that the Arab thinking and actions are rooted in the Koran (the Moslem Scripture), I sought an English translation. I was told that the Koran could not be properly translated or that it was too difficult to explain. I was delighted when I found an English translation of the Koran. I was determined to learn from it so I could better understand them.

Each day, I read a chapter or two of the Koran. It was difficult reading with many footnote references, but I diligently read on. It was enlightening to discover the similarities between the Christian and the Moslem doctrines. Whereas Jesus is the anointed one, the Son of God for the Christians, for the Moslem, Jesus is a prophet, highly esteemed and perhaps second only to Mohammed. In fact, all the old testament prophets are honored as such in Islam. Abraham ("Ibrahim"), through his first son Ishmael, is the father not only of the Hebrews, but of the Arabs as well. Although Christians and Jews had historically enjoyed an inferior status throughout Moslem lands, they were also protected by Islamic law as "Peoples of the book." Mohammed is the last, and greatest, of the prophets, the prophet of 'Allah' (the Arabic word for God, just as the Jews called him "Yahweh" or "Jehovah"). The teachings of Mohammed, as recorded in the Koran, are followed by the Moslems. Unlike Christianity, Islam concentrates on good works on earth. It is believed that the after life will be determined through one's deeds on earth. Moral behavior is a high priority in living. To become a Moslem, one simply must proclaim his belief in God. They believe that everyone is born a Moslem (with a basic belief in God) and later becomes something else by choice.

The sensitivity of the Arabs is often disguised by an outward display of warmth, which can be deceptive. You might offend them and not even know it. It is their custom to be gracious and hospitable. They do their best not to offend. Islam is rather explicit on the duties of the host to aid and protect his guest and not to harm him no matter the provocation. This is especially true when dealing with a foreigner. They will not openly disagree with his views even though they may strongly disagree. If they are offended, they may continue to do business with you but take pleasure in cheating you in business. Depending on the severity of the offense, you might even be blacklisted. If there is physical abuse, you could wind up dead. Conversely, if you are liked and accepted, they will assist you in every way possible. Acceptance can be as simple as giving them respect for their beliefs, a willingness to understand and observe their customs and a genuine concern for their benefit in business dealings.

Reading the Koran earned me much respect from my Arab acquaintances and I acquired a better understanding of them.

Ali noticed the Koran lying on my desk and inquired about it. "It's the Koran, Ali, I wish to understand your religion," I said.

"You good man, Mr. March. You my brother."

The next day Ali handed me a pocket-sized version of the Koran written in Arabic. "This for you, my brother, Mr. March." I thanked him and placed it on my desk.

* * * * *

There was never a dull moment. Each activity brought new insights and the unexpected became the norm.

One evening, Gisela and I were standing in line waiting for admission to the opera. I felt a tugging at my suit jacket and looked down on a small barefoot girl who appeared to be about four or five years old. She held our her hand begging for money. Attempting to ignore her, I turned away but she kept tugging at my coat. She was rather dirty and I was worried that she would soil my suit. I repeatedly told her to go away, but each time I turned from her, she turned with me and continued tugging. I didn't want to look in her eyes simply because I knew if I did, I would feel compelled to give her something.

When I first arrived in Beirut, I was an easy mark for the beggar. Each time a hand was held out, I felt obliged to give something. After awhile, I simply tried to ignore them. This little girl, however, was not to be ignored. She persisted until I reached down to push her away. When I looked into those sad brown eyes, dirty face and straggly hair, I couldn't resist. I reached into my pocket and gave her some money. She bowed, thanking me as she backed away, then went running down the street. I often thought of her persistence. She knew what she wanted and persisted until she got it.

As a family, we tried to fit into the lifestyle of the Lebanese as best we could. Where most foreigners in Lebanon bonded together trying to maintain the social standards of their own country, we deliberately sought the experience of the culture in which we lived. Instead of frequenting western-style grocery stores, Gisela favored purchasing things on the open market.

Bargaining was a way of life. Merchants gave discounts because, "You are a good customer, you are a friend of the family, this was your first time in the store, etc.,"—any excuse to make you feel special to reduce the price. Gisela became quite accomplished at bargaining with the street merchants. She would offer half the price asked. When it was refused, she would turn to walk away, then be called back and provided with a reason why they would agree to a lower price. Christine also became adept at bargaining. She would use the customary twist of the hand to inquire "how much," then raise her eyebrows signifying, "no." The bargaining would continue until both could agree. If you paid the asking price, you were obviously a foreigner and easy prey. The easy prey were those who refused to assimilate, then complain about being ripped-off. The cultural aspects of living in Lebanon touched every member of the family in some way. Sunday at the beach was the highlight of the week. Beautifully tanned bodies were part of the excitement and charm of the beaches. The children would romp in the sand and surf, squealing with delight as the waves rolled over them. I enjoyed playing volleyball with my Lebanese friends who each week would erect a volleyball net on the beach. I'd play until exhausted, then race to the water and wallow in the surf washing the sand from my body and some relief from the heat.

Tourists were easily spotted with their lily-white bodies turning pink, then red; the natives urging them to get out of the sun. Gisela disliked direct sun. She usually sat under a beach umbrella reading a book but enjoying the family's delight at play.

The Lebanese, with all their faults, are indeed hospitable and a joy to be with. They are carefree and enjoy life to its fullest. Contrary to the hustle and bustle of western life with its rigid schedules, they take their time. Family is an important part of their life and they come together, especially at mealtime. The head of the family listens to any problems of the family members and offers solutions. Each one helps the other in business and provides support during hard times. The family is expected to be home for the noon meal where they can relax before going back to work. The quick bite of the westerner, too busy to eat, is difficult for them to understand. One must rest, relax and enjoy the moment. Business can wait. There's always tomorrow.

Chapter 7
Christmas in the Cedars of Lebanon
December 1974

    The winter snow further enhances the picturesque mountains of Lebanon overlooking Beirut and the sea. Within an hour's drive from the city, one can ski and return to the city the same day for a swim. The natives seldom swim during the winter months but tourists, especially from Europe, find the water warm. North of Beirut, near the town of Becharre, are the famous cedars of Lebanon and the birthplace of the Lebanese poet, Kahlil Gibran. Having read his books, we wanted to visit his birthplace and hoped to travel there during the upcoming holidays.

    Christmas was near and I felt a small party at the office would be appropriate. Not yet being in a strong financial position, I decided to have a small gathering of distributors and staff in the office. A wine and cheese party was not the customary Lebanese way of celebrating such an event but it was looked upon with excitement as having an "American-style party."

    We acquired a record player and some hit American recordings. Amin moved about the office keeping his eye on things. He was excited but kept his distance. I encouraged him to join the party but he drank his wine and stayed at his post by the doorway. I was told that he had once been a heavy drinker consuming large quantities of "arak," the strong native drink (akin to the Greek ouzo). Now, with some wine in his stomach, Amin began to tap his shoes and sway with the music. I insisted that he join the others. By this time everyone was feeling good and Amin's presence would not be offensive. Amin began to dance. He reminded me of 'Jed Clampet' of the TV series, "The Beverly Hillbillies." He stomped his feet and danced about Arabic-style with arms outstretched mimicking the words to the music. He was the life of the party. He danced with the girls and it was obvious that everyone was enjoying themselves. However, it was the last time anyone saw Amin so happy and with so much energy.

Albert Tabet, one of my distributors, learned that I wanted to spend Christmas near the cedars and took it upon himself to help me find suitable accommodations. He brought his friend, Mr. Abiad, to see me. After the customary coffee, Mr. Abiad talked about the villa he had in Becharri, which he said he would be pleased to rent to me for the Christmas holidays. I was delighted but wanted more details.

"Is it furnished?" I asked.

"Yes, it has everything."

"Including dishes and bedding?"

"Yes, and it has a fireplace."

It sounded great. I could visualize the family sitting by the fire in a cozy villa but was concerned that a villa might be too expensive. A villa meant a complete house. Apartments were referred to as houses while houses were called villas.

"Is it heated?" I inquired.

"Yes, it has heat and my son lives nearby and will help you if there is anything you wish. Just ask him—he is at your service."

"How much would it cost for five days?" I asked.

"Five hundred pounds (approximately $200)," he replied.

I thought for a few moments then said, "I'll take it."

The long-awaited day arrived. After loading the luggage in a rented car, the family piled in and we were off. The route north took us along the sea. This was the same route some of the world's greatest conquerors had followed, along the 'Nahr El Kalb" (Dog River). We were intrigued by inscriptions on rocks put there by Egyptian, Hittite, Assyrian, Babylonian, Greek, Roman, Arabic, French and English. Some of them dated back over 3000 years.

We passed by Jounieh on our way to Jbail (Byblos). Four thousand years ago, Byblos was already a very old city and an important trading place, especially for the exporting of the expensive cedar wood. We wanted to see more of Byblos but decided that another trip would be necessary to fully explore this historic city and its remnants from the Crusades.

Before reaching Tripoli, the northernmost city of Lebanon, I turned off the highway at Chekka and headed toward the mountains. As we made our ascent it became noticeably cooler. The road was narrow and steep commanding attention to the road. With no traffic, I was able to make frequent stops to take in the magnificent view. White foam from the waves lined the seacoast accentuating the blue water dotted with sailboats and other vessels. It was enchanting to envision the ancient vessels sailing from these shores with their cargoes of cedar.

Excitement mounted as snow appeared in patches, then graduated from a thin layer to heavy mounds of drifted snow creating bare patches among the sparse foliage on the mountainside. Gisela gave the historical narration reflecting on how it must have looked thousands of years ago when these hills were covered with cedar trees. Solomon had used famous cedars of Lebanon from these hills to build his temple. The pharaohs of Egypt prized their wood, which had also been used for making boats and other precious items until the demand for cedar wood left these hills barren. Now only a few hundred cedars from the original forest remain and are protected by the government.

As we approached Becharri, we were intrigued by the winding road leading up, then down again around a huge gorge that at one time served as a natural fortress for the city poised on the side of the mountain. As the sun disappeared behind the mountain, the road became slippery and the driving hazardous as melted snow started to freeze on the highway.

At Hotel Chbatt, I asked for directions to the villa.

"Can you direct me to Mr. Abiad's villa?" I asked. "Mr. Abiad said I should ask here."

"You are Mr. March?"

"Yes, I am."

"I am Josef, Mr. Abiad's son. Welcome to Becharri. Would you like a coffee?"

"No thanks, my family's in the car and we'd like to get settled. Could you please show me the way?"

"We followed Josef up a hill and came to a stop in front of a four-story building. Josef got out of his car and came toward us.

"This is it," said Josef.

I was puzzled. "Are you sure this is the place? I rented a villa."

"Yes, yes, this is the place."

We followed Josef into the building and climbed the four flights of stairs to the top floor. Josef inserted the key in the door and announced, "Ahlan, wa sahlan (Welcome, twice welcome)."

"Shoukran," I replied. Without another word, Gisela and I entered the apartment. It was freezing cold inside and looked empty.

"This is not a villa," I said.

"Yes, yes, it is villa!"

"But Mr. Abiad said it was heated. It's cold in here."

"I turn on heat for you," he replied.

Gisela and I walked through each room and then into the kitchen. It was bare except for a small stove with no butane bottle, and a small table with no chairs. There were only three bunk-type beds in the entire place and the marble floors were bare.

I turned to Gisela and said, "We can't stay here. It's too cold. The children will get sick."

Josef overheard the conversation and said, "It's better you stay at hotel. It's warm and I put money you pay for villa to your hotel room."

I suspected I was the victim of 'bait and switch.' I decided to at least look at the hotel rooms and see what the accommodations would be. Perhaps we could stay the night at the hotel until we could decide what to do.

We returned to the hotel and were escorted to a suite of rooms. As soon as the light was switched on, a huge cockroach scurried across the room. We went no farther.

"That does it," exclaimed Gisela. "I'm not staying here!"

I was irritated and tired. Even though the hotel was warm, I was determined to get what I had bargained for.

I turned to Josef and told him that we would stay in the house. I asked him to turn on the heat, get some beds in the house and butane for the stove. I told him we'd need dishes, and I'd let him know if there was anything else we would require.

Reluctantly, Josef said, "As you wish, sir."

The first task was to get some heat and I asked Josef where I could get some logs for the fireplace. He gave directions to a small store at the edge of the village. I loaded the trunk of my car with twisted roots and other gnarled, ice-covered wood, and purchased some lighter fuel to ignite the fire. After lugging the wood up the four flights of stairs with the help of my son, I set about starting a fire as the family looked on. The fire ignited quickly with the aid of the fuel. Feeding bits of twigs and paper, the children poked at the fire as it snapped and hissed.

Josef brought a bottle of butane and Gisela began preparing some food. I closed the doors to all the other rooms and moved the beds into the living room by the fireplace. The room soon felt warmer but we were not yet ready to shed our jackets. The radiators were banging from the air in the pipes but they were still cold.

In the meanwhile, pots, pans and a few dishes arrived. I asked for a carpet to be placed on the cold marble floor in front of the fireplace and Josef acquired one.

Gisela produced a scanty evening meal from the canned foods we brought with us. Hot soup was like medicine and warmed our bodies as we sipped, slurped and smacked our lips.

We bedded down in front of the fireplace but I couldn't sleep much. I was constantly waking to place more wood on the fire. However, the contented slumber of the family made me feel good.

It wasn't long before the morning sun came streaming through the uncovered window and its warmth penetrated my blanket. I drowsily opened my eyes and looked at the fire. It was smoldering but needed more wood. Grudgingly I got up and quietly placed one of the few remaining twisted objects on the hot coals and poked at it until a small flame began curling around the wood. I then crawled back to my bed to enjoy as much of the time remaining before the children would stir and want their breakfast.

It wasn't long before I heard the children talking but no one got up.

They remained snuggled in their beds; however, the constant babble of voices prevented further sleep.

I got up and went to the window. The magnificent view dispelled any discomfort. Smoke curled upward from chimneys of the small houses below with the windows reflecting the sun on the mirror-like surface of the snow. Viewing the entire village, I imagined how this setting had given Kahlil Gibran the inspiration to write his poetry. The mountains surrounding this peaceful village seemingly protected its inhabitants from the outside world.

My thoughts were interrupted when I heard Caroline say, "I'm hungry, Daddy. When do we get something to eat?"

When I entered the hallway, I was fully awake. The bathroom felt like a cold storage compartment. There was no hot water, so I placed a full pot of water on the stove and lit the fire.

Gisela prepared breakfast and brought it into our makeshift bedroom by the fireplace. After breakfast, sponge baths were also taken by the fireplace, which caused some excitement. The children were enjoying themselves and the inconvenience was no bother to them.

The first full day in Becharre we spent stocking up on food and arranging more living comfort. Then, we embarked on our outing to the ski slopes.

As we drove up the mountain and rounded a sharp curve, there before us was a small grove of old cedars. Fresh snow decorated the branches of these ancient trees, some of which had stood there for more than a thousand years. We stopped for a closer look and walked among the trees. The children romped in the snow and sank to their shoulders where drifts had concealed ravines and ditches.

Just around the corner from the cedars, the barren ski slope came into view dotted with skiers making their way down trails while others were on their way up on the ski lift.

Spills and thrills made it a real fun day. A tired but happy troop returned to the house that night but the excitement of Christmas Eve diminished the weariness. This night we would exchange our Christmas gifts, as was the German tradition that we had adopted from my wife, and the children were impatiently waiting for the moment to arrive.

Gisela served a hot meal. When we finished eating, Duane took Caroline for a walk to look for Santa. When they were gone, I sneaked outside to get the gifts stowed in the trunk of my car. When I made my entrance, the children were singing Christmas Carols by the fireplace. Their rosy cheeks, the sparkle in their eyes all added to the merriment of Christmas Eve.

After we exchanged gifts, the children expressed their sentiments that it was their best Christmas, ever.

* * * * *

Shortly after Christmas, I arrived at the office to find Amin slumped in his chair by the door.

"Marhaba, Amin. Kief Halek?"

"Mniih, ilhamdilla," replied Amin, rising slowly from his chair. He bowed slightly while placing his hand over his heart in salute. He sat back down very slowly and I noticed how tired he looked. Soon my new secretary, Houry Kojayian, arrived. I exchanged greetings with her and couldn't help but again notice her appearance. She was short and chubby with kinky black hair that surrounding her acne-scarred face. Despite her appearance, she was pleasant, efficient and spoke English, Armenian and Arabic. I had hired her for these reasons and also for the low salary she willingly accepted.

I sat down at my desk and busied myself with a backlog of work. Suddenly, Houry rushed into my office.

"I think something is wrong with Amin. Please, you better have a look, Mr. March."

Amin was sitting with his head lying on Houry's desk. His motionless eyes stared straight ahead and his body hung limp.

"Call for an ambulance immediately," I said. "I'll try to make him more comfortable."

By the time the ambulance arrived, Amin had rallied somewhat, but he was holding his chest and I presumed that he had suffered a heart attack. I was not only concerned for Amin's health but what legalities might be involved if he died on the job. I had not considered this before and had no knowledge of the Lebanese law in such an eventuality. However, my first concern was Amin's health.

The ambulance attendants took a long time to reach the office. They shouted and argued among themselves, barking instruction on how and where to place the stretcher. After loud and long deliberations, the attendants finally lifted Amin onto the stretcher and proceeded toward the elevator, a mere fifteen feet from the office door. The elevator was small and the stretcher could not possibly fit inside, except to stand it on its end. They did not consider using the stairwell and with more discussion, they asked Amin to stand up. Amin did as he was told and slowly got himself off the stretcher and walked with the attendants into the elevator. Upon reaching the lobby, the attendants led Amin out of the elevator and then had him lie down on the stretcher again. They carried him to the ambulance, which was parked not more than twenty feet from the entrance. The attendants once again had Amin get off the stretcher, and then helped him climb into the rear of the ambulance.

I stared in disbelief. The whole scene reminded me of something I once saw on the 1960's TV comedy show "Get Smart". It would have been enough to make one laugh if the situation had not been so serious. With handling like this, I thought he might not make it to the hospital. I decided to go to the hospital and make sure he received proper treatment.

I followed the ambulance in a taxi to a Catholic hospital in Ashrafeyeh. For the fourth time, the attendants had Amin get off the stretcher. After he was out of the ambulance, he was placed on the stretcher and carried into the hospital where he was left lying in a curtained-off section of the emergency room. I stood next to him. I wanted to talk to Amin, comfort him, but could not communicate with him in Arabic. However, his eyes told me that he was grateful I was there.

After waiting what seemed a very long time, I walked into the outer office to see if someone would attend to Amin. My appearance, as a foreigner, brought immediate help. A doctor looked at Amin briefly and said he thought Amin had suffered a heart attack but wanted some tests made. Since there were no hospital orderlies available to assist, I wheeled Amin to the various departments for X-ray and other tests and waited patiently in the corridor with him until it was his turn to be seen.

Houry finally caught up with me. "Is Amin all right?" she asked.

"I really don't know. This place is impossible. I think they would have let him lie where he was if I had not been here. Who would have taken him for these tests?"

"Mr. March. Amin is a poor man. Unless they know they will get paid, they will do nothing for him. I think you must pay some money then they will do something."

"Thanks. That didn't occur to me. Whom should I see?"

Houry talked to one of the doctors. The doctor smiled and looked in my direction then walked over to me.

"May I be of some service? I'm Dr. Tabit."

"Amin appears to have suffered a heart attack," I said. "I want him to have the best of care and would you please see that his tests are completed at once. I will assume responsibility for the hospital costs."

"At once, sir. You leave him in my care. I will arrange everything," said Dr. Tabit.

Within a week, Amin was released from the hospital and several weeks later, he was dead.

I was saddened by Amin's death. I had visited him in the hospital and he had expressed his gratitude in the best way he could. His eyes, the gestures of his hands and arms expressed his feelings. Once released from the hospital however, there was no way he could be readmitted without my help. Amin lived in a small village in the hills and word had not reached me that he was again ill. To be sure, Amin was elderly, but the plight of all the poor was the same for those in Lebanon who did not have the means to pay. Social security and welfare does not exist in Lebanon. It is up to each family to care for its own and that family bond is very strong. To be born into a rich family is to have continued wealth and prestige. The poor are left to fend for themselves in a daily struggle for survival with little or no hope for a better life.

Chapter 8
A Change in Attitude
Spring 1975

Most people ignored the deplorable conditions of the refugee camps in Lebanon. When I first became aware of the refugees, I assumed that their plight was of their own making. I didn't understand the full reasons for their presence, and the Lebanese didn't wish to discuss it. Lebanon preferred to be neutral and avoid trouble. It seemed that their attitude was to ignore the problem and hope that it would go away. The Palestinians living in these camps were their brothers and temporary guests. They felt it unwise to speak ill of them, but their presence caused most Lebanese some discomfort since any militant actions by the Palestinian Commandos would provoke Israeli retaliation against Lebanon.

* * * * *

Christine was fond of horses. Riding horseback was one of the things she missed most when we sold our farm in Pennsylvania. For Christine's twelfth birthday, she wanted riding lessons at the Beirut Riding Stable and we granted her wish.

It was a beautiful morning in Beirut. Christine had made friends with a schoolmate who had a horse stabled at a riding club adjacent to a Palestinian refugee camp. This day, Christine was accompanying her friend to the stables along with other students who went for their weekly riding lessons. Duane took Caroline to the ACS (American Community School) playground. Gisela was at the AUH (American University Hospital) coffee shop doing volunteer work and I was at my office.

I was drinking my second cup of coffee, and from where I sat, I could see the crowded street bustling with activity and hear the normal street noise. Suddenly, the air was pierced with the shrill roar of jet aircraft streaking low overhead. I rushed to the window and caught a brief glimpse at three jets before they disappeared from sight over the buildings. I first thought the sounds of explosions were from the planes breaking the sound barrier, but then noticed heavy smoke accompanied by the sound of gunfire.

I stood frozen by the window. The smoke was rising from the general area of the riding club. All too quickly I realized what had happened. The planes had bombed the Palestinian camp and Christine was practically next-door at the riding stables.

Sirens started blaring and the telephone went dead—deliberately cut for security reasons. There was no way to communicate with Gisela and access to the riding club would be cut off, making any attempt to get there useless. A feeling of helplessness possessed me as I walked aimlessly around the office trying to remain calm and wondering what to do. Within a short while the 'all clear' siren blew, and the telephone functioned when I tried it again. I was told that Gisela was not at the hospital but was on her way home. There was no answer to my call home and my emotions were starting to get the best of me. In my exasperation, I blurted, "If they have hurt my daughter, I'll fight them myself." At that moment, the telephone rang.

"Have you heard anything from Christine?" asked Gisela.

"No, have you? Do you know what happened?"

"The Israelis just bombed the Palestinian camp next to the stables." Gisela's voice was choked as she continued. "Some of the school officials are on their way to the stables now. They said they would bring all the students back with them. They will be permitted access to the area. I wish there was something we could do."

"There's nothing we can do, sweetheart. Don't worry; I'm sure everything will be all right. Why don't you stay by the phone in case anyone calls. I'll come home. I'm leaving now. Don't worry!"

I knew my words were useless, and I too was worried. The ambulance sirens only increased my apprehension. All roads leading to the area were blocked-off allowing only emergency vehicles to pass. The taxi made a detour from the heavy traffic and got me home without much delay.

Gisela met me at the door and threw her arms around me. Silently we held each other. Her tears wet my shirt and I fought back my own emotions with the helplessness of the situation.

As we waited for the telephone to ring, my outrage toward Israel for this air raid made me think of my changing attitude. I remembered my feelings in 1967, while working for IBM. We all rooted for the one-eyed General, Moshe Dayan, exclaiming how he should kill "those damned Arabs, those trouble makers." Reading the papers each day, we had all applauded Israel's military conquests, having no idea what the troubles were about, nor did I take the time to find out. We all reacted to the news. The United States supported Israel and as a patriot, that was enough for me.

It seemed a long time before the telephone rang.

"Mr. March?"

"Yes?"

"Christine would like for you to pick her up. She's here at the school."

"Is she all right?"

"Yes, she's fine but rather shook up."

"I'll be right there," I said, and immediately left the house.

I found Christine waiting for me on the school steps. I asked her if she was OK.

She nodded her head, yes, but said nothing. She remained silent on the way home. Her face was white and she just stared with a blank look. I wanted to say something but couldn't find the words. Arriving home, I placed my arm around her shoulder and walked her to the door where Gisela was waiting. She threw her arms around Christine, holding onto her, sobbing with relief.

For several days, Christine seemed to have no appetite. When she was ready, she told us what happened. Here is how she described it:

"Everyone saddled up after grooming the horses and we went to the exercise ring. I sat on a bench and watched. Everything was going as usual when we heard a series of shots. It sounded like loud firecrackers and then it stopped. The horses were fidgety and nervous and not very cooperative."

"Then, all of a sudden, there was an explosion of machine gun fire all around us. The riders half jumped, half fell, and we all stood looking around in confusion trying to make sense of what was happening. Then we saw them. There were three jets screaming above us. They were so low that we could see the cockpits and the heads of the pilots. I saw one of the jets spraying bullets on the Palestinian camp. I saw the trace of the bullets as they fell from the sky."

"I turned to my friend Laura, who was crouching under the tree next to the bench where I had been sitting, trying to hold onto her horse. I looked at her and yelled, 'what is happening?' She said, 'We're being attacked!'"

"At this point I was still in a state of confusion and I yelled, 'did this ever happen before?' What I meant was, did it ever happen to her before, and she yelled, 'No!' That's when I began to feel a helpless fear, mixed with trying to make sense of what was happening."

"We crouched under that tree what seemed an eternity. There was so much noise and confusion. The screams of the women and children coming from the camp, made it even more frightening. People were running around in panic and men were shooting their rifles at the aircraft. So much happened all at once."

"Then, everything quieted down and the riding instructor yelled for us all to make for the main house. Laura and I ran like crazy for the entrance to the ring, and just as we rounded the corner, we almost ran into a gunman, with his head wrapped in a koufieh, holding a rifle. Laura took one look at him, handed him the reins of her horse, and we both ran into the house. All the others were already there, sitting against the stonewall of the house. We sat with them. We could hear the bombing and gunfire as the planes circled and continued shooting. We hoped that the bombs would not fall on us."

"We didn't talk much. We mostly stared at each other. Our hopes would be raised, and then the shooting would start again."

"I don't know how long it lasted, but when the men who defended the grounds came and told us the jets had finally flown away, we tried to get through on the telephone to the school for them to send cars for us. This took awhile because they wanted to be sure that the bombing had stopped. The Palestinian camp was horrible. Bodies lying there that didn't move. The screams of the wounded were horrible."

This incident influenced a major change in our attitudes.

Local newspapers reported the number of dead and wounded while the American and European press reported Israeli comments about their retaliatory raid against Palestinian commandos inside Lebanon. The outrage I expected from the international press for Israel's intrusion into the heart of Lebanon and for the killing of innocent women and children was not forthcoming. For the first time, I felt empathy for the people of Lebanon and the Palestinians living there. Many questions now occupied my thoughts. What was the reason behind all this madness? Were press reports about commando raids into Israel factual, or was more of the story being suppressed? Who was retaliating against whom? The Palestinians would certainly retaliate for this raid, which would provoke another raid by the Israelis. When would it end? Why was there so much hate between the Palestinians and the Israelis? I wanted to know.

Through friends, I was introduced to Osama, a Palestinian who had lived in the Palestine city of Nablus, now in Israeli-occupied territory. I wanted to hear his story and was determined to be objective about what he had to say.

The story began to develop slowly. Historical dates and events creating the state of Israel were unclear to me. Osama told me about massacres, of being ousted from his home by the Israelis, of being threatened if he and his family did not leave. Osama described how their homes and possessions were taken, leaving them with only the clothes on their backs.

"How would you feel, Mr. March, if you had a home and land and then someone kicked you out? Wouldn't you fight back? If your mother and father were killed, wouldn't you want to avenge their deaths?"

As Osama described these events, I could only imagine what it would be like. In my mind, I thought that if those things happened to me, I would certainly be compelled to do something.

"We live here in Lebanon. The Lebanese don't want us but where are we to go? We are people without a country. Most of our people live in shacks with no toilet facilities, no water, and many are sick. Have you seen where we live?"

"I have passed by some of the camps and have seen them from the road," I replied, remembering the stench. "Why do your people resort to hijacking airplanes and killing instead of a more peaceful approach?" I asked.

"Mr. March," he said with a sigh. "There has already been too much talk. For years we have been trying to tell our story but no one would hear us. Nothing we say seems to matter. It was only after we began doing drastic things, like hijacking, that world attention began focusing on our situation. We dislike doing these things. We seek only our homeland and peace."

"I know it's difficult for the westerner to understand us because they don't know our heritage and our way of life. We are simple people. We live off the land. Our ancestors were shepherds who moved freely from place to place where there was grazing land, and where they could find food. They cultivated the soil and grew things. Where they settled, we lived. We built our houses and worked hard on our lands to provide food for our family and leave an inheritance to our sons. Now, all this is gone. Many of our people are old. We wish only for our children to enjoy our beautiful Palestine and live in peace. We do not wish to be Lebanese, or Syrian, or Jordanian, we're Palestinians!"

He said that with such force and emotion that I knew he would never be satisfied with any other identity. Osama was not an ignorant man. He had studied at the University in Jerusalem, worked for the British, and his English was spoken with clarity.

Osama continued, "You ask me why we resort to acts of violence, why we create international incidents. It's very much like your own situation in America with the Black people. Did they not burn cities and terrorize people for attention? You do not have to answer that, Mr. March. They did, and today they have a better life. Their own situation would not have changed if they had not acted, and I believe their cause was just. Do you not think so, Mr. March."?

I felt uneasy, but replied, "Yes, they did have a just cause and they are still working for more equality."

"You see, Mr. March, if we just make raids into our own occupied lands to avenge ourselves, it does not help us enough. Your newspapers only show us to be troublemakers and do nothing to help our cause. If we are to be known as trouble makers, then we must make trouble in a way that attracts world attention."

I asked, "Why do you object to Israel? Don't they have a right to their own land as well?"

"Mr. March, you have asked a very important and difficult question, but I should try to answer it as briefly as possible. The piece of land carved out of Palestine was against our wishes but we could do nothing about it. The United Nations decided to give them that land as a home and so it was. As a race the Israelis claimed that they were entitled to a land of their own. But was it right that they should have ours? You see, Mr. March, they are not a race. They are a religion. What the United Nations did was create a religious state. We are not against the Jewish people; we are against the fanatics, the 'Zionists,' who call for Jews from all over the world to come to Israel. There was not enough room for all of us to live there, so they kicked us out and now they invite all Jews to come there. You see, there was not enough room for all these new Jewish immigrants and for the many more they expect to come. They wanted more land, so they began to create troubles with us, just as they continue to make trouble with the Palestinians still living there. They wanted us to leave. This is when all the trouble started. As you know, they have expanded their borders many times, always taking from us, our land."

I interrupted, "But they took this additional land by winning it in war."

"Yes, this is true. With the powerful United States supplying Israel with weapons, what chance did we have?"

"But who started the fighting?" I asked.

"This is difficult to answer. You see, our people were being evicted from their homes and they resisted and fought back. When you resist the police or the army, you are always branded as the guilty one. The Zionists only needed an excuse to fight, and with each struggle, we lost more land. When our Arab brothers were getting close to forcing the United Nations to act on our behalf, another war would start. Now, instead of talking about 1948 borders, they are talking about 1967 borders. I will not be surprised if there is another war and new borders become the subject of contention. But, Mr. March, this time the fight will be to the finish. We cannot be pushed any farther."

"I want to thank you for talking with me," I said. "You have given me an entirely different perspective from what I had. I intend to learn more about the problem and I do have a better understanding of how you must feel. I may not agree with your methods, but I do believe you have a just cause. I only hope a solution is found so the killing stops."

"The solution is simple, Mr. March. Let us live in our Palestine in peace."

I could not be sure of the accuracy of Osama's account of past events and that he was telling one side of a complicated story, but he made me realize that there was an other side to the ongoing conflict that I had never heard. I needed to learn more. I had only begun to realize how much I did not know. I was raised in a very religious Christian family and our life was centered on the doctrine of the church. It was a natural thing to associate anything Christian with good, and non-Christian as bad. Now I found myself reevaluating many things I had once believed as a matter of course. I felt that if justice is right, then injustice must be wrong regardless of religious or political affiliation.

Chapter 9
Middle East Business Mentality
Summer 1974—Spring 1975

Everyone seemed willing to help and I was elated. In my eagerness to begin business, I failed to gain an understanding of business customs and that failure caused problems for me. By accepting friendly offers of assistance, I became indebted.

There was an unspoken, but very important business tradition, that one was expected to return a favor. The Lebanese were traders; therefore much of their income was derived from commissions they earned by performing services. What the westerner would consider a favor, to the Lebanese it was business. The return of a favor was in the form of cash or an equivalent service. Simple introductions to the right people were a service. When I looked for a place to live, all I needed to do was mention it to someone and before long I was presented with a number of options by that person. When I sought office space, I was besieged with possibilities and help, which resulted in a commission, paid by the landlord, to the person who successfully consummated the deal.

I loved the optimistic attitude of the Lebanese. If, for example, you asked them if they would be interested in a new venture, usually the answer was "Yes, yes, what is it?" Everything appeared to be possible if one had the right connections and was willing to pay.

Introductions were always an embarrassment to me. The party being introduced was excessively lauded. Should the introduction result in a business deal, a commission was expected. Successful introductions elevated the influence of the person making the introduction and his worth as a contact person.

I accorded each person I met with the respect for the important position he was alleged to have. Most always, I was promised help, but that help was commission-oriented with no permanence attached to it. Each situation where assistance was needed involved commission negotiation for the service they were expected to perform. It occurred to me that being the outsider, the foreigner, I would forever be vulnerable to bad judgment or misinformation as long as I remained an outsider. My money was rapidly being depleted and real progress was yet to be made. One solution that seemed fitting, was to find a Lebanese partner and become an insider, but first I would have to find the right person.

Business in Lebanon was unlike anything I had ever experienced or imagined. Although I had worked in countries outside the USA, there was no comparison to Lebanon and the other Arab markets. Negotiation was part of every business activity, whether that be a simple purchase or making a sale.

Establishing a company in Lebanon had not been an easy task. There were several options open to me but each required substantial amounts of capital and 51% Lebanese ownership. It also required that the company be managed by a Lebanese managing director (the equivalent title of a U.S. company president), which I found unsuitable. There were, of course, ways to circumvent these requirements. After all this was Lebanon and anything was possible—for a price.

It took time until all the formalities to register my business was completed. I found an attorney who was well connected and for the appropriate fee, would find a way to satisfy my wishes. He devised a way for me to retain control of my company by restructuring. I established the Lebanese company as a wholly-owned subsidiary of my American company. The Lebanese managing director I was legally required to appoint, would own 51% of the Lebanese company, but my attorney would have him sign a private paper which turned ownership back to me. As a major stockholder, I would be able to obtain a residence permit and be available to direct the efforts of the company.

As with any start-up company, keeping expenses to a minimum also applies to the wages one can afford to pay. The only person I had an acquaintance with in Lebanon was Edgard Zehil. He was my immediate and only logical choice to initially appoint as managing director. Edgard was delighted at the idea of becoming managing director and signed the papers turning back ownership to me without hesitation. He would have worked without compensation to hold that title. Being obsessed with saving money, I failed to provide the incentive a manager needs if he is to work for the best interests of the company. Edgard delighted in making purchases for the company and his pockets jingled with the commissions (kickbacks) he received from the merchants. Instead of following the marketing plan I had outlined, Edgard made his own special deals with distributors and retailers that were of financial benefit to him. When I learned of this practice, I had no choice but to remove him from my employ.

I replaced Edgard with Joseph Akoury, one of my independent distributor/representatives. Joseph had proven himself to be an extremely conscientious representative, always expressing promotional ideas to benefit the company. In his younger days, Joseph had studied for the priesthood but had to leave that calling to help provide family support for younger brothers and sisters. He was a man with high moral values and principles, which instilled confidence in those with whom he met.

During my first months in business, my initial efforts to promote my products had not been easy. I sought distributors and product representatives for direct sales in order to generate cash flow. To earn spending money, my twelve-year-old son Duane wanted to sell products. I gave him a cosmetic demonstration kit containing a full line of skin care products and some fragrances, then sent him on his way without any sales instructions; I expected nothing and thought it would give him something to do. That same night, he informed me that he needed more products and handed me the money for his sales with his commission clearly deducted. I asked him how and where he sold the products. He told me he went door-to-door. He took Caroline with him and she thought it fun to knock on doors. Speaking no Arabic, he simply showed the products and pointed to the price marked on the bottles. Whether the people bought because they felt sorry for these young people, I'll never know. I can only imagine the surprise on the customer's face, seeing two American kids pushing products on the streets of Beirut.

To my chagrin, Duane was my top retailer in my first month of business. During the summer of 1974, Duane would recount his adventures in selling cosmetics almost daily. He realized that he must have appeared to many of the wealthier Lebanese as a poor boy selling for his livelihood, and he willingly exploited this pretense. It was probably no accident that his best sales days occurred when he took Caroline in tow. One family, to whom he returned several times, insisted on feeding him on each visit. I felt embarrassed at first and was concerned that people would think I could not feed my own children, but few customers knew who my son was and I was proud of his initiative.

I soon came to realize that if I was to be successful in business, I had to conduct my business in a manner that was acceptable to the Lebanese. I could insist that my western program was better and continue my uphill struggle, or I could do things my way, but in their manner. I therefore altered my marketing program. I cancelled my fixed-price policy on retail sales, on which I based commissions, and implemented a program where the distributor/representative would purchase from me at a fixed-price and he could sell it at whatever price he wanted. This allowed them the freedom to negotiate which was the natural course of business. In America, this would have been deemed unfair by other representatives who would complain about unfair competition. In Lebanon, it was standard practice.

Part of the western influence I introduced, dealt with the excitement of belonging to an organization. The contests, awards and recognition designed to inspire achievement, resulted in increased sales. The concept of organization sales was new to them and required training.

I conducted monthly sales seminars for my new recruits. Part of the seminar was devoted to product knowledge: The proper care of the skin, make-up application and how our products worked to help nourish and beautify the skin. Another part of the seminar was devoted to our marketing program. This too was a new and exciting concept. They could build an organization of their own sales people and elevate themselves within the organization to a top distributor level. This direct sales concept is quite common in the USA but was new to them.

I had conducted motivational seminars in Canada with large seasoned sales groups, in Greece with fertile minds, but here it was necessary to begin with simple basics. I adapted the training to fit their mentality, but more importantly, to expand their thinking and outlook on life. Simple concepts as the power of positive thinking and the power of the mind were enlightening. Self-esteem caught hold and it was exciting to watch them develop and grow.

Each seminar grew in numbers as the word spread. Some people just wanted to attend even though they had no interest in joining the company. I began charging a fee for the seminar and it was open to everyone. I felt that if they attended and became motivated enough, they might want to join. Most did.

It was at one of these seminars that I met Amin Issa Jouma. He was a Jordanian who was now living and working in Saudi Arabia. He had brought his family to Beirut for vacation and, after attending my seminar, became interested in representing our product in Saudi Arabia. On the last day of the sales training seminar, Mr. Jouma, who was traveling to Jordan to visit his relatives, invited Duane to go with him. Duane was excited about the experience it afforded and I granted him permission to go. Upon his return, Duane recounted his adventure.

They left Beirut traveling along the Beirut-Damascus highway and reached the Syrian capital in the early afternoon. Compared to Beirut, Damascus is an intensely Islamic city. It is located in the middle of an orchard oasis that opens up into the plains and the desert. To the west of Damascus are the Anti-Lebanon Mountains. After lunching, they traveled south and reached the Jordanian frontier at night. Duane did not have a visa, but since Jouma had a Jordanian passport, Duane was given a twenty-four visa and was instructed to obtain an extension in Amman, the capital city of Jordan.

Jouma's family received Duane in a small concrete dwelling outside Amman on the desert's edge. As their guest and an oldest son, Duane was offered the bedroom of the family's head. Duane accepted, but when he learned that the entire family would sleep on the roof to take advantage of the cool desert night, he told them, through Jouma, that he would join them.

Meat was a rare treat for the family, and Duane's presence gave his hosts an excuse to prepare a rather scrawny roast chicken. Duane had first choice and took what looked like the juiciest piece. When he realized that his piece had a beak at one end, he attempted to return it unnoticed. The men spotted him, however, and had a hearty laugh at the sheepish twelve-year-old American boy's expense.

The night under the desert stars was very restful. In the morning, Duane and Jouma set off for Amman in order to obtain a visa. As they entered the city, Jouma spotted a limousine that he recognized and signaled. As luck had it, the car contained the Jordanian defense minister, a personal friend of Jouma. In minutes, Duane was granted a special visa, courtesy of the defense minister.

That afternoon, they visited more of Jouma's relatives in Amman. During their visit, Duane had to use the bathroom and was shown what looked rather like a large shower stall. It was Duane's first encounter with an Arab-style lavatory that consisted essentially of a large hole in the floor and a water hose. One used it by squatting over the hole and then cleaning oneself with the water hose. Herein lies the explanation of the Arab custom of eating only with the right hand: The left hand was used for cleaning oneself in the lavatory and was considered unclean and unfit to use in eating. Herein also lies the explanation for the Islamic punishment of cutting off the right hands of thieves: Without a right hand, one could not break bread with his fellow Moslem, making him a social outcast.

Duane managed to cope with the strange facility, but his efforts were not made any more comfortable by the faces of the household's children peering through the door window who were probably curious to see how a westerner handled himself.

The next day, Jouma and some of his relatives took Duane to the ancient city of Jerash. The most impressive remains there are Roman, and these greatly fascinated Duane who already had a strong interest in ancient history.

On the day following, Duane and Jouma returned to Beirut via Damascus. The trip had a great influence on Duane's perception of the Middle East. He had now seen areas more predominantly Moslem and had spoken with many of Jouma's relatives who had been driven out of Palestine. Thus, Duane's attitude changed as mine had, and he conceived a more sympathetic perception of his Arab neighbors.

I traveled to Saudi Arabia, Syria and Jordan that brought large bulk cosmetic orders. The business was beginning to expand, although slowly. With the exception of Lebanon, where there were no rules regarding the mingling of male and female, all my contacts in these countries were with the male sex—a bit unusual for cosmetic sales. Understanding the quality or effectiveness of the product was not as important as the package appeal. Cosmetic purchases were made primarily on the appeal of the bottle or the label. Price was unimportant. An order from a single customer could be quite large if it were from a sheik.

If product was purchased by a sheik that had more than one wife, he purchased the same item and the same amount for each wife. A sheik tries to treat each wife equally and show no preference. Therefore, his purchases were usually in case lots. Once the product got into the hands of the local merchant, further sales had a different turn. One-of-a-kind products would go to the highest bidder. I heard outlandish stories about products sold by my representatives. A bottle of perfume that cost me $2.50 had sold for more than $200.

Lebanon is located at the western edge of the Syrian desert, and by its location it was an oasis and the vacation spot for many Arabs coming from the desert and surrounding regions. Their arrival in Beirut meant a bonanza for the retailers. One sheik in particular traveled to

Beirut yearly in his caravan of eight Rolls Royce cars, each car carrying one of his wives, obviously a bulk purchaser.

My business progress was slow and my resources limited. I was still the outsider and continuously preyed upon by commission seeking advisors. I needed to find a way to represent my company as Lebanese. Having a puppet managing director was not the answer.

Chapter 10
Business Struggles
Spring 1975

"There are two gentlemen here to see you, Mr. March."

I looked up from my desk. Houry was standing in the doorway with her hands on her hips blocking the entrance. It was not unusual for people to pop in on me without an appointment and expect to be seen. Often they would stroll right in unless stopped.

"Who is it? What do they want?" I asked.

"I don't know. They said they wanted to see you and were about to walk right in, but I stopped them."

"Alright, show them in," I said.

Houry stood aside and invited them in.

"Saba el khier," I said in greeting.

"Good morning," replied the one while the other acknowledged my Arabic greeting.

"What can I do for you?" I inquired.

"I am Elie Bassil and this is Philipe Trouboulsi. Mr. Trouboulsi not speak English. I translate for him."

"Please be seated. Would you like some coffee?"

"Medium, please," replied Elie.

Houry took their order while I leaned back in my chair waiting for Elie to talk.

"We wish to discuss your business. We may wish to place money in it," said Elie.

I was puzzled. "I don't quite understand," I said.

Elie turned to Philipe and began talking to him. Then he faced me and said, "We want to invest in your business."

I made an effort to control my reaction. It could be the answer to my problem. I needed a Lebanese partner and I needed capital to expand the business.

"How did you hear about my company? What brought you to see me?" I asked.

Elie spoke once again to Philipe and then said, "Mr. Tabet told us about your company and the good business you make."

"Oh yes, Albert Tabet is one of my distributors, a very good man," I replied.

I wanted to get right to the heart of the matter but thought it better to wait until after they had their coffee. It would not be to my advantage to appear too anxious.

"You are native to Lebanon?" I asked.

"Yes, I was born here," said Elie. "My family is very large and well known in Lebanon. Mr. Trouboulsi comes from the village at Baalbek. You have seen Baalbek?"

"Yes, it's very beautiful and very old," I said. "I can't understand how the Romans managed to build such magnificent structures with primitive tools. They must have been great architects."

"You have been to Byblos?" asked Elie.

"I have only passed through the city but I understand it has many historical things to see," I replied.

"Yes, it is very old. You will come with me to Byblos and I show you the city, yes?"

"I'd like that," I said. "Perhaps when the weather becomes cooler."

"Yes, yes. You will like it," said Elie.

Ali entered with the coffee. "You're welcome sir," he said. Ali used that phrase coming and going. He placed the small cups of Turkish coffee and a glass of water next to each of my guests. With Turkish coffee, a glass of water was practical. Bowing, Ali said, "You're welcome sir," and departed.

As they sipped their coffee, I said, "You wish to know about my company and product, I'm sure."

"Yes, can you tell us about the company?"

"I'll be glad to, and then I will ask you about yourselves and why you wish to invest in it."

"But of course," said Elie.

"As you already know, I'm in the cosmetics business. It's a great business. There isn't a woman in the world that does not want to become more beautiful and she will buy any product if she believes it will help. This is why the cosmetics industry is so large. It's a multi-billion dollar industry and it increases each year. The great thing about the product is that it's consumable and therefore a repeat business. We specialize in skin care. Our product contains a special formula, which aids the skin in retaining moisture. It's the moisture content in the skin that gives it that healthy look and makes a woman look younger, longer. Do you think a woman would buy our product if she thought it would make her look younger?"

"Of course. Any woman would," said Elie.

"When product is simply placed on the shelf in a store, a tremendous amount of advertising is necessary to entice the woman go into the store and buy it. Advertising is very costly. I believe the best advertising in the world is by word of mouth. If a woman likes the products, she will tell others about it and they too will want to buy it. That's why I've created a special marketing program to do just that. Instead of selling the product directly to the stores, which I mentioned would require much advertising dollars, our representatives sell direct to the consumer. They are trained to give facials. When the lady received a facial, which feels great, and she is told how good she looks, she buys the product."

Stopping from time to time, allowing Elie to translate, I continued.

"Another important aspect about our business is the opportunity it presents for people to make money. From what I've observed, there are many Lebanese who need more money and look for ways to earn it. For the most part, the women of Lebanon do not have the opportunity as men do, to make money. Well, we're changing that. We let the business part of the business to the men, and the selling to the consumer, we leave to the women."

Elie liked that. He quickly translated what I said to Mr. Trouboulsi and together they laughed approvingly.

I told them that I had the formulas for the product and that perhaps one day it could be manufactured in Lebanon. I went on to discuss the great potential of my product for the entire Middle East market, how the arid temperatures of the region caused the skin to age prematurely. I also explained that I had a Men's line of products which was catching on in the states and that men were becoming as vain as women. The few trips I had taken to other countries and the orders that resulted, proved that the potential was there. Additional capital would accelerate expansion of the business with a larger staff. And, with the right connections, the business could develop beyond our wildest dreams.

When I finished my enthusiastic presentation, I said, "Perhaps you have some questions."

"We like to know how much you want for fifty percent of company."

I was stunned. I had not even considered a value for my company, nor had I anticipated such a forthright question. Besides, I didn't want a fifty-fifty arrangement and I felt that whatever price I would quote, they would likely cut in half. Therefore I said, "I'm sorry that I cannot tell you the price at this moment. I first want to know more about you and your associate. Perhaps you can tell me about yourselves."

Elie translated all this to Philipe as I waited and observed his reaction. They talked among themselves for a while and then Elie said, "Tomorrow we will bring you a dossier which explains everything. You will find we have much holdings in Lebanon and we have good connections." They then stood up and we shook hands.

"It was a pleasure meeting you," I said.

"It was our pleasure, Mr. March. Ma es salaameh."

"Ma es salaameh," I replied.

That same afternoon and late into the night, I considered all facets of my business and its potential. Without additional capital it would take considerable time to grow and there was always the concern about help. Who could be entrusted to carry out directions and open other markets? I could not do it alone. With an Arab partner, the interests of the company would be better protected and with the right connections, expansion could occur more rapidly.

I prepared an "Income and Expense Projection" sheet encompassing the Middle East markets that contemplated sales of fifteen million dollars within the next two years. If I were to give up fifty percent, I must secure my own position in the event things went wrong with the partnership.

The next day Elie and Philipe returned as promised. Though only twenty-seven years old, Elie was a major stockholder in the Byblos Bank of Lebanon that had eight branch offices throughout the country. Philipe had been a financial advisor to Elie's father before he died and had helped him enter the banking business. Now Elie and his uncle owned the bank and Philipe wanted Elie to have western connections and become experienced in other businesses. I was impressed with their financial resources and saw a willing pupil in Elie. As he learned western business methods, I could learn more about the Arab ways of business.

"I like what I see and hear," I said.

"Thank you. We like what we know about you also," said Elie. "Have you set a price on your business?"

"Yes, I have," I said.

I first went over the projection figures while Elie translated to Philipe. I forecasted figures, based on population, for seven Arab countries. By selecting major exclusive distributors in strategic locations within each country, and by requiring a minimum purchase of products to maintain their exclusivity, the figures I presented were realistic.

"If I am to give up fifty percent of my company, I want two million dollars for the shares of stock. The amount required for working capital will be additional. If you can arrange letters of credit with your bank for product purchases, that will satisfy the working capital requirement."

I waited and watched for reaction as Elie translated what I had said, to Philipe. They showed no visible reaction. They talked together and then Elie said, "The amount you ask is much. We must study it. We will give you our answer soon. Perhaps we will offer a different possibility."

After they departed, I was concerned that I might have asked too much. On the other hand, I thought, they would undoubtedly make a lower counter proposal.

I went about my business and for the next week, heard nothing from Elie. Then Elie called and said he was busy with other matters concerning the bank but that within another week, he and Philipe Trouboulsi would like to arrange another meeting.

My apprehension was mounting. Now that I considered having a partner and increased working capital, the fear that it may not materialize was distressing. To keep the company afloat, I was not taking any money for my personal use and my own bank account was nearly depleted. Working capital to a business is akin to food. It is necessary for survival and the survival of my business was at stake. As I considered alternatives, my thoughts were interrupted with the ringing of the telephone.

"Hi Abe, this is Dan."

"Dan? Dan Peters?"

"Yes, I'm calling from Japan. I'm coming to Beirut and I'll be arriving on Friday at 1:20 PM. Would you pick me up at the airport?"

"Yes, of course. It will be good to see you again. What brings you to Beirut?"

"I want to discuss business with you. I'll fill you in when I get there. See you on Friday."

I hung up the phone and was puzzled. What was Dan up to? I knew Dan was in Japan and had heard he was doing extremely well in that market. Dan was heading the Japanese operation as president of the cosmetic company there.

Although Dan had been my close friend and mentor, I had declined his invitation to join him in Japan. I was concerned that his promises to me in Japan might duplicate those he had made to me in Canada. For this reason, I declined his offer to join him; also I wanted to have my own business, unencumbered by any affiliation or association that could control me. Dan once remarked, "As an employee, you can make thousands' but as the head of your own business, you can make millions."

Dan's flight was thirty minutes late. After clearing customs and greeting each other, we proceeded to the Holiday Inn where I had a room reserved for him.

"How long do you plan to stay?" I asked.

"As long as it takes," he replied.

"What do you mean?"

"Just that. I came here because I want to do business in the Middle East and since you're already here, I want to talk terms that will benefit us both. Let me get some rest and then we'll have dinner and talk."

I was curious and elated that Dan was here. There was no certainty that Elie Bassil would invest in my company, and the possibility of working with Dan was exciting. Any misgivings I felt about our past relationship in Canada were pushed out of my mind.

Dan weighed nearly two hundred-fifty pounds and stood six-feet-six inches tall. He was a great salesman and almost always got his way. He was very intimidating, and I knew forming a working relationship with him wouldn't be easy.

For the first two days, we reminisced about the days when we were distributors. We spent time eating, drinking and seemingly avoided the purpose of his visit. Dan asked about business conditions in the Middle East and its potential. I was delighted to provide the information he sought. Finally, on the third day, I brought up the subject.

"When are you going to talk about the purpose of your visit?"

"Right now if you like," he replied.

"How do you see us working together?" I asked.

"You know my track record. I can make you a lot of money. I've built the Japanese operation and have about thirty million dollars in our company's bank account. I'm expanding into Hong Kong and Malaysia. I also want to get into the Middle East. My biggest problem right now is getting our money out of Japan. I have equity interest in the Japanese operation and having the money tied up there doesn't do me or the company much good. The government has so many restrictions on the money that I must seek alternate ways to justify moving some of it out of the country. International expansion is one way. I can supply the Middle East operation with all the product it can handle."

I was impressed, although I felt there must be some exaggeration on Dan's part, but I also recognized his dynamic motivation and drive.

"Every operation I get involved with, I want at least fifty-one percent," said Dan. "That's the only way I operate."

At this statement, I was rather disappointed, but then realized there were other shareholders in the company Dan managed who would insist upon control if they were to place the company's money here. Giving up fifty-one percent to Elie would occur only if I got enough up front cash and I knew Dan wouldn't spend that kind of money up front. Having laid all the groundwork, I only needed some additional working capital for expansion. On the other hand, I thought, a smaller percentage of something big would be better than a large percentage of something small. With a large company behind me, aggressive expansion could take place at once.

Dan interrupted my thoughts. "You said you were in need of cash. How much would it take to get things moving?"

Since I was talking to a friend, I made the fatal business mistake of letting my guard down and admit weakness.

"First of all, I require some money to live on. I personally financed this operation and have nearly depleted my resources. Secondly, there needs to be an injection of cash into the company as operating capital."

"How much operating capital are we talking about?" asked Dan.

"My best ball park guess is about $200,000 with additional reserves."

"What's the least amount you could manage with to get things rolling?" he asked.

"Unless we can inject at least $100,000 into the business with the immediate availability of more, when requested, then the operation will continue at a slow pace. The money is needed for expansion to other countries and to provide a more solid base of operations here with additional personnel and some inventory."

"How much money do you personally need?"

"That depends. What I need to live on, and what I'm giving up is another matter."

"Of course. As I stated before, I'd want fifty-one percent."

"So you want to know what I want for giving up fifty-one percent?"

"That's right. Just keep in mind what I told you. I can turn this operation around very quickly. You'll stand to make more money than you ever dreamed of. If I duplicate here what I did in Japan, you'll be rolling in the dough."

"You must realize, the Middle East is not Japan," I said. "Things are different here. If the business is conducted according to the Arab mentality, it can advance rapidly. To answer your question, I need a better place to live and I also need a car. There are other obligations that I have been neglecting as well. A minimal sum would be $100,000 cash. I would expect to be on your payroll and be compensated accordingly. I would also expect to be in charge here to run the Middle East operation."

"There's no question about your running the operation. I want you to be in charge. I'll send whatever help you need. Do we have a deal?"

"I'm not sure. What exactly are we agreeing to?" I asked.

"Assuming there is no outstanding company indebtedness..."

"There is none," I interrupted.

"Good. In that event, I'll provide the $100,000 as working capital and see that you get $40,000 to help get you squared away personally. You will of course be compensated on a monthly basis for running the company. That amount can be anywhere from five to ten thousand dollars, depending on the company's cash flow."

It certainly was less than I wanted and it did not come close to covering what I had spent, but considering my present situation and the potential this collaboration offered, I said, "It's a deal. Just for my personal information and to avoid any future misunderstanding, would you just jot down your understanding of what we have agreed to?"

"Sure," he said.

Dan used the back of a napkin and wrote down the amounts to be paid and the fact that I was to be in charge.

"That OK?" asked Dan, handing me the napkin.

I looked at it and said,"Sure."

"As soon as I get back to Japan, I'll send my comptroller to go over the books. He'll bring with him the funds we agreed on. I will also send

John Morgan to give you a hand. John has been a right arm to me and you'll find him to be a great help."

"That's fine with me. I can use the help," I said.

The next day we relaxed by the pool and discussed plans until it was time for Dan's departure. I was excited about the prospects of working with Dan, and Gisela shared my enthusiasm.

In the meanwhile, I sent word to Elie Bassil that I was delaying the meeting between us for a week or so until a business deal I was working on was finalized.

John Morgan arrived the following week. I welcomed him and attempted to familiarize him with the local operation as well as indoctrinate him on the local customs, etc. John was aloof and appeared uninterested in what I had to say. He asked me to arrange a meeting with all the distributor/representatives and, in good faith, I arranged the meeting.

John opened the meeting himself after telling me he preferred to take it cold without introduction. John welcomed everyone and then began his speech:

"My name is John Morgan. I'm here on behalf of Mr. Dan Peters, a multi-millionaire who owns this company. Most of you here know Abe March. Mr. Peters sent Abe to Lebanon to lay the groundwork and now Mr. Peters is ready to begin. Mr. Peters has placed me in charge to run things and…"

I was alarmed at what I was hearing. As John continued, I suddenly realized that Dan meant to take the business away from me completely. The comments John was making could not be his own; he was obviously carrying out instructions. As John talked, some of the salesmen were looking at me questionably. They believed that the company was mine and that I had come to Lebanon on my own. That was true. Now, however, they were being led to believe otherwise. My integrity and future credibility would suffer with these people who had worked diligently with me. It was incomprehensible that Dan would approve this type of introduction without discussing the transition with me.

When the meeting ended, I took John by the arm and said, "I want to talk to you—now!"

I found a private corner adjoining the meeting room and was rather indignant as I began to talk.

"This is the most outrageous and unprofessional approach to our collaboration I could have imagined. You have discredited me in front of these people with lies. What right have you to barge in here and tell these people that Dan sent me here to lay the groundwork? You implied that Dan owned this business from the beginning. These people that I have worked with will now question my integrity. Besides, we haven't even signed an agreement and this is not in line with what Dan and I discussed and agreed to."

"Don't get yourself all bent out of shape," said John. "I'm only following instructions. Dan knows what he's doing. You've got nothing here. If anything happens here, we will do it."

"You have no idea of the struggle to open this business nor of the difficulties in operating here in this part of the world. If you think anyone can get off the plane, waltz in here and commence business, they've got a lot to learn. I didn't lay everything on the line to have someone—anyone for that matter, make me out to be some flunky. Who put you in charge, anyway? This is still my business!" I said.

"Dan did. He sent me here to take charge. As far as Dan's concerned, you're nothing but a pussycat," he said with distain.

I did my best to contain my rage. If that's what Dan really feels about me, I thought, then I will be out in the cold. I left John standing and walked away. I immediately placed a call to Japan. I was in luck. Dan was in his office.

"Dan, this is Abe."

"Hi, Abe, how are things?"

"Not good. I'm furious about John as well as confused and concerned about your intentions here."

"What's the problem?"

"I would think that your approach to starting here would have been discussed beforehand. Neither you nor John understands the mentality of these people. Trust is of prime importance. These people were just told a fairy tale about how you sent me here to lay the groundwork and now you're ready to begin, and that you have sent John to run things."

"So what's the problem?" asked Dan.

"First of all, it's not the truth. Secondly, it's not what we agreed to. John made me out to be some flunky here today. If I'm to run things, as we agreed, my own integrity and credibility have been jeopardized by what John told these people. You said you were sending John to give me a hand. This kind of hand I don't need."

"You worry too much Abe. John knows what he's doing. I'll talk to him. Leave him to me. I'm glad you called. By the way, Bob Williams, my comptroller, will be arriving tomorrow to get things settled between us. Don't worry, we'll work this out."

Well, I was worried. I decided to wait for Mr. Williams before taking any further action.

After Bob Williams arrived and was settled in the hotel, I took him to the office. Mr. Williams reviewed the books and appeared satisfied that all was in order. He then produced a contract for me to sign. I began reading the contract agreement. As I read, I became more perplexed. According to the agreement, I would own shares in the company—nothing more. No guarantees, no mention of my position or of any compensation. Bob handed a pen to me.

"Sign here," he said.

"Not so fast, Bob. This agreement does not contain the conditions that Dan and I agreed upon. Did you bring any money with you?"

"Yes, I have a check for $40,000 for the company's operating funds."

"What about the $100,000?" I asked.

"You don't need that much. I also have a check for John Morgan for his salary and expenses in the amount of $16,000, and there's a check here for you in the amount of $11,000."

"Eleven thousand dollars! You've got to be kidding. None of this is in accordance with the agreement Dan and I made. This is totally unacceptable!" I exclaimed. "Here! Look what Dan wrote on this napkin."

Bob looked at the napkin and laughed. "That doesn't mean

anything. Look, Abe. I don't see that you're in any position to turn it down. You have no choice. You know Dan, he'll do right by you."

"I'm not so sure I know Dan at all or perhaps I'm just beginning to know Dan. There's too much at stake for that kind of blind trust. I've already invested over $200,000 in this business. To accept these crumbs would be asinine. I'd rather go it alone under these conditions."

"Abe, if you don't sign this, we'll come into the Middle East anyway. We'll bury you!"

To these remarks, I said, "The last time I heard comments like that was between Nikita Khrushchev and Jack Kennedy. It didn't work then, and it won't work now. The deal's off!"

"Why don't you talk with Dan?" asked Bob.

"No, you talk with Dan! If he wants to talk to me, he knows where I am," I said.

I dropped Mr. Williams at the hotel, and then went home. I explained the situation to my wife.

"The way it appears to me, if I go along with Dan, I'm back to square one. I'm once again working for someone else—completely at their mercy. I don't believe I can handle that. We've sacrificed too much."

Gisela was upset. "How could Dan do this to us? After you worked so hard for him in Canada. What are we going to do? We were counting on the money," she said.

"Do you remember the article I read to you about courage?" I said. "In it, there was a passage that read, 'I'd rather die on my feet than live on my knees.' If you're with me, I'm definitely turning Dan down."

"I'd rather you said no to Dan than to accept what he offered. If he has already gone back on his word, how will you ever trust him in the future? We'll make it somehow," she said.

"Good. I just wanted you to be aware of the potential consequences. I think I'll call Elie Bassil. Maybe he'll invest in the company if I make a better proposal."

I immediately placed the call and reached Elie at his home in Byblos.

"Are you still interested in investing in my company?" I asked.

"Yes, of course. I thought you were no longer interested in me," said Elie.

"I'd like to see you as soon as possible. I have a proposition for you, provided you're prepared to act immediately," I said.

I arranged to meet Elie the following morning at my office. Elie came alone and after the customary pleasantries, I said, "I have just been offered a proposition by a Japanese company to buy into my operation here. They wish to come here and launch a big effort with cosmetics in the Middle East. The man heading the company is an American friend of mine. Personally, I'd rather continue the business alone or together with someone local who knows the market better. My problem is that I must give an answer within the next twenty-four hours. That's why I called you. I know it's short notice but if you're serious about joining me, I'll tell those people no, and have you join me, provided we can agree on terms."

"What do you want?" asked Elie.

"As you know, based on our previous conversation about the business and its potential, I place a lot of value on it. I have exclusive agreements from three major suppliers, one in Canada, one in West Germany and the other in the United States. I not only have the exclusivity of the products they produce but the formulas as well, and that's worth a great deal. I have registered the brand names of each of the products under my company. This protects us against any circumvention the suppliers might attempt. Since I've been here, I have proven the acceptability of the product in the marketplace. To do this was costly in time and money. Everything is in readiness to aggressively expand the business. All that is required now is money."

Elie interrupted and said, "Our bank has the resources."

"That's good and that's also why I'm interested in our collaboration. I am willing to give up thirty-nine percent of my company for one million dollars. Due to the short notice I've given you as well as my preference in you as a working partner, I propose the following: I want $10,000 per percentage point of equity. That comes to $390,000. The balance is for working capital. You need not put up the operating capital in cash but rather provide a line of credit with your bank in the amount of $610,000. This credit will be used primarily for the purchase of product. Should you agree with these terms, I'm prepared to enter into an agreement with you at once. I will, however, require the $390,000 by tomorrow. We can have your or my attorney write a simple agreement that spells out these terms."

Elie was silent for a few moments. Then he said, "Let me talk with my advisor, Mr. Trouboulsi, and I'll let you know in the morning."

I went home full of hope and much anxiety. Later that same evening, Bob Williams called to say he was leaving for Japan in the morning. He said that Dan would be calling me.

The next morning I was up earlier than usual. I hadn't slept much and the importance of the day weighed heavily on me. I knew that my work and efforts were on the line. I went to the office early and attempted to occupy myself with work but couldn't concentrate on anything. At 10:05 AM, the telephone rang.

"This is Elie. Marhaba."

"Marhaba," I replied. "Kief Halek?"

"Mniih, ilhamdilla" (Fine, thanks to God), he replied. "Mr. Trouboulsi and I would like to come by your office and see you. Are you available now?"

"Yes, of course. I'll make time for you."

"We'll see you in a few minutes," said Elie.

"I look forward to it," I said, and sincerely meant it.

I paced the floor as I waited for them to arrive. Would they buy in? Perhaps I asked too much. I can always reduce my demands. Something is better than nothing. I'll just have to wait and see. My mind rambled on.

Elie and Mr. Trouboulsi arrived at 10:35 AM. Coffee was ordered and I exchanged amenities doing my best to remain calm. I didn't want to show my anxiety nor tip my hand regarding my desperation and willingness to compromise. Elie spoke first.

"Please explain to Mr. Trouboulsi your proposal. He wants to be clear about it."

I restated the terms I made to Elie the day before. Elie and Philipe conferred in Arabic while I waited. The tension I felt brought perspiration to my forehead, and I felt the sweat running down the inside of my shirt. Would they agree, or would they make a counter offer? Elie turned to me and began speaking.

"We like you, Mr. March, and we like the business. There are other business possibilities we can make together. These other possibilities we will discuss later. We have decided to accept your offer."

I could hardly believe my ears.

"When did you say you required the money?" asked Elie.

"If it's possible, I would like it today." My heart seemed to stop beating! "You must understand that if I am to decline the Japanese offer, I must be certain that we definitely have an agreement."

"But of course. You have my word. We do agree. I'll arrange for the check and we'll meet with your attorney. It's Claude Chaiban, I believe."

"Yes, that's right. You know Claude?"

"Yes, we know of him and he's a good man."

I was elated. I could hardly contain myself. Could this really be happening? Maybe something would go wrong and they would change their minds. My thoughts continued to express doubt.

After they left the office, I called Gisela. She shrieked with joy when she heard the news.

"When will it happen?" she asked.

"I've arranged a meeting for this afternoon at 3:30 PM. I've already instructed Claude, while they were still in my office, to draw up a simple agreement spelling out the terms."

"It sounds too good to be true after what Dan had proposed," said Gisela. "Now perhaps we can find a better place to live."

"You may also be able to take the kids and visit your father in Germany for awhile."

"That would be wonderful," she said. "Let me know when you finalize things. I'll be on pins and needles until I hear from you. Please let me know as soon as you can."

"Don't worry, Schnuck (a German term of endearment which I often used), you'll be the first to know," I said.

Everything went without a hitch. Claude had prepared two

agreements, one in English and one in Arabic. Minor clarifications were made to the agreement, and the changes were initialed by both parties. Elie then presented me with the check made payable to Abe March.

The moment they left the office, I called Gisela and told her the news. I went immediately to my bank to deposit the money, then purchased a good bottle of wine and went home to celebrate.

Why Elie bought into my company, I could only speculate. Major companies were increasing trade, particularly in Saudi Arabia, and having western connections became an important asset to traders and bankers alike. Having huge sums of money pass through their hands was something they all sought. For the westerner to have confidence in an Arab banking institution, he must feel comfortable in doing so. I suspected the future business Elie spoke about had something to do with banking.

Early the next morning while I was eating breakfast, the telephone rang.

"Hello, Abe. This is Dan. I just talked with Bob Williams. Apparently he got my instructions mixed up. I can understand that you were upset. I'm preparing a new agreement which I'm sure you'll like."

"I'm sorry Dan. It's too late. I've already taken another investor and now have the funds to do things on my own."

"You haven't signed anything yet, have you?"

"Yes, it's signed and I already have the funds."

"What kind of a deal did you make?"

I explained the details with much satisfaction. When I finished, there was a long period of silence on the phone. Finally Dan said, "Congratulations. I'd still like to work with you. What if I do the training and run the sales force for you? We can work a separate arrangement and work together with you." One had to admire his persistence.

I smiled to myself. There's no way I would place the sales force in someone else's hands. The person who controls the sales, controls the company. I knew that and so did Dan. Does he think I'm that naive, that much of pussycat? I wondered.

"I'm sorry Dan but that won't work," I said. "I have a partner and he would not go along with it."

"I'm sorry to hear you say that, Abe. I just want you to know I intend to come to the Middle East in any event."

The conversation ended and I pushed Dan out of my mind. I was engrossed in planning our expansion throughout the Middle East market. John Morgan was still in town. He called me to see if there was any mail at the office since he had given my office as his address. There was some mail and John came by to pick it up. He inquired about the new 450 SEL Mercedes Benz that was parked outside. I was pleased to tell him that I had just purchased it. The smirk on John's face indicated mischief. It was only after I received a call from one of my salesmen that I became disturbed. John had contacted this salesman and told him that I would soon be out of business but if he wanted to work with John, he would have a place for him.

Several days later, I was interrupted when two men pushed their way past Houry and came barging into my office. The men wore uniforms and ignored Houry's efforts to stop them. Realizing that I didn't speak Arabic, they then conversed with Houry.

Houry turned to me and said, "These men are from the security police. They say that they were informed that you have started a company here and are taking money from people and have no product. They want to see if we have product."

I opened the door to the product room where the shelves were stacked to the ceiling with skin care products, perfumes and makeup items. The brand names were all in English, and I wasn't sure if they could determine that they were cosmetics or not. A men's line named "Stud" aftershave and cologne, a women's line of perfumes named "Nefertiti" and "Santosha," as well as a skin care line named "Herb Garden," and many others.

While they were in the stock room, I called Elie.

"There appears to be some kind of a problem. The security police are here. It seems someone has given them bad information and according to Houry, they have orders to shut us down."

"Tell them to wait. I'll be right there," said Elie.

Houry informed the police that Elie Bassil was on his way and offered them coffee while they waited.

Elie arrived and listened while the police explained their orders. Elie picked up the phone and made a call. He then instructed the security police to wait until his call was returned. They obeyed.

Elie turned to me and said, "Apparently someone called the security police and told them we have no product and that we are taking money for orders without any products to sell. The police also said something about this company not being legal in Lebanon. I know this is not true. I checked on this before I invested. I have just called my friend, Tony Franjieh. You know Tony?"

"He's the President's son, isn't he?" Suleiman Franjieh was President of Lebanon.

"Yes, and he's also a minister in the government and a close friend. He's calling the security chief right now to find out what this is all about. I also want to find out who made this complaint."

I said nothing. I could hardly believe my luck! I was thankful I had Elie as a partner.

"Do you know who might have done this?" asked Elie.

"I have an idea but I don't want to make accusations without proof."

I went on to explain that John Morgan was still in town and that Dan had insisted they were going to do business here.

The telephone rang. It was for Elie.

Elie listened intently, saying, "Nam, nam, (Yes, yes)," then passed the phone to one of the security officers. When the officer was through listening, he passed the phone back to Elie. Elie conversed briefly with Tony and had a grin on his face. When he hung up the phone, the police had already left the office.

"Tony called the chief of security," Elie explained. "Tony told them that their men were investigating his business. He told the chief that I was his brother and that he wants this investigation stopped or his head would roll. He also wants to know who made these accusations. Tony will call me back soon."

I understood the close ties associated with the term 'brother,' and in their eyes, if anyone attacked their fraternal brother, it was the same as if he were a member of the family.

An hour went by before the phone rang again. It was Tony Franjieh. When Elie hung up the phone he said, "The man who called security wouldn't identify himself. It was a foreigner who, they think, had a British accent. Don't worry, Mr. March, they won't bother us again. Could the man be John Morgan?"

"It sounds like it. John is Australian but his accent could be interpreted as British. I can't imagine anyone else who could have done it. He is obviously trying to make trouble for us," I said.

With a slicing motion across his throat, Elie said, "You say the word, Mr. March. For two pounds, I can have him eliminated. He'll never bother us again."

"No, no," I said. "I don't want the man killed. I'd just like to see him out of the country."

"It is done. He will be out of Lebanon in twenty-four hours. Just leave it to me," said Elie.

Within twenty-fours, I was told that John Morgan was no longer in Lebanon. I was not told, nor did I wish to know, how he was removed. Elie then showed me a document that had been transmitted to the Lebanese Consulate in Japan. It specifically banned Dan Peters and John Morgan from obtaining a visa for Lebanon.

"They will not be allowed to enter Lebanon," said Elie. "If we find they go into another Arab country, I will have them black listed."

Having the protection of Tony Franjieh was invaluable. Lebanese politics ran in the family and betting odds were that Tony would eventually become president himself. His family was very powerful. The realization of the clout I now had with Elie's connections gave me the courage and fortitude to move forward in a bold manner.

* * * * *

The sacrifices made by my family were now rewarded with a better life style. We found a new home and were beginning to enjoy the fruits of our labor. Gisela took the children to visit her father in Germany, and when she returned, she did volunteer work at the American University Hospital and with the women's auxiliary in the hospital's coffee shop.

She would push a cart with magazines and other sundry items for the patients. Patients from all over the Middle East came to this hospital. The flirtations of the patients were taken in stride. She was most amused when one of the male patients asked, "Did I not meet you before in Benghazi?" Christine and Duane helped out occasionally waiting on tables and pouring drinks in the coffee shop, thanks to Mrs. MacDonald who headed the women's auxiliary and was in charge of the coffee shop.

We enjoyed exploring the historical places throughout Lebanon and the surrounding countries. The business was progressing well and the future looked very bright. I envisioned millions of dollars within a short period of time. Elie was making contacts in other Arab countries and it appeared that our business was on the brink of dramatic expansion. However, there were political problems and beginning in the Spring of 1975, trouble began to brew between various elements within the government. Threats were made by dissidents and some incidents of armed reprisals were reported.

One day, Elie and Mr. Trouboulsi requested a meeting with me to discuss the sponsoring of a bank in Lebanon. "We would like an American or Canadian bank", said Elie. Do you know of a bank that we could talk with who might wish to establish an operation in Lebanon?"

"There are many banks in the U.S. There are already some of the major banks here. I have no idea what other banks might have an interest but that possibility could be explored," I said.

"To open a bank in Lebanon, the foreign bank must have a sponsor. We would like to sponsor a foreign bank. Most of our business is here in Lebanon and with some of the other Arab countries but we wish also to become involved in the American market. There is much business now with America and the Middle East. We think sponsoring an American bank will give us the possibility for western trade."

"That makes sense," I said. "I'm sure there must be banks that would be interested in coming here, especially since Beirut is the banking center for the Middle East. The only problem I foresee, is that they may wish to wait until the troubles here settle down."

"We believe the troubles will end soon and don't want to wait. We believe a bank wishing to do business here would feel more comfortable if an American was involved. What we propose, once we find a bank that is interested, is to make you the president of the bank."

"Me? The president of a bank!" I laughed. "I know very little about banking. Besides, what about our business here? Who would run it?"

"You need not to worry about the banking business. Our people would do the work. You would not be required to do much," said Elie.

"In other words, you're looking for a figure-head."

"What means figurehead?" asked Elie.

"Someone with a title but no responsibility," I said.

"Something like that, yes. But we compensate you, of course. As we trust you, Mr. March, we believe a foreign bank would have more trust in us if you were the president."

"It sounds exciting," I said. "What would you like me to do?"

"Perhaps you can make inquiries in the U.S. and in Canada to see what bank would be interested. We can discuss the requirements that the bank needs once we have someone interested."

"Let me see what I can do," I said. "I'll write a few letters first, and if necessary, I'll travel to the states to make further inquiries."

"This is only the beginning, Mr. March. We will make big business together," said Elie.

Troubles, however, were spreading throughout the country. Skirmishes between the various factions in Lebanon were increasing. As time went by, Elie stayed away from the office more since he had to pass the trouble spots enroute to the office. Then a cease-fire would occur and the hopes of everyone would soar, believing that things would get back to normal. I was excited about the future and ignored the problems within the country. I was confident, as were the Lebanese, that the troubles would end soon.

Chapter 11
Iranian Connection
Summer 1975

More cosmetic products were needed, so I made a trip to our supplier in West Germany. During this buying trip, I was introduced to a man who had a twelve-year relationship as a consultant to the Shah of Iran. He was searching for a company to collaborate with members of the Iranian Royal family in establishing a cosmetic manufacturing facility in Iran. The Iranian consultant, Mr. Schmidt, heard about my cosmetic operation in Lebanon and sought to interest me in the Iranian project. The German cosmetic company also expressed an interest in participation. Mr. Basil Walsh, who served as managing director for the Germany Company, was anxious to involve me in the project and arranged a meeting with Mr. Schmidt.

Mr. Schmidt indicated the desire of the Royal family to build more business enterprises in Iran. They had money but needed foreign expertise. To make a joint venture with a promising cosmetic company that is already doing business in the Middle East was very interesting. For the right project it would entice other business people as well. However, based on their business practices, Mr. Schmidt stated that $150,000 was required as seed capital. Five million dollars would be raised by Iranian investors, which included members of the Royal family.

When I returned to Lebanon, I discussed the project with Elie. He expressed great interest and wanted to meet both Messrs. Schmidt and Walsh. Within two weeks, a date was set for Elie and I to meet with them in Frankfurt, West Germany. We met, and after several days of deliberation, an agreement was reached whereby our Lebanese company would own thirty percent of the proposed Iranian operation and our German partners would own twenty percent. Our Lebanese company would be responsible for establishing the cosmetic factory and providing the expertise in managing the operation. As a commitment, we were to place $50,000 as capitalization in an account in West Germany to form a German corporation. Mr. Schmidt would earn a fee for his consulting services for putting the deal together and he would also be given an equity percentage from the Iranians.

A German architectural firm was engaged to draw-up the plans for the cosmetic factory. It was to be the first complete cosmetic manufacturing operation in the Middle East. The plans were elaborately drawn to include on-site guest quarters at the proposed cosmetic facility.

Mr. Schmidt arranged a trip for Elie and I to vist with our prospective Iranian investors.

The day before our trip to Iran, I went to the bank to withdraw some travel money. That night, as every night at bedtime, I placed my wallet on the top shelf of my closet with the door standing open. When I crawled into bed, I took off my wristwatch and placed it on the floor next to it. As usual, it was a warm night in Beirut and we slept with little or nothing, covered only with a sheet.

When I awoke the next morning, I reached for my wristwatch but couldn't locate it. I sat up and looked under and around the bed, but no watch was to be found. Perhaps the cat had played with it, I thought, and had pushed it down the hallway. The marble floors would have allowed the watch to slide easily. I walked down the hallway, past my son's room and into the foyer, and noticed that the door to the apartment was standing open. Then I spied my wife's purse lying on an end table by the door with its contents strewn about. I immediately went back into my bedroom and looked on the shelf for my wallet. The money was gone.

I called the police. They came and took fingerprints as a routine matter, but gave no hope that the thief would be found. According to the police, the thief entered through the open window of my son's bedroom and must have sprayed some substance that caused us to remain sleeping. We found burnt matches on the floor. I told Gisela that the thief must have been rather poor not to have a flashlight and needed to use matches. Gisela seemed pleased by this and said, "At least he wasn't able to get a good look at us while we slept with nothing on." For weeks after this happened, Gisela searched the street vendors that sold wristwatches to see if she could find mine. When she was asked, "Would you like to buy a watch?" She replied, "No, I'm just looking for the watch that was stolen from my husband."

Upon our arrival in Teheran, Mr. Schmidt met us at the airport and escorted us to the Intercontinental Hotel. Western businessmen pursuing trade with Iran patronized this hotel. It bustled with activity and was filled to capacity.

Iranian oil money was radically changing the country and its way of life. Women were unveiled and wore western-style clothing. Bars and nightclubs were commonplace, which was rather unusual for this fanatically Moslem country. The industrial development was proceeding at a rapid pace and westernization of the country was evident. The Shah held great power, but dissention among the zealot supporters of the exiled Khomeini was beginning to create problems for him. The Shah was ruthless towards dissidents and governed with an iron hand. The years of repression toward those he governed was soon to be felt. In retrospect, revolution was inevitable, but who could know this in 1975?

The businessmen at the Intercontinental Hotel rubbed shoulders with each other seeking new contacts and eager to meet anyone with high-placed connections. Business in Iran was primarily transacted between power brokers who could influence the acquisition of contracts for products and services. They were paid a commission for their services.

Mr. Schmidt arranged a dinner meeting with two members of the Royal family: Abbas Guilanchah, Chambellan De S.M.I. Le Chahinchah (Secretary to His Imperial Majesty the Shah), and his brother who was the general in charge of security for Iran. I found Abbas Guilanchah to be a refined gentleman while his brother, a fierce disciplinarian, had crude manners. Abbas Guilanchah spoke no English; however, he spoke perfect German. The general spoke a little English and I learned that his son was married to a girl from Oil City Pennsylvania. When he discovered that I was from Pennsylvania, he became a congenial host and conversed amiably with me.

The meeting went well. They were anxious to become part of the cosmetic operation and pledged their support. We reached an agreement about their participation. Mr. Schmidt was to look after their interests in the project and coordinate matters on their behalf.

Abbas Guilanchah was interested in visiting the factory in Germany, mostly out of curiosity. His Austrian-born wife would accompany him. We agreed on a tentative date for the visit and our meeting ended.

Returning to the hotel, we went to the bar for a drink. We were immediately inundated with questions. They were curious about the government limousine that had picked us up that evening, who our important contacts were, and could they get an introduction. They bought us drinks, supposedly to loosen our tongues, but we refused to discuss our dinner meeting.

On the morning of our departure, a special package arrived at the hotel containing caviar bound with the Royal Seal—a departing gift from the Guilanchah's.

A month later, I traveled alone to West Germany in advance of the scheduled visit by the Guilanchah's. I carried in my attaché case $50,000 in cash, fulfilling our part of the agreement, and turned it over to Mr. Walsh. I also placed an order for more than a half million dollars worth of cosmetics, to be paid by letter of credit. The merit of the letter of credit insured that the money would be paid only after the goods were in the hands of the shipper and the shipment matched the product order.

The meeting with the Guilanchah's took place at the 'Hotel Forsthaus' in Gravenbruch, near the Frankfurt airport. Among the distinguished guests were representatives of the German Government and the opera singer, Dr. Felicitas Weathers. Later, our private discussions led to a concrete arrangement to proceed with the project.

A German contractor would supervise the construction of the cosmetic facility and I would make myself available, when needed, to organize the company's development. I then returned to Lebanon.

Chapter 12
Violence Escalates
Spring/Summer 1975

The taxi driver weaved his way through the June morning traffic, joining the chorus of beeping car horns. The wailing of street peddlers pushing their carts, blended with other familiar street sounds as the taxi entered Beirut's Hamra district. The street noise muffled the rumble of intermittent explosions and gunfire nearby. Hamra's sidewalks were no longer visible. The mass of morning shoppers wandering from store to store, haggling with merchants on both sides of the street, brought traffic to a standstill. What used to be sidewalks were now cluttered with makeshift stores run by displaced merchants who laid territorial claim to sidewalk space. Loud voices raised in argument could be heard between small street merchants and the shop owners whose store entrances they blocked. Mercantile competition was always keen, but now there was a sense of urgency, which increased the pitch, and intensity of the vendors' appeal to every potential customer.

As the taxi edged its way along the street, I viewed the scene in disgust. Driving through Hamra had always been difficult when things were normal, but now, with souks lining the sidewalks and overflowing into the streets, it was exasperating. The bombing of the Bourj area not long before had created this mess and since the police were practically nonexistent, there was chaos.

I wondered how these people could be so indifferent. They obviously heard the gunfire yet they seemingly disregarded and danger for the sake of making a sale. As long as they were not directly threatened, they did not seem to give a damn about anything other than business. "Typical Lebanese attitude," I concluded, oblivious to my own mental state.

The taxi picked up speed, then made a sharp turn leaving the Hamra district, and stopped.

"Where you want go?" said the driver turning his head sideways.

I pointed north and said, "That way. Go straight ahead."

The driver shook his head. "You not go that way. They shooting there."

"Look, I want to go that way—so go!"

The driver now shook his head vigorously, "I not go there."

It seemed only a few short hours ago that my plane had landed. The return trip from Frankfurt had been full of anxiety. It was reported that a barrage of rockets had fallen in and around the area of my office and I needed to know the extent of damage to my office and products stored there.

"I'll walk then!" I shouted. "How much to here? Hadeesh?"

The driver held up his open hand and said, "Five pounds."

"Five pounds!" I exclaimed. "What do you mean, five pounds? It's only two pounds anywhere in Hamra!"

The driver shrugged his shoulders and raising his outstretched arms in a gesture of resignation, said, "Troubles sir. Price now five pounds."

I thrust a five-pound note at the driver, grabbed my briefcase and slammed the car door. I started walking briskly toward Rue Fouad Chehab.

I usually wore a suit even in the hottest weather and today was no exception. Beads of perspiration appeared on my forehead and my armpits were wet. I had not walked far before I became uneasy. No cars were moving on this street and the absence of people was noticeable. I looked back and forth surveying the street ahead. Scattered debris, from what had been a cheese shop, now littered the sidewalks and street. Glass crunched under my feet amplifying the sound of my footsteps in the uncommon silence of the street. All was too quiet. I began to think that the taxi driver may have been right but I determined not to let myself be intimidated. I believed that no harm would come to me since I was a foreigner.

Perspiration was running down my chest and my shirt clung to my body. The day seemed exceptionally hot, or was it me? Suddenly, a movement across the street caught my eye. My heart pounded as a man appeared from a doorway and stepped onto the sidewalk. I recognized the black and white spotted scarf as the "koufieh" worn by Palestinian commandos, and then my heart skipped a beat when I spotted his gun. My thoughts raced as another gunman stepped out and joined the other. I considered stopping, but decided that would show fear. "If I run, they might shoot. Better to keep a normal movement," I thought.

Everything was in focus. Their rifles were held waist high from shoulder straps and the gun barrels pointed directly at me. I struggled to keep my inner turmoil hidden; I knew that I appeared calm on the outside. Stress produced a protective shield even when I had butterflies in my stomach or my knees were ready to give way. Instinctively and with only a slight change of pace, I stepped off the curb and walked directly across the street toward them. They stood still with their eyes and guns fixed on me as I approached.

Stepping onto the sidewalk in front of them, I said, "Marhaba. Kief Halek?"

A look of bewilderment showed on their faces, but they made no response to my greeting. I continued walking by them. My senses cried out to run but I concentrated on maintaining an even pace. "Don't show fear," I thought, while breathlessly alert to any sound from my rear.

I came near the end of the street and resisted the impulse to run with each controlled step. The staccato of machine gunfire could be heard ahead, but my mind was on the impending sound of gunfire behind me. Each step brought me closer to the street corner and safety. I forcibly maintained the same stride and on reaching the corner, I leaped quickly out of sight, flattening myself against the building wall. The moment I disappeared from view, the gunmen opened fire. Bullets ricocheted off the pavement and glass shattered as they sprayed the street and surrounding buildings with their automatic weapons.

I leaned against the building and abandoned all thoughts of going to my office. I desperately wanted to get back to Rue Hamra and the Al Manara district where I lived. As I considered my next move, the firing stopped. I remained motionless and listened. I could hear the car horns several blocks to my left and sporadic gunfire to my right. The nearest route home was across the street that was sprayed by bullets only moments before. It was quiet now.

I inched my way to the edge of the building and peered around the corner. No sign of the gunmen. "Now's my chance," I thought.

Gripping my briefcase in my left hand as a shield, I dashed across the street. As I leaped onto the far curb, the gunmen opened fire but with two more strides, I was out of sight in the safety of another building. I kept running until I reached the end of the block. Ahead were the St. Charles City Center and the Holiday Inn. I continued in that direction and then turned left onto Rue Hamra toward the downtown area. As I approached the center of town, the tension slowly began to leave my body. Weakness and exhaustion made me aware of my physical condition. My shirt was soaked with sweat and I noticed the large perspiration rings under the arms of my jacket. My feet were hurting. It was not the day to wear the fashionable elevated shoes I had purchased in Frankfurt. They were uncomfortable to walk in and certainly not meant for running. My whole body ached.

I stopped, removed my jacket, and let the breeze cool my body. There was always a breeze coming off the Mediterranean that made the extreme summer heat more bearable. As I rested, I thought about the troubles in Lebanon and how it might disrupt my business. But then, as always, I dismissed it with the feeling that it was only temporary and would pass.

After a brief rest, I decided to go to the American University Hospital. Gisela would be there and I could sit with her in the coffee shop and have a cup of American coffee.

Gisela saw me come in and immediately went behind the counter to get me a cup of coffee. She knew that I liked the coffee here not least of all because of the congenial atmosphere and hometown-like feeling. She enjoyed her volunteer work with the Women's Auxiliary that ran the coffee shop. She also enjoyed the camaraderie of new friends she met while waiting on tables twice each week and the feeling of being needed.

Our friends, Josephine MacDonald and Ray Ruehl were there as usual. I grabbed a chair from an adjoining table and greeted "Jo" and Ray as I sat down. Jo was a long time resident of Beirut and a mother to the wives of foreign businessmen. Since the death of her husband, a noted administrator of the American University Hospital, she had remained in Beirut contributing her time to the Women's Auxiliary, which she had organized. Ray Ruehl, a bachelor, was the Art teacher at the American Community School (ACS). He enjoyed meeting the parents of his students who dropped-in at the coffee shop, and Duane was one of his students. Hamburgers, french fries, milkshakes and other typical American fare were on the menu and the familiar catsup bottle sat on each table.

Gisela placed the coffee in front of me, kissed me lightly on the cheek and eyed me carefully as she sat down. I reached for the cup but quickly returned it to the saucer, my trembling hands spilling coffee on the table.

"Are you all right?" she asked.

"It's just the heat," I replied without looking at her.

"You're all wet. Where have you been?"

"I've just been walking and I'm tired. Besides, it's terribly hot out there."

Gisela was no fool, and I knew she suspected that something was wrong and would not let up until she had an explanation. As I attempted to make light conversation, I was aware of her blue eyes following my every movement. Her youthful appearance did not reveal her thirty-seven years, and although her German accent was still detectable, she was not aware of it. At a petite five-feet two-inches, she made a striking figure. Although underestimated by most people, she was strong willed and usually got her way.

Gisela placed her hand on Jo's arm and said, "We'll have to be going now. I've already spent too much time here today, and there's still much to be done at home before dinner." Her curiosity was getting the best of her.

"You're right, Schnuck," I said. "We should go. I'll meet you outside."

'Schnuck' had become a word of endearment between us. Before we were married in Germany, I had tried to find some German pet word and had come up with 'Schnuckiputzilein,' whose meaning more closely resembled 'sweetie pie.' This I shortened over the years to 'Schnuck' and it was the only name I now used with her.

I bade Jo and Ray goodbye and went outside to wait and have time to think. I didn't want to worry her, but I knew she would not be fooled by a fabricated story. I would have to tell her something without alarming her unnecessarily. As I contemplated what I would say, Gisela appeared beside me. She took my hand and said, "Now tell me what happened!"

As we walked up the hill to Rue Hamra, I gave a brief description of my encounter while downplaying the potential danger and avoiding the display of gunfire. When I had finished, she stopped, turned to look directly in my eyes and said, "The next time you attempt to go to the office, I'm going with you!"

During the next several weeks I kept seeing the same face. It seemed that wherever I went, I saw this man who would try to preoccupy himself whenever I looked in his direction. I became aware that he was following me. When I went home, the man positioned himself where he had a clear view of the entrance to my house. Each day when I left the house, he followed me. I thought the man might be part of the security police and finally decided to confront him. On my return home this day, I entered the house, waited a few moments, then went back outside and made my way along the street careful to keep out of sight. When I reached the spot where the man stood, I walked up to him and said, "Can I help you?" He just looked at me and said nothing.

"Why are you following me?" I asked. Again the man did not reply, so I turned to leave and said, "I don't plan to go anywhere tonight so you can have the night off."

I don't know whether he understood me or not, but his surveillance must have stopped for I never saw him again.

* * * * *

During the spring of 1975, troubles in Lebanon had begun increasing while the availability of goods and services were decreasing. The sporadic outbreak of hostilities caused people to stay home from work and important services like the collection of garbage were disrupted.

One day that summer, Gisela decided to visit her friend, Elham Samara, the daughter of the minister from southern Lebanon, who lived several blocks away from our house. I had gone out in search of food, so Gisela went alone. She told me how she stepped over the trash on the sidewalk, covering her nose with a handkerchief to keep from inhaling the awful smell of burning garbage that had been set afire to prevent the spread of disease. She heard a pinging and popping sound, which she thought, came from cans and bottles exploding among the burning piles of rubbish. When she reached the end of the block, she could see Elham's house on the other side of the wide intersection. The streets were empty, so she stepped off the sidewalk and started across the middle of the intersection. As she approached the center of the street, shooting broke out on both sides, catching her in the crossfire. Bullets began pounding the street and ricocheted around her. She froze in her steps not knowing which way to turn. She glanced at Elham's house and caught sight of someone frantically waving to her. She recognized Elham and started to run, and then she fell.

The impact of the fall temporarily knocked the wind out of her. She must have slipped or tripped on something, but then it had happened so fast, she couldn't be sure. Her chest was hurting from the impact of the fall. The firing continued as she lay there deciding what to do.

Upon seeing Gisela fall, Elham thought she had been shot and screamed for her brother, Hassan, to help her. Hassan ran down the stairs to the ground floor. By this time, Gisela had recovered and was about to get to her feet when she saw Hassan coming out of the building. She realized he would be in danger if he came to her, so she jumped up and waved him back as she ran to him. He caught her as she stumbled onto the sidewalk.

"Are you all right?" Asked Hassan with deep concern.

"Yes, I'm O.K."

Just then, more shots were fired. Hassan quickly pulled Gisela inside the building to safety. Elham was waiting inside and embraced her. They both cried.

As they began to climb the stairs, Gisela felt the pain in her ankle that was already swelling badly. She now knew why she had fallen. It must have been a pothole in the street that caused her to overturn the ankle and fall.

Chapter 13
Warring Factions
Spring/Summer 1975

Situated at the major crossroads of East and West Civilization, Lebanon has been overrun time and again by conquering Armies. The inhabitants of this coastal strip have been known throughout history as Canaanites, Phoenicians, Syrians and Lebanese. They have always been merchants, not warriors. With few exceptions, they have always waited to determine which way the battles would lean, and then sided with the expected victor.

Centuries had not changed the Lebanese. They maintained neutrality in the international arena except when the Arabs were at risk with other nations. Then the bond of language brought the Arabs together. True Arabians are few and exist in Saudi Arabia and in Sheikdoms throughout the Gulf region. Simply stated, an Arab is one who speaks Arabic and is of Arab—Semitic descent, the majority of which are Moslem. The exceptions were to be found in Lebanon.

Lebanon acquired its independence in 1945 during the French Mandate which stipulated that the President of Lebanon must be a Maronite Christian, and the Prime Minister a Sunni Moslem. According to the recorded population statistics at the time of the Mandate, there were more Christians than Moslems living in Lebanon. This ratio changed in the years that followed and now there are more Moslems than Christians.

The Government was comprised of various factions, each representing its religious sect. The Christians were known as the Phalangists, or the Kataeb, the predominant faction of the 'Rightists,' while the predominant faction of the 'Leftists," were the Nasserites (Pan-Arab) and the Progressive Socialist Party, comprised mostly of Moslems.

Camile Chamoun and Pierre Gemayel led the 'Rightists' while Kamal Junblatt headed the 'Leftist' movement, supported in part by the Palestinians.

Trouble surrounded every election. The Leftists wanted more representation in government while the Rightists opposed any such move to weaken their dominance. The Rightists referred always to the Mandate and insisted on their 'majority rule' even though they had now become the minority. The Moslems wanted to institute change in the constitution to reflect the demographic situation. It was in this environment, as the elections of 1975 drew near, that the Civil War began.

The political division was not a simple split between Moslems and Christians. Many Rightists were Moslem and many Leftists were Christian. In truth, the champions of the poor were the Leftists; the Rightists represented the rich and were primarily concerned with preserving their power and wealth.

The Palestinians living in Lebanon were, essentially, people without a country. They had fled Palestine or had been forced out when Israel was created as a country and the Jews took possession of a specified area in the land of Palestine. Arriving in Lebanon, the Palestinians had been accepted as brothers and were afforded temporary living areas while negotiations continued at the United Nations for a resolution that would permit them to return to their homeland. The several ensuing wars with Israel however, brought more Palestinian refugees into Lebanon and it became the headquarters for the Palestine Liberation Organization (PLO). The PLO used Lebanon as a base to launch raids into Israeli-occupied Palestine. Those Palestinians who were fortunate to arrive in Lebanon with money, were now living among the affluent, holding good jobs, while those who came with nothing lived in camps at a sub-human level.

Western influence in Lebanon was evident everywhere. The business community headquartered major companies from all over the world, the majority of which were from the west. The continual disputes over territorial rights between Israel and her Arab neighbors, together with the knowledge that the Unites States supported Israel, led the Lebanese from a pro-Arab posture to a more neutral position. It was evident that they would wait once more to see who the probable victor would be before choosing sides.

Public opinion in the U.S. highly favored Israel's position as publicized by the many Jewish organizations, influential Jewish business leaders and well-organized news propaganda. The Arabs had not yet learned to use the power of the press nor had they used their wealth to gain favorable influence among the American people. American political candidates vied with each other to gain the support of the Jewish vote and their financial backing, by promising support for Israel. Religious organizations gave their support based on Biblical ties. With this popular support, Israel flaunted her strength and chose to ignore UN resolutions when it suited her and invoked those resolutions when it was in her best interests. Violations to UN resolutions became a matter of record but were not known to the American people at large. It was unpopular to speak out against Israel for fear of being labeled anti-Semitic. The irony is that Arabs are a Semitic people also.

The first incident leading to the Lebanese War was in April 1975. A busload of Palestinians was massacred by the right-wing Phalangists, a result of irreconcilable antagonisms between the predominantly Christian Phalangists and the masses of desperately poor Lebanese and Palestinian people. Both Christians and Moslems who aspired to end the right wing dominated political system and wanted an end to their subjugation and poverty, were included among the Leftists. Surprisingly, there was no armed reprisal by the PLO for this massacre. However, the Leftists wanted revenge for their slain brothers.

After this incident, a real power struggle came into play. I heard conflicting views about the massacre from the few who openly discussed it. Hoping it would be forgotten, the majority shrugged it off. I knew it was important not to become involved in the internal affairs of Lebanon and remained silent. After all, I was a foreigner and it was not my concern.

Skirmishes broke out on the outskirts of Beirut. Earlier, when there had been trouble, the people stayed home from work in fear an all-out war would develop. After deployment of Lebanese security forces, people went back to work. Clashes continued, however, and spread throughout the countryside. Although hostilities were increasing, the population as a whole went about their work with the attitude that it would pass. Cease-fire after cease-fire was continuously broken while the severity of these skirmishes increased.

Public outcry for an end to the fighting was expressed in the newspapers and pressure was being placed on the President of Lebanon, Suleiman Franjieh, to do something or resign from office. The President made speeches expressing his desire for an end to the fighting but took no direct governmental action with the Army or Security Forces. The Army was predominantly Christian (Phalangist) and would not act against their own factions. The Security Forces roamed the streets in Armed Vehicles but had no authority to use force. Armed men of all factions walked the streets and went about setting up their own defenses. Bombings of the commercial establishments of opposing factions escalated throughout the city. Merchants paid protection money to prevent destruction to their properties while 'Mafia-type' strongmen gave rise to new lawlessness when the government failed to act. Homes were being burglarized and the police were of no help; they would investigate, but no action would be taken to apprehend the criminals. No one wanted to do anything to provoke reprisal.

The President's son, Tony Franjieh, used his ministerial powers and led the Phalangists in the north of Lebanon against opposing factions. It was obvious that the ruling party did not have a sincere desire to end the hostilities unless the Rightists could expect to be victorious.

Before too long, another actor arrived on the scene. The first incident occurred when an auto rental agency unwittingly rented a car to persons with false European passports. The cars were rigged with rocket-propelled explosives and time devices, and then parked near the PLO headquarters building frequented by the PLO leader, Yassir Arafat. The explosives detonated after the perpetrators had already left the country. In reprisal, the auto agency was bombed for its negligence in renting the car and not properly checking the identity of the people. The belated descriptions of the infiltrators identified them as Israelis.

Confusion existed everywhere and lent itself to further infiltration by Israelis into Lebanon. The PLO was now for the first time becoming involved in the armed clashes and assisting the Security Forces in their efforts to maintain the peace. The PLO was also being used to negotiate cease-fires between the factions because their power was well known and respected by the Lebanese. The PLO was well armed and had enormous supplies of ammunition. Their presence was soon acutely felt and they began to appear as a threat to the Rightists while providing comfort to the Leftists. Although the PLO had supplied the Leftists with arms, to this point in time they maintained a neutral position.

* * * * *

Another cease-fire had just been broken. I was visiting the home of a government minister from southern Lebanon, Raif Samara, whose daughter Elham was Gisela's close friend.

"What happened?" I asked. "I thought this cease-fire would hold."

Mr. Samara had just returned from an emergency meeting of the Cabinet and looked tired.

"We are not sure," he said. "Both sides had reached an agreement and promised to control their men and insure that no one would take action against the other. We have been in session for the past two days endeavoring to learn how this new fighting got started. The reports we received indicate that a third element is involved. This new element fired on the one group and the other assumed it was the rival faction, so they returned the fire."

"Who was it? I mean who is this new element you referred to?"

"Mr. March," he paused, cleared his throat and chose his words carefully. "We think it is Israeli infiltrators but cannot prove it. If we make this accusation, it will be promptly denied, but the fact remains that our daily reports show persons coming through the border in the south, from Israel."

"Why hasn't anyone stopped them?" I asked.

The minister lit his pipe, then said, "The Israelis move their fences into Lebanon daily. They have already advanced about two kilometers inside our territory."

"Why doesn't the government take action to stop them?" I asked.

Again the minister adjusted his seat and appeared uncomfortable as he formulated his thoughts.

"You see, Mr. March, there are certain factions in our government who don't wish to cause any problem with Israel by taking any action or making any accusations that would jeopardize their promise of support. Right now, the troubles are in the northern provinces and all attention is focused in that direction."

I asked my next question cautiously.

"Sir, I'm afraid I don't understand. You mentioned something about Israeli support. What does this mean?"

Mr. Samara moved forward in his chair and said, "Mr. March, your wife and my daughter are good friends, and I consider you a good friend and member of our family. I trust our conversation will remain confidential."

"Sir, you can be assured of that. I will say nothing that would reflect adversely on you. My family loves Lebanon and wish to remain here. We are naturally concerned about the developments here since it not only affects our business but our safety as well. I don't wish to pry into your country's affairs but I am naturally curious to know and understand exactly what is happening here. You may feel free to discuss anything with me."

Mr. Samara sat back in his chair and said, "I felt this, of course, but I must not be quoted on what I say at this time. I'm sure you understand these matters are sensitive and most confidential."

"You have my word, sir," I said.

"The Israeli government, through private channels, has offered assistance in the way of arms. Some have already been received and are in use. Now do you understand?"

"It certainly explains a lot. But aren't you concerned about becoming indebted to them? For example, I understand they've always wanted control of that river in the South."

"The Litani?"

"Yes, that's it. If they're moving their fences in the south, perhaps that's a move to get it. What do they expect in return for their support?" I asked.

"They have only expressed their willingness to help in our struggle here. They fear the Palestinians will exert more control here, and with their strength, take over the government of Lebanon."

"Why all the concern about the Palestinians? They are not involved in the fighting, are they?"

"Indirectly, yes. They are supplying arms to the Leftists and could easily become actively involved themselves should the Rightists have a major victory. It appears only a matter of time now before they are drawn into the fighting. I fear for my country and my people. I wish there was something more I could do, but I am only one person and the situation is most complicated."

This and other discussions afforded me greater insight about the problems and the complications surrounding the troubles. I felt it was only a matter of time before all-out fighting would take place, but then another cease-fire was arranged and the hope that it would hold, brought optimism.

I received word that Elie had been wounded while trying to come to the office. A bullet passed through his chest but he was out of danger and recovering at his home in Byblos. He did not want me to visit him since it was too dangerous to travel there. Under the circumstances, I felt my presence was needed in Lebanon, so I called the cosmetic company in West Germany to inform Mr. Walsh that the Iranian project should be placed on hold for the time being. To my dismay, I was informed that Mr. Walsh had fled the country and taken the money I had placed in his care. For the moment, I was powerless to act. Perhaps when Elie recovered, I thought, we would both go to Germany to see what action could be taken. In the meanwhile, I must give my full attention to protecting the business in Lebanon.

* * * * *

Gisela was spending more time with me at the office. Her

knowledge of cosmetics was helpful in determining the right mix of products for this market. Her study of history, especially history of the Middle East, was also an asset. Due to the unacceptance of women in a business role outside the country of Lebanon, she confined her assistance to that of advisement. She performed various liaison duties with representatives and distributors within the country and was an inspiration to other Lebanese women who sought change from their sheltered lives. Her background as an IBM systems analyst could not be utilized as yet, but we had hopes of automating our operation and she was already planning for an appropriate system.

* * * * *

What started out as a peaceful day at the office was suddenly interrupted by gunfire. I ran to the window and saw people scattering in every direction. As the gunfire continued, the unrelenting sound of car horns added to the noise as people fled the area.

"We better go home," said Houry. "It's not safe to stay here."

"Go if you like," I said. "Tell the others they may also go if they wish. I'm staying. The shooting will likely stop as soon as everyone leaves."

The staff departed and other offices within the building also closed, but Gisela and I remained. The streets were soon deserted and we alone continued working. I got up and left my desk, I don't remember why, when a bullet crashed through my office window, piercing the back of my chair, ricocheted around the office walls until it spent itself. What was I doing here? I carefully went to the window, cautiously peered around the corner of the window, endeavoring to locate the source of the gunfire. Across the street windows were being shattered by rapid machine gun fire. The sound of bullets ricocheting off the street and concrete buildings was frightening. Having second thoughts about leaving with the others was a little late. It had been foolish to place ourselves at risk like this; besides, we could no longer concentrate on work. I was especially concerned about Gisela's safety, always feeling I could manoeuver better alone.

In a short while the gunfire became sporadic, so I decided it was best to try leaving while it was still daylight. My car was parked behind the building and I could get there without being seen by using the back door where high walls provided cover.

Crawling under windows to keep out of sight, we cautiously made our way to the elevator. It was not working; the electricity had been turned off. It was necessary to take the stairs, which were in total darkness. Gisela stayed close behind me keeping one hand on my shoulder as I felt my way down each step. The stairwell was narrow, and each floor landing, different, but we managed to reach the lobby without mishap. Shadows followed our movements on the Lobby walls in the small amount of remaining daylight. We cautiously made our way to the back door. The door was locked.

"What do we do now?" asked Gisela.

"We'll have to go out the front door," I said.

"We can't. We'll be seen!"

I could see she was frightened and knew I had to appear calm. It was imperative that we leave the office building now, before nightfall, or we may be trapped overnight.

"Listen carefully," I said. "I'll make my way to the corner of the building, and if it's clear, I'll motion for you to follow. Stay close to the building and remain as inconspicuous as possible."

"OK, but please be careful," she pleaded.

Pillars lined the front of the office building. Stopping by each pillar for a few moments before continuing to the next, I slowly made my way along the front of the building. I reached the corner and looked around. At ground level, we were shielded from view by a wall next to the garage entrance. The overpass in front provided protection from the building across the street.

I motioned for Gisela to follow while I scrutinized other buildings for any sign of movement. I waited until I felt her hand on my back. Seeing no sign of movement anywhere, I said, "I'm going to run to the car. Wait until you hear me start the engine, then come running. I'll have the door open."

I ran along the building and kept low until I reached the car. It seemed forever to get the key in the lock. I unlatched the door, jumped in, pushed open the other door for Gisela, and then started the engine. Gisela came running and jumped into the car, slamming and locking the door.

"Stay down," I said. "I'm going to make a run for it and I'm not stopping for anything. Keep your head down and don't look up. OK?"

Gisela nodded her head and slid down in the seat. I eased the car into gear and slowly moved toward the street. I looked at the underpass directly in front of me and glanced around for any sign of gunmen. It looked clear. I jammed the accelerator to the floor. The powerful Mercedes engine roared to life with the tires squealing. They continued squealing as I rounded the corner of the underpass leading to the ramp that would take us onto the main road to the downtown area. Before I could navigate the turn onto the ramp, gunfire erupted. I kept the accelerator pressed to the floor and crouched low in my seat. White puffs of chipped cement exploded around the car, but within seconds I reached the main highway traveling at high speed. My thoughts raced as I watched the road ahead for any signs of a roadblock. The road was clear. I breathed a sigh of relief and braked quickly as I approached the curve leading to the St. Charles City Center. After negotiating the curve, I tapped Gisela on the back and told her it was safe to get up from the floor. She sat up but remained quiet as we made our way home.

Chapter 14
Abduction/Detention
Late Summer/Fall 1975

    The civil unrest was increasing and spreading to more areas of Beirut as new factions entered the skirmish. The U.S. Embassy issued its first warning, advising Americans to leave if they had no pressing business in Lebanon. I had no thought of leaving and remained hopeful that cooler heads would prevail and that it would end as suddenly as it began. For employees and families of foreign companies, it was a simple matter to pack up and go. They had an income and a job back home. Any losses they sustained would be compensated by their employer. For the entrepreneur, it was not that easy. I was determined to stay and find a way to hang on until things settled down; otherwise, I stood to lose everything I had saved and worked to accrue during the past fifteen years.

    Ready for work, I left the house and walked to my car. It was gone. There was no mistake in parking the car since I had my own private parking space and that's where I always parked it. I immediately called the police. They were sympathetic but gave me no hope in recovering it. As they explained it, a car like mine was probably already out of the country with its serial number changed. The insurance company added to my misery. Due to the militant actions within the country, the 'acts of war' clause was in effect and they were excused from paying any claim for theft. It wasn't the fact that it was a Mercedes Benz that caused me grief; I had owned three of them before. It was the $50,000 I paid for the car that concerned me. With the troubles in Lebanon, business had slowed considerably and money was once again very tight. Now, with the 'acts of war' clause in effect, the risk to all businessmen would be much greater.

I decided to go to my office by taxi and Gisela insisted in going along. I flagged a taxi and held the door for her to climb in. She brushed the seat before sitting down. The hot plastic-covered seats easily soiled one's clothes when they became damp with perspiration.

I slid in beside her and directed the driver to Rue Fouad Chehab. He nodded, beeped his horn, then edged his way into the traffic. On hot days like this I would miss the air conditioning of my own car.

The slow movement of traffic produced very little air as the taxi maneuvered its way onto Rue Spears. I was apprehensive. Would the driver take us to my office or would he refuse to go into that area? One nice thing about taxis in Lebanon, you didn't give a street address of your destination. You only indicated the locale or the street where you wished to travel.

There was little talk of troubles in the news the night before and on the surface, people appeared more relaxed.

As the taxi approached the intersection leading onto Rue Fouad Chehab, the driver gave a twist of his hand, a sign of inquiry, as to the direction I wished to go.

"Straight ahead. Bisharra Al-Koury Street," I said.

The driver hesitated, then shrugged his shoulders and continued. This was a metered taxi and I wasn't concerned about haggling over the fare. During these troubles, the metered taxi was the most reasonable since the others charged whatever they wished or could extract with sympathy.

We were now approaching an overpass that bridged an unfinished roadway below. On the other side of the overpass, rocks and other debris were scattered over the highway, blocking the road. The driver slowed the car and was preparing to stop when I noticed an opening to the extreme left that looked passable, and pointed to it. At that moment, movement from a balcony overlooking the highway, caught my attention. A woman was frantically waving her arms in an effort to signal the driver. Before I could alert him, Gisela grabbed my arm and shouted, "There're gunmen, over there!"

"Where!" I shouted.

"Over there, to the side of the road!"

She was pointing to the stairwell at the edge of the road leading onto the overpass. Four gunmen approached the car forcing it to stop and immediately surrounded it. They looked at Gisela and me in the back seat, and then motioned for the driver to backup. He obeyed at once. The gunmen then motioned for the driver to move the car toward a side street. The car moved slowly with the gunmen walking alongside. One of the gunmen gave instructions to the driver, which he obediently followed.

We were escorted into a narrow alleyway. Two gunmen took their position in front of the car and the other two walked behind. Gisela was holding tightly onto my arm without saying a word. I was growing anxious wondering where we were being taken. News reports of people being abducted and killed came to mind. I tried to dismiss these thoughts. After all, we were foreigners, and none of the reported incidents had involved foreigners. Perhaps, I thought, we were being shown a safer route around the area and we would still be able to get to the office.

The driver said nothing and maintained the gunmen's slow pace by letting the clutch in and out as we continued. Just before the end of the alleyway, we turned into an old courtyard. It was then that my anxiety turned to alarm. The courtyard was filled with gunmen—perhaps forty or more with even more heads appearing from doorways

The entire group of gunmen now surrounded the car. They were young and appeared nervous, pointing their guns menacingly at us. This nervousness could cause one of them to unwittingly pull a trigger, I thought.

I looked at Gisela. She was visibly shaking. I took her hand and said, "Don't worry, everything will be alright."

Gisela held her stomach. "I think I must go to the bathroom," she said.

"You can't go now. Just sit tight, we'll be out of here soon. Don't worry."

She looked up at me and said, "When you say don't worry, that's the time I worry."

I attempted a chuckle but it caught in my throat. The driver was being ordered out of the car.

The gunmen looked carefully at the driver's identity card while others searched him. The driver was talking excitedly. He kept up a constant babble, gesturing with his hands and pointing to Gisela and me in the back seat of the car. The gunmen then ordered him to open the car trunk. After searching the trunk, they came to the back door and motioned for me to open it. From what I could determine, they wished to see my identity papers.

I reached toward the inside pocket of my suit jacket but stopped immediately when I saw the reaction of the gunman who moved his gun barrel to my head. I pointed to the pocket of my coat and said, "I.D., I.D." The gunman then motioned for me to get the I.D., which I produced very slowly and handed my passport to him. The gunman took the passport, then using the point of his gun with his finger on the trigger, motioned for me to open my briefcase.

I nervously obeyed. The gunman poked around inside until he was satisfied there were no weapons, I presumed. The gunman then took my passport and left without searching Gisela's purse.

Shouting now occupied my attention. The gunmen were yelling at the taxi driver and prodding him with their weapons. He kept opening his arms with the palms of his hands up, seemingly gesturing, 'What did I do?' He would then point again and again to the back seat of the car toward Gisela and me.

The seriousness of the situation began to take hold and my mind sought a plan of action. I drew a blank.

A gunman now opened the car door and motioned for me to step out. For the first time, I was truly afraid. I was not about to go anywhere without Gisela so I grabbed her hand and pulled her out with me. I determined not to leave her alone with the gunmen at any cost.

After some discussion among the gunmen, all three of us were ushered through a small passageway that opened into a tiny room. The stench of urine was strong and the room was dimly lit. A small table with one chair stood in the center of the room and a bunk was positioned against the wall.

The driver was ordered to the chair and Gisela and I to the bunk. Three guards stood by the doorway with their guns slung over their shoulders. Waving his gun back and forth as he talked, one of the gunmen began immediately to interrogate the driver. Gisela and I sat quietly and watched. We couldn't understand what was being said. Their talk was very rapid, but their actions needed little interpretation. The driver was wailing as though in anguish, pleading his case—whatever it was.

As we sat there, watching, I began to wonder what our abduction would lead to. Many thoughts crossed my mind. I could have acted differently, stayed at home, packed it in and left the country, only to reach the conclusion that there was too much at stake—our financial livelihood. At that moment, however, I was more concerned about staying alive.

The first sigh of relief came from Gisela when true to Arab tradition, one of the gunmen said, "You like coffee?"

Almost in unison, we replied, "Yes."

Standing his gun against the far wall, he left the room. The offer of coffee appeared friendly enough but I realized this gesture was so rooted in tradition that one could not draw any conclusions from it. I eyed the gun that had been carelessly left behind. It was an M-1 type, which was familiar to me. It was the same type I had used in basic training when I was in the U.S. Air Force. If it became necessary, I thought, at least I could use it. A disciplined soldier would never have let his gun stand there. However, we were not being held for routine questioning by the Lebanese military. The shabby and diverse military garb worn by the gunmen had no uniformity whatsoever. They were obviously members of one of the factions, but which one?

The aroma of coffee reached us even before the man appeared. He entered the room with two small cups held on a slab of wood and offered it first to Gisela, then to me. "Only in Lebanon," I thought, "would gunmen hold us hostage and offer their hospitality!" The taxi driver was not offered any. It did not look good for him.

"Shoukran," I said.

At this, the gunman spoke rapidly to me in Arabic.

"Do you speak English?" I asked.

"Yes, I speak little English," he said.

"I speak Arabic, swayaa (a little)," I replied.

The gunman grinned with a pleased expression on his face and I took this opportunity to ask him a question.

"What is the problem? Why are we being held here?"

"No worry, every-ting OK," he replied.

I was about to inquire further when the gunman who had taken my passport walked into the room and came directly to me. He opened the passport and pointed to the word, 'Pennsylvania.'

"Venezuela?" he inquired.

"No! Amerikaner! United States! Amerikaner!" I shouted.

The gunman left once more with my passport and my concern deepened. There were reports that Israeli infiltrators were using Venezuelan identities and with a name like Abe, it wouldn't help much if they couldn't read too well. I hoped they were not part of a militant PLO faction and get me confused as an Israeli. I was thankful that I had changed the name in my passport from Abraham Firestone March to Abe F. March. They would have tried to make some connection, I thought. In Lebanon, one could not distinguish identity by one's appearance because of the great number of foreigners. This added to the confusion within Lebanon itself. Identity primarily depended upon your name and the area in which one lived, not where one was born.

Gisela sat quietly, holding onto me, and sipped her coffee. Her thoughts had also been racing ever since the taxi was forced to bring us here. She wondered what she would do if they took me away. Would she scream or just hang onto me. She was determined to put up a fight.

The interrogation of the taxi driver continued and he was sweating profusely. He now sat in a state of resignation and his eyes would wander toward me as if pleading for help. I had no way of knowing to which faction the driver belonged and decided it best not to interfere. But as time passed, I felt compelled to do something.

Pointing at the driver, I said, "He was taking us to our office. What do you want with him? He did nothing wrong. We are Americans working here in Lebanon and don't know what these troubles are all about. I have a Lebanese business partner. Perhaps you wish to speak with him."

From the look in the interrogator's eyes, I knew he understood very little, if any, of what I was saying, but there was obvious appreciation from the driver. The driver then repeated, in Arabic, what I had said to the interrogator. As he was talking, the door opened and the man with my passport entered once again. He wanted to see my Lebanese identity papers. I produced my work and residence permit, which he took and once more departed. I now began to wonder if I would be physically searched. I had my wallet in my pocket and my Pennsylvania Drivers License had my full name, Abraham Firestone March on it. A short while later, the man who took my papers returned and spoke with the interrogator. They talked together while leafing through my papers and glancing intermittently toward us. After a while, the interrogator abruptly left the room.

The man with my papers walked up to me and with the aid of the gunman who spoke some English, said, "We sorry for you—you be here. You go now. Every-ting OK. We treat you good, yes?"

I stood up and said, "Yes, you treat us good. Shoukran."

The gunmen stood aside as we were then escorted from the room to the taxi. The gunmen in the courtyard remained where they were as we walked by them. The Taxi driver was smiling and obviously relieved. Gisela climbed into the car and said, "Would you believe it! The meter is still running." I had no trouble believing anything at that point.

"Don't worry," I said. "He probably won't charge us. If it wasn't that we were foreigners, the driver might still be held. In fact, this is one time I'm glad you were along. There is no way they would want to be accused of abducting a woman. You probably saved me from a lengthy confinement."

"Perhaps they didn't think we were important enough to keep," said Gisela.

As the taxi backed out of the courtyard, the gunmen stood aside, watching. The driver was directed to proceed farther up the alley and return toward the city-center via another route. They conversed together in Arabic, smiling and acting as though nothing had happened.

The stench was terrible on the back street from sewage running thru the gutters. People walked through the muck and sludge making no effort to avoid it. Children played with make-believe guns, aiming them at the taxi, shouting, "Boom, boom."

As soon as we were clear of the area and approaching the more modern part of town, the driver turned half-way in his seat and said, "You very lucky. They know me. They let you go because they know me. I tell them you live in Moslem sector. It not good to keep you. You good people. Not good to cause trouble."

I was uncertain whether he was telling us the truth or if it was just a ploy to extract more money for the cab fare. Three hundred and twenty-seven pounds registered on the meter for a ride that would normally have cost five pounds. The driver continued making comments regarding the good fortune that he was the driver, which I tried to ignore. I had only thirty pounds in my pocket, so I instructed the driver to stop and let us out. I handed the thirty pounds to him to avoid an argument and said, "This is all I have."

"It OK," he said.

It didn't seem important at the time to report this incident to the Embassy. After all, I thought, we weren't harmed, so why bother. Within a short time, however, the significance of our abduction took a different turn. It was apparent that the gunmen were looking for a foreigner with stature and U.S. Ambassador Malloy and his aide were abducted. The foreigners in Lebanon now had reason for alarm once this precedent had been set. My belated information to the embassy was regrettable.

* * * * *

As the fighting intensified, weapons and supplies were of prime importance to the differing factions. The splinter groups within the Moslem community were comparable to the various political groups among the Phalangists who had their own individual armies. Tony Franjieh sought to strengthen his own power base and acquire weapons for profit at the same time.

Elie Bassil, having recovered from his wound, came to see me with a list of weapons that Tony wanted to acquire. He asked if I knew someone in Germany who could get the weapons. I told Elie that offhand, I didn't know anyone. He said that Tony would be most appreciative if I could help him get these weapons. I felt very uncomfortable at the thought of dealing in weapons. Would I be contributing to the on going fighting if I consented to help? Our personal losses were mounting, and I felt I owed Elie some consideration, so I told him that if I were to go to Germany, I could inquire and perhaps locate a source.

"Good. When can you go? Tony wants to spend five million pounds. If you can arrange it, there's a five percent commission in it for you."

"Suppose I find the source," I said. "How will the transaction work?"

"We want the arms brought in by boat near the Lebanese coast. Our people will meet the boat and pay for the arms in cash, in whatever currency they want, once we verify that the guns are all there," said Elie.

"If this is urgent, I'll make arrangements to leave at once. Perhaps I'll be able to do something about our $50,000 that Mr. Walsh absconded with."

"Yes, if you find where he is, we have many connections. We can get it from him," said Elie. "The weapons are important. Tony will be very generous if you can get them for him."

I made immediate arrangements to fly to Frankfurt. I'll make the arrangements, I thought, but I want no part in the transfer of arms. I could imagine two boats meeting on the high seas, exchanging arms for cash, then taking the money back by force.

Without consciously realizing it, my concern for money overruled my convictions. I told myself that I was doing Elie a favor. If they wanted to kill each other, that was their affair.

On my arrival in Frankfurt, I made discreet inquiries with business associates who gave me the name of a man who dealt in small arms and who reportedly had connections in Belgium. I called the man known as Werner, and we arranged to meet at a convenient place for lunch.

Werner was prompt and after exchanging greetings, we selected a table that afforded privacy.

"You are American?" asked Werner.

"Yes, I'm an American living and working in Beirut, Lebanon."

"That seems to be a trouble spot at the moment," he said.

"Yes it is. Hopefully, the troubles will end soon so things can get back to normal," I said.

"What brings you to Frankfurt?" asked Werner.

"My business here is two-fold. I have my regular business to conduct involving cosmetics and toiletries, however, I'm here for another reason and that's why I asked for this meeting. I understand you either handle arms or have connections where they can be obtained."

"Who wants arms?"

"I think that's rather obvious, knowing where I'm coming from. I'll provide more details if I know I'm talking to the right person. Are you in a position to supply weapons?"

"Depends on what kind you want," said Werner.

I produced the list Elie had given me. "These are the items my client wishes to purchase. Would you be able to get them?"

Werner studied the list, and then said, "There are some items here that might be difficult to get. Perhaps they could be substituted for something similar?"

"That's possible. I'd have to check on it," I said.

"If I locate these articles and you pay for them, I really don't care what you do with them," said Werner.

"That might pose a problem. My client wants the goods delivered. Upon verification, the money will be paid in cash."

"I'm sorry, Mr. March. I won't get involved in shipment of arms beyond the German border. Some of the articles that would originate in Belgium would also have to be picked up there."

"Do you know of anyone who would handle the shipment for a handsome fee?" I asked.

"Fortunately or unfortunately, I don't. This is a risky business. I can supply the goods but it's up to you or your client to take possession. Also, we'd want to be paid before we release the goods."

"I understand," I said. "I'm only trying to help a friend. Perhaps I'd better drop this matter completely."

"That would be my suggestion. Getting the arms is not too difficult, but transporting them across international borders can be a big problem. Those people who regularly deal in smuggling operations are the ones to contact. There is honor among these people. You may have heard the expression, 'honor among thieves.' Well, if they cheat, they die," said Werner.

I concluded the meeting and decided to pursue the matter no further. The risk was not worth it, I decided. I would simply tell Elie that I was unable to arrange transportation for the goods according to his terms. If Elie wanted to arrange transportation, then I would have him contact Werner directly.

I tried unsuccessfully to locate Mr. Walsh. I was told that the company he headed was in serious financial difficulty and that he had suddenly disappeared. It was rumored that he had taken much of the company's money to Switzerland before he left. Since he was Australian, it was thought that he might have gone there. I contacted Mr. Schmidt who was also trying his best to extract some money from the German company for fees owed to him for his efforts in the Iranian cosmetic operation. According to Mr. Schmidt, the Iranian project was still viable but it would require more upfront money and the backing of some western businessmen who could participate. We could not rely on the Iranians to put the project together. Under my present circumstances, I told him he would have to look elsewhere for assistance.

I returned to Lebanon and informed Elie about my trip. I told him I had found a source but was unable to arrange transportation. He wanted to know how he could contact Werner so I gave him his telephone number. Elie said he would inform Tony Franjieh and let him handle it from there on.

Chapter 15
The Foreign Exodus
Fall 1975

The Souk area, center for the Moslem merchants, was falling to ruin from the day and night bombardment of rockets and mortars hurled from the Christian stronghold of Ashrafeyeh. The Port of Beirut had seen some of the toughest fighting with each faction striving for control of the port. Ships waiting offshore with badly needed supplies were unable to dock. One by one, these ships departed for other Middle East Ports to unload their cargo. Syria, Jordan, Egypt and Saudi Arabia welcomed the ships with the hope that they may replace Beirut as the center for commerce.

As told to me by the minister from southern Lebanon, the Lebanese government was receiving arms from Israel. Israel also sold arms to those Rightists factions who had the money to pay. Elie told me that Tony Franjieh was getting his arms from Israeli sources.

The numerous cease-fires appeared to be a convenient method for each side to regroup, resupply, rest and plan their next move. This lull in the fighting also enabled the citizens to get money from the few banks that would open for a few hours each day. Hoarding of food caused prices to soar and in many instances, stores were completely sold out.

Broken water mains caused much of the town water to be shut off and the small amount of water that was available, was contaminated. Using Clorox or other purifying substances together with boiling the water, made it safe to drink.

Most of the foreigners and many of the affluent Lebanese had fled the country. Those who remained, stayed because of family ties or business interests. Their departure would mean looting and confiscation of their property.

In the meantime, the American Community School opened for the new school year. Although everyone could hear shelling day and night, the fighting had been limited to central and East Beirut. Until the end of September, West Beirut was relatively quiet. It was the Moslem section of the city. Most westerners lived there and the school was also located there. Cinemas and shops remained opened and held normal hours. One could almost imagine that everything was alright. Despite our misgivings, Duane and Christine began the new school year by walking almost a Kilometer to the ACS everyday. After a short while everyone became used to the sound of distant shelling and gunfire. "It's over there," people said, and our children appeared to give it no second thought after a few days.

Gisela and I deliberated time and again whether to leave or stay. We remained hopeful that the fighting would cease so we could pick up the pieces and continue our business. But our hopes diminished as the skirmishes continued and our losses mounted.

The money I had earned was once more tied up in the business and in the possessions we had acquired in Beirut. A half million dollars worth of goods that I had purchased and paid for arrived in the Port of Beirut but we were unable to get it. Now with the bombardment of the port area and the looting, it became doubtful that anything remained. Traces of our product, with the German labeling, began to appear on the street market. There would be no insurance coverage for these losses. I learned later that most of the wealthy had been shifting funds out of the country for safekeeping.

Safety was now the prime concern. Many of the wealthy Lebanese now lived in major European cities and were continuing their business as traders. Others had fled to summer homes in the mountains; a few remained in the city along with the poor who had no hope of leaving.

In the spring of 1975, when serious fighting started, the U.S. Embassy had "suggested" Americans leave if they had no pressing business in Lebanon. In the fall, this advice was changed to "advise you to leave," which was the step next to evacuation. The families of U.S. Embassy personnel had already departed leaving only a skeleton crew to administer official business.

I was virtually without money. Most of my money was deposited in the Royal Bank of Canada, located at the St. Charles City Center. The bank was completely closed down and severely damaged. The cash I had was insufficient to purchase air tickets and my credit cards were not being honored since there was no way to check their validity. The only form of payment was cash and U.S. dollars were preferred.

Our business had become inactive. The only attention it got was our attempts to protect the small amount of stock remaining at the office. Elie stayed near his home in Byblos and did not venture into Beirut. Our communication became less frequent as telephones were often inoperative. During our last telephone conversation, he told me he was trying to move assets out of Lebanon. Later I learned he had departed for Columbia, South America. Then the Royal Bank of Canada, along with a few other banks, were raided and all the cash and gold looted.

Perhaps the U.S. Embassy could help, I thought. If the Embassy were considering evacuation, perhaps they would provide the transportation from the area. I decided to call them.

I asked the consular official if they were planning to evacuate American citizens.

"Not as yet," was the reply. "So long as the airport is open and the roads are passable to the airport, we will not evacuate. However, we do advise you to leave."

Armed vehicles were escorting convoys of foreigners to the airport on a daily basis and I knew I could leave if I had the money. I was embarrassed by my financial situation but decided to ask assistance from the Embassy, anyway. It was important to get my family to safety.

"I've got a problem," I said. "Very simply, I'm out of money and don't have the means to purchase tickets for my family. Could you advance me the money for transportation or provide me with tickets?"

"I'm sorry, but we do not have the facility nor the authorization for this type of request. We will, however, send a message by telex through the State Department to someone in the States who could send you money. What about your company? Can't they help?"

"I'm here independently. There is no company back home to help."

"I'm sorry, sir."

"You mean there's no other way?" I asked.

"We can send a telex but that's all we can do," was the reply.

"What would happen if you decided to evacuate? Wouldn't you furnish transportation out of here?"

"Yes, but we would take you only to the nearest European city and from there, you would be on your own."

"Thanks for the information," I said.

Now what to do? I didn't wish to impose on my family in the States; I knew my father didn't have the money. Perhaps if I were able to get the children out, then I could figure a way for Gisela and myself. As much as I hated to do it, I would seek help from some of my friends who still remained in Beirut. How ironic! I thought. The first time I have ever asked help from my government, and I can't even get the price of an air ticket, while U.S. foreign aid to Israel is in the billions of dollars. Some of my tax dollars even provide the arms contributing to the fighting here!

In the beginning of October, the situation worsened, and the American School closed—temporarily, it was hoped. It was dangerous to go outdoors now. Nights were filled with the sound of explosions. The ever-present fear that we could be hit by indiscriminate shelling prevented sleep. We huddled together in our master bedroom and attempted to distract our attention from the shelling by playing cards and reading. When nearby explosions shattered the air and shook our building, we held each other until the sounds faded away.

Although Gisela had endured this kind of fear as a small child during the Second World War in Germany, there was no getting used to it. As a mother, she remarked about how her mother must have felt at that time. She further commented how she felt as a small girl growing up in post-war Germany. No one had wanted to know or speak about the atrocities inflicted upon the Jews. Although most German people had known little or nothing about these atrocities when they occurred, the people bore the shame for crimes inflicted in their name. Those who did know what was happening were punished for not speaking out against it. Gisela wondered now if the Jewish people in America were really aware of what was happening here and of the atrocities which had been inflicted upon the Palestinians by the Israelis. "If they know, why don't they speak out? Don't they know that all Jews will be held responsible for Israeli deeds? Perhaps they are too ashamed to say anything. I can understand how they must feel but one would think that the leaders would do something."

"I don't believe the American people really know what's happening here," I said. "It will take time for the truth to come out. The people only know what they read in the papers. You knew my feelings when we first came here. Israel was the victim. Now I see that the Palestinians are victims also. Lebanon is caught up in this mess and we are all suffering."

As the days passed and our resources dwindled, the children became very frugal with the food and watched out for each other. The plight of the family brought us closer together. The children were frightened, yet these events cultivated an inner strength and we were proud of them.

Jo MacDonald was leaving Lebanon after twenty years. She had remained during other periods of conflict, but had finally had enough. Ray Ruehl was also leaving. Jointly they provided the money for air tickets for our children. Jo was traveling to the State of Washington and would escort the children.

The Carlton Hotel was in a relatively safe area by the sea in Raouche. An airline ticketing office had been established there to accommodate the foreigners leaving Lebanon. It was from this hotel that transportation to the airport would depart with military escort. I located a telex owned by The York Corporation with its head office in York, Pennsylvania where my parents lived. The Lebanese manager sent the telex to The York Corporation who relayed the message to my parents. They were informed where and when to expect the children.

The Carlton Hotel lobby was filled with people loaded down with all the things of value they could carry. A head of a dog or cat stuck out of flight bags while the murmur of voices spoke of precious possessions left behind. Tears were flowing as departure time drew near and families were separating.

Christine held on tightly to her cat. Fearing it would be shot; she had refused to leave without it. Jo MacDonald obtained the cat's inoculation papers that would be necessary for the immigration authorities in London where they would layover. In packing their bags, the children made difficult decisions on what to take and what to leave behind. The Paleolithic artifacts and donkey skull Christine found in Syria and prized so highly, had to be left behind. Only one large piece of luggage per person was permitted. Armed with the thought that someday soon they would return, they took with them only the necessities.

I saw them to the airport. The bus was crowded, but I managed to squeeze on. Gisela was crushed as she said goodbye to the children. She continued to weep as she waved at the departing bus.

I struggled with my own emotions and tried to maintain my composure and provide comfort to the children. I held onto the overhead rack to maintain my balance, watching the children as they held their bags and clutched the cat. Although I hoped this separation was temporary, I couldn't help but think that it might be the last time I saw them.

The bus route took us by bombed-out buildings and tank positions where armed men roved about in a state of readiness. The military escort led the buses off the main highway and over a makeshift dirt road in order to detour an armed Palestinian camp.

The airport terminal building was a scene of madness as people hoping to gain passage out of the country, fought their way to ticket counters. Passengers who had been stranded at the airport were taking any flight out of Beirut, regardless of destination. Many flights had been cancelled and some airlines had discontinued all service in and out of Beirut.

I was glad that I had managed to get on the bus. I elbowed my way to the counter for boarding passes while Jo MacDonald assisted the children with the customs documents. With boarding passes in hand, we made our way toward customs and the security area. Carrying the bags and trying to keep everyone together was difficult as we pressed through the crowd.

Security, as such, did not exist. After looking at the boarding passes, they just waved people through. Luggage had to be carried directly to the plane.

I hugged my kids, one by one, trying to cheer them up, making jokes about the cat. I looked at each of them as though it were for the last time. I held Caroline in my arms and dried her tears promising that daddy and mommy would be joining her soon.

I watched as they departed the security area, struggling with the luggage, each one helping the other to get to the plane. Then the announcement came over the loud speaker that the escort bus was leaving immediately to return to the hotel, and I was unable to witness the departure of their flight.

* * * * *

Now that Gisela and I were alone to contemplate our own departure, we spent time reveling in nostalgia about the good times we had in Lebanon with our family. Together we would stand on our balcony watching the ocean spray and listen to the pounding of the surf on the rocks. The night breeze always carried with it the intoxicating smell of the sea. We wondered how the children fared on their flight home and whether they arrived safely, but there was no way of knowing. Our beautiful home with its marble floors, spacious rooms and baths, all beautifully decorated and furnished, now seemed empty without the children. In Duane's bedroom stood the lifelike statue of himself that he had made in his art class—the likeness was uncanny. Clothing, toys and other items belonging to the children were constant reminders of their personalities and their absence.

We talked about the American Community School and how enthusiastic the children were to attend. The students admired their teachers who made learning so interesting and enjoyable. In Christine's room lay the artifacts and the donkey skull she left behind. It reminded us of the field trip Christine had made with her class to Syria where they had slept in tents among the Bedouins. This experience would give her a lifetime of memories. Of all the schools our children attended, they enjoyed the ACS in Beirut best.

* * * * *

Restlessness and hunger forced people into the streets in search of food and diversion from confinement. Dangers were ignored as people darted here and there looking for vendors who may have gotten through from outlying regions with fruits and vegetables. Whiskey and cigarettes were plentiful; small boats brought these items from Cyprus generating huge profits for these voyagers since custom duties and restrictions of any kind were abandoned or ignored. Whiskey soothed the nerves and smoking was part of one's perpetual nervous consumption.

Guns and ammunition arrived in small boats all along the coast. Large shipments, supplying the Phalangists, were unloaded in Jounieh. Gunmen roamed the streets at will with no attempt to conceal their weapons. Looting and theft were commonplace. No one blamed or even attempted to punish people for their acts of lawlessness.

The hopelessness of the situation caused me great depression. There didn't appear to be an end in sight. The basic causes of the problems within the country were placed on hold. The struggle was now for dominance of power with a military solution. To complicate domestic matters, the Israeli-Palestinian problem was becoming more and more a part of it. Israel sought to eliminate their Palestinian adversary by aiding the Rightists as was revealed in future events. My own struggle was for my livelihood and I saw no way out.

Chapter 16
End of the Line
September/October 1975

The once plush hotel district had been under siege for sometime. The St. Georges hotel and the Phoenicia hotel were in ruins. The Holiday Inn loomed against the skyline like a skeleton, with its walls scarred with gaping holes, blackened by smoke.

Opposing factions to the conflict had taken positions in these hotels and blasted away at each other. Nearby stood the tall-unfinished structure of the Muir Tower building whose strategic vantage point provided an excellent position for snipers and for the launching of rockets and mortars.

Beirut was finished and I realized that I was as well. Everything I worked for, accumulating the money to get to Beirut, putting it all on the line, finally succeeding - all had literally gone up in smoke. To think of starting over again, placed me in a deep state of depression. Even if the fighting stopped, the financial means to continue were gone.

In my mind, I relived the struggle to make it: how my wife and I had worked and saved; how we sacrificed and did without things over the years to accumulate money and have possessions, the perpetual struggle to "make it," and having finally become a millionaire, to be flat broke. All this hard work and struggle, for what? Where would I go and what could I do? How would I support my family? I thought of assets, but there were none. I was wiped out. I had liquidated all my possessions to accumulate the money to start the business in Beirut. I thought of the farm that I had sold; the wonderful memories and the satisfaction of achieving my goal to own a farm. I thought of my office building, the cars, the good times. Everything now lost, due to this senseless war.

The only thing of some value was my life insurance. "That's it!" I thought, "That's the solution. If I were killed, at least there would be money for Gisela to get a fresh start and care for the children." Planning my death now possessed me. I'll get a gun, or maybe I'll just jump off the cliff at Pigeon Rock where distraught lovers often jumped to their death. Would my insurance pay in case of suicide? Could I actually pull the trigger or make the jump? If I only had my car, I'd ram it into a tree or building. I suddenly recalled the loss of my car to thieves and my depression deepened. Suddenly an idea occurred to me. What if I were to get shot? My insurance policy has a double indemnity clause in case of accidental death. The more I thought about it, the more it seemed to be the solution to my predicament. I was unaware of my insanity in my depressed mental state.

On impulse, I decided to go to the battle area and let it happen. Oblivious to my surroundings, I was obsessed to do something drastic to fix my financial problem, yet I knew that if Gisela suspected my intentions, she would stop me.

When I left the house, I appeared calm telling her I was going for a walk. I began walking toward the hotel district where the sounds of battle were the loudest. I walked down Rue Hamra, the main street of town, allowing the sound of gunfire to direct me. At the east end of Rue Hamra, I passed tanks and soldiers that were positioned near the Etoile Cinema to defend the Hamra business district. The soldiers did not challenge me when I passed them. All was quiet as I neared the Myrtom House, a small Viennese restaurant that had been our favorite eating-place. I recalled the good food and the pleasant atmosphere of the restaurant. I remembered the evenings we spent there as a family, the business dinners, the laughter, the camaraderie of friends—all gone now. Burned-out cars and other debris littered the street mixed with remnants of the restaurant. I spied a human hand lying next to a pile of rubble; it did not effect me.

I proceeded down Rue Du Mexique and stood for a moment looking at the building that had been our first home. I visualized the pots and pans we used to collect the drinking water. The barrels on the roof for collecting bath water were no longer visible. I recalled standing on the balcony with Peter Jennings, the soon-to-be-well-known news correspondent, who had visited us. Peter had wanted the vantage point of the balcony to photograph a wedding that took place in the church across the street, and we had chatted over a cup of tea while he waited for the wedding party to emerge. There were no windowpanes left in the house, and the balcony where Peter and I stood, had vanished.

I turned right onto Rue Clemenceau and passed the press building peppered with bullet marks; its sidewalk cluttered with shattered glass. Sand bags once used as bunkers were strewn over the next intersection. The street was cratered and a stream of water coursed through the gutter winding its way around debris and into the craters, leaving a trail of sludge.

The battle in progress seemed to be just around the next corner. Shots from the Muir Tower were answered from the Holiday Inn. The gunfire echoing through the streets grew louder. I hoped the shot meant for me would happen suddenly and without my awareness.

I turned left at the next corner. At the end of the street, part of the Holiday Inn became visible. A pool of blood with a sandal lying next to it caught my eye. The trail of blood continued a short way and then disappeared from view at the edge of the next building. I followed the trail and stopped for a moment staring at the motionless body swarming with flies. The stench filled my nostrils and I wondered if my end would be like that. I continued walking and studied the Holiday Inn looming larger in front of me. The only movement I saw was the curtains flapping in the breeze through the broken glass of the hotel windows. As I got closer, I could see a tank protruding from the lobby. The skeleton of another tank blocked the driveway in front.

I suddenly realized that the shooting had stopped—the silence got my attention. I sensed I was being watched. "Why don't they shoot and get it over with," I thought. As I neared the end of the street where I expected the fatal gunfire, my thoughts turned to my family. I visualized the faces of each of my children and my wife. I saw them weeping for me. The emotion of love I felt for them overwhelmed me and I wanted to be with them. "What am I doing?" I thought. "We can make it! We'll find a way! If we have love, it won't matter if we are without money." I stopped abruptly.

I was seized with desperation to get out of my dangerous predicament. I stood frozen in the open street directly in front of the Holiday Inn. As my eyes darted from building to building, I spied a red and white 'koufieh' at the top of the Muir Tower. Movement from the windows of the Holiday Inn also caught my attention.

I turned away from the hotel and began walking fast along Rue John Kennedy, the long street leading to the American University. I then broke into a run; my only thoughts now were to get out of danger. There was no alley to turn into and all the buildings were boarded-up. The only way to get out of sight was to reach the end of this long street and turn the corner. The impending gunfire I expected caused my feet to fly over the pavement. "If I can only make it to the end of this street," I thought. "I've got to make it." When I reached the last building, I knew I would make it. As soon as I turned the corner, I stopped. The sound of gunfire meant the battle had resumed but I was safe. I stood leaning against the building wall, weak and shaking. Why they stopped shooting and permitted me to escape could not be comprehended. Overwhelmed by this harrowing experience, I remained by the building a short while, allowing my emotions to subside and took control of my senses. I then gave myself a mental lashing for my stupidity. Life was too precious to be thrown away. I would find a way out of my predicament.

I then walked home to be with the woman I loved.

Chapter 17
The Last Days
October/November 1975

The telex rattled in the background as Gisela and I sat down at the Commodore Hotel bar. News correspondents used this hotel as their headquarters and were busy transmitting their daily news stories to home offices around the world. A lone Japanese man sat at the bar drinking and talking to the bartender.

I looked around the room at the many empty tables and chairs. Through the partially drawn drapes, the light from the bar made a reflection on the remaining water of the swimming pool. It was dusk and the sky was filled with heavy clouds rumbling with thunder. Rain would be good after the long hot summer, I mused. In another month it would be Christmas, and then a new year. What would 1976 have in store for me?

Frustration and boredom had prompted us to walk the six blocks to the hotel. Gisela carried an umbrella as it seemed likely to rain before we returned home, and it appeared imminent now. Another man walked into the bar and was greeted warmly by the lone Japanese. The bartender greeted the man and then came over to us.

"Welcome. What would you like?"

"I'll have a Bloody Mary and my wife…"

"I'll have a Dubonnet with one ice cube," interrupted Gisela.

"She always insists on one ice cube," I said. "Perhaps she gets more to drink that way."

"Perhaps you're right. I'll see what I can do," said the bartender.

The drinks were delivered and we raised our glasses and said, "Cheers."

"Cheers!" resounded from everyone sitting around the bar.

As we sipped our drinks, we listened to the conversation between the Japanese and his friend. The Japanese man's accent with his broken English was amusing.

Lightning flashed and a loud bolt of thunder suddenly shattered the quiet. We all jumped as the rumble of thunder echoed across the sky. The first person to speak was the Japanese, who exclaimed, "Every night we go to sleep with sound of music."

Everyone laughed as the rain began pelting the windows and a heavy downpour got underway. Loud explosions were common at night but certainly no music to one's ears. However, the harmless thunder placed everyone in a jovial mood.

"Play some-ting on piano. We need music and more drink. A drink for ev-lery body," shouted the Japanese while his friend went to the piano.

As the man played, we listened to the music and sipped our drinks, each deep in one's own thoughts while the rumbling of thunder and pounding of rain continued.

"You are remaining in Lebanon?" I asked the Japanese.

"I go home soon—Tokyo. I only one here. All Japanese company, they leave. My wife, she go one month before. Now I lonely. Need woman," he chuckled.

"We'll soon be going also," I said. "It doesn't make sense to stay any longer."

"No, I tink war continue. Not finished," he replied.

The pianist finished playing and motioned for the Japanese to come to the piano.

"Play a Japanese song for us!" shouted the pianist.

"No, I not play good."

"Play!" shouted everyone.

He sat down at the piano and slowly picked his way through an oriental song. When he finished, everyone applauded and shouted, "More, more!" He shook his head and returned to the bar.

"Japanese music—so sorry," he said.

We all laughed and he looked bewildered until his friend explained the difference between sorry and sad, then he laughed uproariously.

Gisela was contented. A stray cat had rubbed against her leg and it now nestled in her lap being stroked. Then the lights went out, followed by more lightening and thunder. The bartender lit some candles and placed them on the bar. The talking subsided as attention was drawn to the flickering candles placing everyone deep in thought. The thunder stopped and the sound of steady rain made me drowsy and I felt it was time to leave.

We bade everyone goodbye and started home. There were no street lamps working and it was very dark, but in our cheerful mood we had little apprehension. We slowly made our way through the rain sharing the umbrella and joking that the war, this night, had been rained-out.

The following day, I telephoned the U.S. Embassy and spoke once again to the consular official who was now living at the Embassy.

"What's the situation?" I asked.

"No change in our status. We advise everyone to leave Lebanon."

"Do you think you will order an evacuation?"

"It's possible, however I still don't see how that will help you."

I became irritated. "Certainly you have emergency funds to help stranded U.S. citizens. I'll repay you."

"I'm very sorry, Mr. March, but we must follow regulations and we have no authorization to help you in this way. As I told you before, we can assist you by sending a telex via the State Department to someone in the U.S. who can transfer funds to you."

I thought for a few moments. I had tried to contact Elie but he apparently was still out of the country. Perhaps my brother-in-law, Harry Miller, who lived in York, Pennsylvania, could help.

"OK, send the following message for me," I said.

"Before we can send your message, you'll have to come by the Embassy and sign an authorization slip."

"But there's snipers down there, aren't there?"

"In front of the Embassy, yes, but if you come around to the back of the building, we can let you in."

"You mean, unless I sign this form, you will not send the telex?"

"I'm sorry, but that's the regulation."

"OK, I'll try to get there," I said slamming down the phone.

"Can you believe this?" I said to Gisela. "I've got to go to the Embassy and sign some damned form before they'll send the telex. They're so wrapped-up in regulations that no one can make an independent decision to act, even in special circumstances, to bend the rules. These people need a signature to cover their ass even if it could cost someone else his life."

I left the house and walked down the hill to the waterfront and made my way along the sea toward the Embassy. It was a long walk but the exercise felt good. Lebanese soldiers, who were posted near the Embassy, barred any traffic around it. As I approached, a soldier stepped forward and asked for my identity papers. Upon seeing my American passport, he waved me on. Just before the Embassy building, a sign had been tacked on a tree, which read, "Do not go beyond this point. Snipers!"

I proceeded to the rear door and knocked. The door was opened by a US Marine. I showed my passport and said, "The consular is expecting me. I'm Abe March."

The Marine frisked me and then called the consular's office. He then instructed me to wait until someone came to escort me upstairs.

The consular officer was wearing an open-necked short sleeve shirt. He saw me coming and said, "You must be Mr. March."

"Yes, that's me. Where's that damn form you want signed?"

"Right here. I'm sorry about all this, but you do understand regulations."

"I'm trying to, but I think this is carrying it a bit far."

He did not reply. After I had signed the form and written my message, I asked how long it would be before I could expect the money, assuming that my brother-in-law could make the money transfer.

"You should have it within twenty-four hours. The State Department will give it top priority," he said.

I asked him to call me as soon as it arrived. "I want to get out of here," I told him.

"I'll call you the moment we get it," the consular promised.

I was escorted to the rear door and returned home using the same circuitous route. Nothing to do now but wait.

I thought about the difference between an employee of a large company and that of a self-employed entrepreneur. The employee has little to worry about. He would be compensated for his losses and his travel paid for, as well as a continuous income. Whereas the entrepreneur has everything on the line. Surely the government that I pay taxes to, should help. As I was later to discover when I returned to the States, the IRS wanted its tax from me and refused to allow deductions for any losses which I was unable to prove. With records destroyed, there was little I could prove and I had to pay, although I was granted an extension due to my financial circumstances.

When the twenty-four hours were up, I called the Embassy.

"No, nothing yet, but it could come in at any moment. We'll call you as soon as it arrives," was the reply.

The following day, I received the same story. Moreover, our plight had grown more serious. The cupboards were completely bare and there was no more food in the house. I had only a few Lebanese pounds remaining and no stores were open that day. The gnawing of my stomach matched Gisela's as they seemingly growled in unison. As much as we tried, sleep eluded us.

"Would you like a drink?" Gisela asked.

"I'd love one."

"Hot or cold?"

"As you like," I replied, wondering what she was up to.

Gisela went into the kitchen and boiled some water. Some butane still remained in the stove but it was very low and wouldn't last but a few days. In one of the drawers, she found some sugar cubes that the children had at one time picked up from some restaurant and stashed away.

Gisela entered the room with a tray, held like a waitress, and said, "For you, Monsieur."

"Merci," I replied. "Won't you join me, Madame?"

"But of course, Monsieur."

We sipped the hot sugar water and sat together holding hands, our eyes fixed on each other, no words were needed to express the feelings we felt for each other. Together, we found sleep.

* * * * *

Gisela packed her suitcase with care to squeeze in as much as possible. She folded her evening gowns and oriental dresses that she prized and placed them neatly in the closet. The children's beds were stripped, clothes washed and packed neatly away. The oriental rugs were rolled-up and placed under the beds. My suitcase lay open. I was able to fit only two suits into my luggage and would have to make a decision about the selection. It would be cold in the States and a heavier suit would be practical. I glanced at the large selection of tailor made suits I had collected from various countries and selected two.

Unknown to me, Gisela had traded some of her jewelry for food and now surprised me with a meal of Arabic bread, some rice and a bottle of wine. It was delicious. Tomorrow was another day and we would worry about tomorrow when it came.

I was up early. It was the fifth day since I had signed the authorization form at the Embassy. Each day I called and pleaded with them to do something for me. As I thought what to say this time, the telephone rang.

"Mr. March."

"Yes?"

"This is John Girard at the Embassy. We received a telex this morning and have authorization to give you money. It looks like your friend came through for you and transferred the funds."

"I'll be right there!" I said.

Gisela heard the telephone ring and was standing in the doorway looking bewildered as I tucked in my shirt.

"I'm going to pick up the money and arrange for our tickets. I'll be back as soon as I can."

"Finally!" she said. "Did they say what took so long?"

"No, and I don't care just now. I just want to get the money so we can get out of here."

I said goodbye while she exhorted me to be careful. I took the same route to the Embassy as before. This day there were more military troops on the road with tanks and armored cars. "Something is brewing," I thought, "but with luck we won't be here when it boils over."

I knocked on the back door of the Embassy and a Marine invited me in. After the frisking routine, I was escorted to the consular's office.

"I'm sorry Mr. March, but we don't have any dollars to give you. The official pouch has not arrived yet. Perhaps we'll have some in a few days, but we can give you the money in Lebanese pounds, unless of course, you prefer to wait."

"I can't wait a few days. I need the money now! You fail to understand that I'm completely out of money. I can't even buy food!"

"Take this authorization slip to the paymaster and you'll get your money. Good luck with your trip."

"Thanks. With Lebanese pounds, I'll need it."

Travel Agents were only accepting dollars for tickets. I knew I would lose money in conversion to dollars, but I wanted out of Lebanon and I also wanted to eat, so I made my way to Rue Hamra in search of a moneychanger. Banks were not open, so the street merchants were conducting local banking business.

After searching and making numerous inquiries, I located a moneychanger on a side street. I negotiated the best possible rate of exchange but still lost money.

A small travel agency was located just around the corner. I knocked on the door and it was opened by the proprietor. He wrote the tickets for a one o'clock departure the following day.

"Be sure you go to airport early if you want seat. I only write ticket," he said.

There was some money left over, so I went in search of food for our last night in Lebanon.

It was early afternoon when I returned home. Gisela admonished me for taking so long and causing her worry. She smacked her lips at the bottle of wine, the bread and the fruit I had brought.

After our meal, we decided to go for a walk along the sea. It would be our last chance to indulge in this pleasant experience.

Right next to the roadway in Raouche, stood Pigeon Rock. It was named that for the many pigeons that swarmed around it and nested there. It loomed majestically from the sea just as it had thousands of years before with the water lashing around and through the natural tunnels hollowed out by the waves over the centuries. The high embankment next to the rock was knows as "Lovers Leap" where jilted or distraught lovers ended their sorrow by jumping to the rocks and waves below. The sidewalk cafes and restaurants overlooking the rock were all closed. Businesses of every kind were closed; their owners having fled the country.

The joys of the past now remained only in our minds. We walked arm in arm with the sorrow brought by war ever present. Tomorrow would bring the joy of freedom. The future and what it would bring was unknown, but we would face it together.

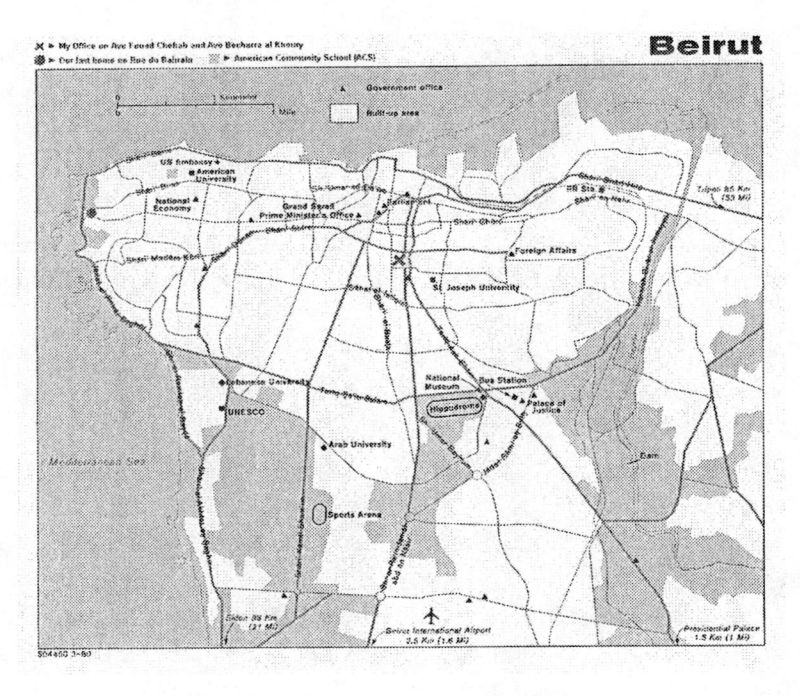

Beirut, 1980

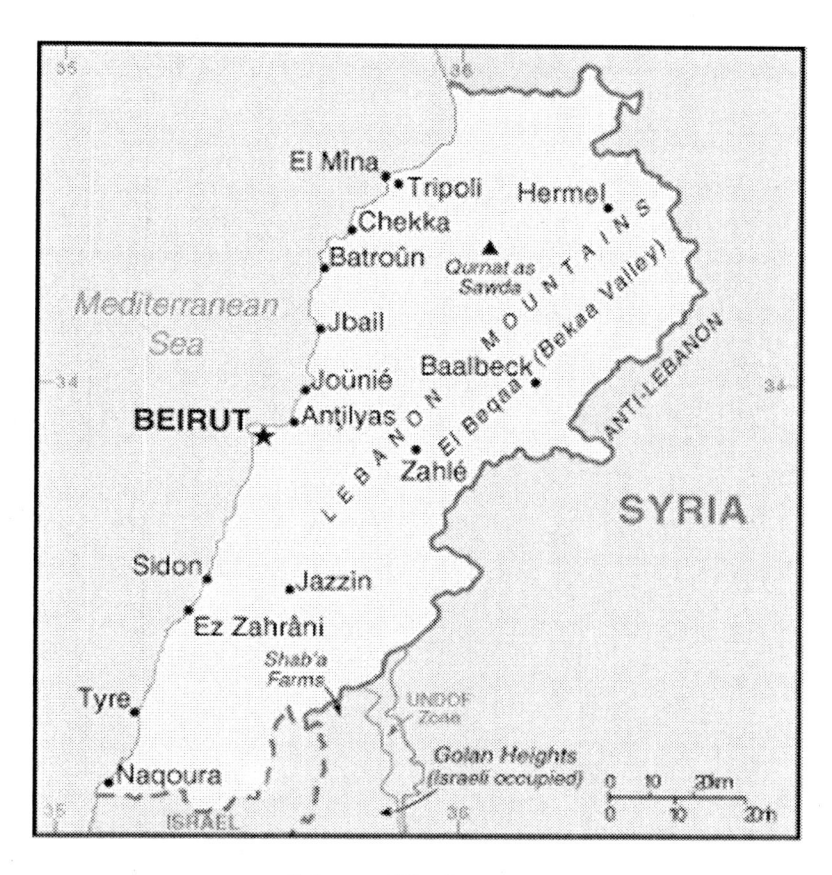

Map of Lebanon

Ducked Bullets, Business Ruined

Yorker Back From

By JOEL MICHAEL

Yorker Abe March and his German-born wife, Gisela, may have been the first civilian Americans in strife-torn Beirut, Lebanon, to be kidnaped and released. A day after their capture, U. S Embassy officials were kidnaped and are still being held by commandos.

March returned to York Saturday, penniless and with no prospects, but happy to have escaped safely with his family from Beirut where they've lived the past two years. There March had established his own wholesale cosmetics business before his offices were suddenly wiped out in a rocket barrage, a half-million dollars-worth of merchandise stolen, pilfered or burned at dockside and his new Mercedes Benz taken.

March, Gisela, whom he met and married in West Germany while in the Air Force, and their children Duane, 13, Christine, 12 and Caroline, 6, are living with March's parents, Mr. and Mrs. Richard March, 1490 Monroe St., West York, until March can find employment and begin another career. Gisela began working Wednesday as a clerk at York Mall. The children have begun classes at West York Area School District.

The seven-month-long civil war in Lebanon and especially in its seaport capital of Beirut not only has costs 4,000 lives and 8,000 wounded since clashes between Moslems and Christians, but has cost March his livelihood and his adopted Middle East headquarters in what could have been a financial success story in the best tradition of American enterprise and ambition.

The beginning of the end of the Marches' stay in Beirut happened on Oct. 21 when he and his wife were yanked from a taxicab by a band of gunmen as they tried to drive through sniper fire to their offices in downtown Beirut.

March recalled Wednesday in an interview with this reporter that the day after their capture by commandos, two Embassy officials were similarly pulled from their car in a Moslem stronghold and apparently kidnaped. Their whereabouts are still unknown.

By October this year, internecine fighting and sniping among rightwing Christians, Moslems and leftwing Palestinians had spilled into Beirut's center city where March had his cosmetics headquarters. On that midmonth Tuesday after his Mercedes had been stolen, March and his wife took a taxi to the office, driven by a Lebanese cabby.

Halfway there, the cab encountered a roadblock — piles of rocks and concrete strewn over the road. The cabby indicated he could drive around the impasse, but March and his wife saw people in the shadows of buildings waving frantically for the cab to turn around and leave.

But before the driver could back up in the narrow street, gunmen suddenly surrounded the taxi and forced the cabby to pull into an even narrower alley that effectively was a dead-end. The first group of commandos were then joined by some 15 others who searched the cab and its occupants.

March said one of the gunman in looking through his passport saw the word "Pennsylvania" and read it aloud to the others as if saying "Venezuela." March paled visibly because Venezuelans are not well liked in Lebanon and he feared that he and his wife would have no chance to leave unharmed if the Moslems thought them Venezuelans.

"No, Amerikani, Amerikani," March said he shouted as he pointed to the word "Pennsylvania," pronouncing it correctly to try to resolve the

Article appeared in the York Daily Record, York, PA., in 1975

Beirut Kidnaping

misunderstanding. Whether or not March made his point, the three of them were hustled into a small room in an old house and guarded by some of the commandos, one of whom spoke a little English.

That man assured the Marches and the cabby that there was "No problem, no worry," but Mrs. March whispered to her husband that the time to worry is when one is told not to worry.

After unseen and unheard discussions by the commandos, the trio was released four hours after being picked up. March recalled that the taxi driver was the most shaken, that he feared for his own life, not the Americans. But he argued just the opposite and tried to convince them that had it not been for him, they surely would have been shot. He demanded more money for having saved their lives. March said he paid him more, but only because his taxi meter was running during their kidnaping.

When sniper fire and indiscriminate shelling became heavier downtown and started threatening the fashionable Raouche section of Beirut where the Marches and many foreigners live, March began seriously to consider the U. S. Embassy's advice to get out of Lebanon.

March had become used to crawling on his hands and knees on his office floor downtown to avoid bullets sometimes sprayed through the windows. He had even managed to walk away from a group of gunmen by stuttering through his pidgin Arabic, "Hello. How are you ?" They said nothing and he kept walking. When he turned a corner, they sprayed the street with automatic weapon fire.

Then, three weeks ago, with all communications out of service and no obvious way to contact his parents in York to let them know the family was safe, March discovered a telex machine in a Beirut hotel that had a direct line to the York Division of Borg-Warner Corp. March got permission to use it and sent word through the corporation's York plant to his folks that the family was all right but that he was sending the kids from Beirut and that they would be on a plane landing in Baltimore.

Borg-Warner kindly telexed back to Beirut that the message was delivered personally to March's parents and, in turn, used the corporation's communications machine to send a message from the West York parents. March said Tuesday he visited the York Division offices and thanked the company for its aid.

Though March is looking for a job here, at least temporarily, he still wants to go back to the Middle East. He's developed some important business contacts there and has made the acquaintance of some important military and governmental officials who could be valuable to him as the representative of a firm with international markets.

Beirut is not now a happy or safe place to live. It is one of the few cities on earth where water costs more than gasoline, where you can be shot down for stepping out of your house and where you can't tell the good guys from the bad. It is a place where one sleeps during the day because most of the bombs and rockets go off at night.

Still, March wants to return, someday. On his own initiative and with his own brain child, he was making money before all of it was ripped off. "You win some and you lose some," March smiled. "We'll bounce back, and we'll bounce back higher."

First American Back
Yorker To Reopen Beirut Business

(Special To The Daily Record)

BEIRUT, Lebanon — The pioneer spirit still burns strongly in the heart of Yorker Abe March, the first American businessman back in Beirut.

At a time when most people are waiting to see whether the 57th cease-fire in this country's 18-month old civil war will hold, Abe March, 37, of Taxville Road, York, Pa., is back and starting anew.

Undaunted by past experiences which would frighten lesser men, having had his cosmetics importing business completely wiped out, March just says, "This is where I lost all my money and this is where I am going to make it back."

March, who is the son of Mr. and Mrs. Richard A. March, 1419 Monroe St., West York, returned from Beirut to York over the weekend. He will spend Christmas here with his wife and children at their Taxville Road home.

March came to Lebanon almost three years ago, with his German born wife Gisela and their four children, to enjoy the excellent opportunities that the Middle East offered to anybody with a product to sell and the will to do it.

Hardly had he got the business started, when civil war broke out. March decided to stay on, but it fast became apparent to him that his own life and that of his family was continually in danger. He sent the children home but his wife elected to stay on.

They became the first Americans to be kidnapped by leftist Moslim gunmen. After four hours and some tense moments they were freed, others were not so lucky. American ambassador Melloy was to be murdered in a similar incident and other foreign nationals were held for long periods.

Going out to lunch early one day, March returned to find that a sniper's bullet had gone straight through the back of his office chair.

On another occasion, he and his wife found themselves pinned down at the office, with a raging gun fight going on outside between rival Christian and Moslim gangs. "It was like the wild west," he said, "with both sides just blasting away at each other."

Realizing that they had to get away before a stray bullet parted them forever, one at a time they dashed for the car which was parked at the back of the building. Forcing Gisela to lie prone on the floor, March hurtled at top speed up the street, followed by a stream of machine gun fire. Shaken by the experience but unharmed, he later said, "I guess I must have seen how to do it in the movies."

The last straw came when a large consignment of goods which had been stuck at the docks was hit by rocket fire and set alight. He had his brand new Mercedes stolen and a rocket went clean through his office wall, destroying everything.

March decided that to stay on was madness and cutting his losses in November last year he returned to his home town a ruined and worried man. "Last Christmas was a real mean one for me and the family."

After a few frustrating months, with his wife having to curtail her charity work and take a regular job, March had managed to draw up a portfolio of products with good sales potential in the Middle East.

In the early summer of this year, he had formed International Trading and Merchant Corp. with the backing of some York businessmen.

Within hours of the Syrian Army enforced cease-fire being announced, March was on his way back to Lebanon. This time via Amman in Jordan, where he checked into the Inter-Continental Hotel shortly before the Palestinian commando raid, in which eight people died and many others were injured.

On Sunday, Nov. 21, a year and a week after his hasty departure, Abe March was back in Beirut, to be hailed as the first American businessman to return.

But his troubles were not yet over. On arriving at his apartment he found that everything had been looted and that there were some Leftist gunmen and their families squatting there, with little intention of moving out.

Ignoring their threats and hoping that nobody would pull a gun on him, he refused to be intimidated by them. Within hours they were gone, leaving his once beautiful home as bare as the day he had moved in three years before.

Since then March has been busy re-affirming old contacts and making new ones. It looks as if his early-bird tactics will pay off handsomely for him.

He said, "I believe that this cease-fire will hold. The Lebanese are anxious to forget the last two years and get on with the task of rebuilding their battered country. I am lucky enough to be in a strong position to help them, and being the first man in improves my chances."

March intends to move his family back here as soon as it looks safe to do so. "Both my wife Gisela and I are eager to return in spite of everything which happened to us during the first months of the fighting. I shall soon be going back to York to join the family for Christmas, which is going to be a whole lot happier for us all than Christmas last year!"

Rocket Scars

Yorker Abe March points out a gaping hole blasted through his downtown Beirut, Lebanon, office. The rocket gutted with fire the entire floor.

Article appearing in the York Daily Record, York, PA., 1976

Part Two

Chapter 1
Starting Over
Winter 1975-Spring 1977

(Retrospect) The reunion with the family was very special. We learned about the children's flight back to the USA and the difficulties with the cat at Heathrow airport in London. They had to stay overnight and the cat was restricted to the airport and placed in quarantine. On their departure the following day, they were unable to retrieve the cat from quarantine since it was required to remain there for 48 hours. Several days after the children arrived at their grandparents, their grandfather received a call from Emery Air Freight advising him to pick-up the cat and pay a $150.00 shipping charge. Grandpa told them that he was not paying since the cat should have accompanied the children free of charge. If they did not wish to release the cat to him, then they could keep it. Within a few hours they called back and said that he could pick-up the cat—no charge.

Returning to the USA was difficult. Although financially broke, it wasn't a sense of failure but the perplexity of how or where to begin that concerned me. I tried desperately to find employment in my home area but was considered over-qualified. Prospective employers felt that I would not be satisfied with what they could pay me, or that something better would come along and I would leave their employ. Without employment, I was unable to support my family and was forced to apply for welfare. This was not only humiliating, but the money was insufficient to pay for rent, food and clothing. Living with my parents had been pleasant for a time, but the lack of privacy and the need for independence compelled Gisela to take whatever job she could find. Her IBM programming background was no longer 'state of the art,' and she felt inadequate in pursuing that field. She sought something temporary, always with the belief that we would be returning to Lebanon. We had hoped that Gisela's part-time job at minimum wage would help make up the difference we needed to live on, only to discover that the welfare payments were decreased in proportion to her income. I could understand why many welfare recipients would prefer not to work unless their wage income was sufficient to offset what they received from welfare.

How I could get involved in international business again, particularly in the Middle East, consumed my thoughts. I had no money and no equity to borrow against since all my assets had been liquidated. Even if I had equity, it would be difficult to borrow against it without showing proof of income or other means of repayment capability.

Accepting the fact that the war in Lebanon would be prolonged, I borrowed my father's car and visited various manufacturers whose products I felt could be marketed in the Middle East. My intention was to become their representative, or if that failed, provide them with consulting assistance in promoting their goods in the Middle East region. I met with skepticism and resistance. Most companies were content to sell their products on the American market and were not interested in exporting since they felt it was "too complicated, too much red tape." A larger company said that if they decided to enter the Middle East market, they would use their own personnel who were familiar with their products. My objective in pursuing this course of action was based on my knowledge of the region, its tremendous potential, and my need for an income. As an entrepreneur, it was difficult to comprehend their complacent attitude or lack of foresight in not looking beyond the American border. Our government was experiencing a balance of payments deficit, and although it encouraged exporting, it did little in the way of simplifying procedures or educating small to medium-sized businesses in how to go about it. Here I was, walking into their offices, telling them it was simple to export and that

I could develop the foreign market for their product. "If it is so simple," as one executive put it, "why isn't everyone doing it?"

As in any business or endeavor, there are leaders and there are followers. Somewhere, I thought, there must be someone who can see the potential I have to offer. My advocating to be first in the market, to take advantage of the huge sums of oil money that was available, fell upon deaf ears. I knew that if they ever intended to enter that market, it would require more than product knowledge: it requires contacts and knowledge of the area. If they were willing to spend several hundred thousand dollars for their own people to acclimate themselves, then they could do it. I only requested a small consulting fee to get them connected. Most businessmen told me that I could sell their products if I wished, and they would pay me a commission, as would most any company. However, without a commitment on their part and no serious desire for export, they were poor candidates to work with.

The risks taken by independent commission salespeople are often overlooked. They are expected to spend their own time and money promoting a company's products, and if they're successful, they receive a commission. If they fail, they also sustain the loss. The company has little or no risk, and often when the salesperson succeeds, the company replaces him or her with someone else who can continue what was started, for less money. Unless a company is willing to make some form of commitment, it cannot be relied upon.

In order to provide more comfortable living space at my parent's house, Gisela and I would spend the night with a friend in his log cabin. The cabin bordered the farm property I once owned and the logs for its construction had been taken from the farm woods. I had sold this cabin to Nelson Weaver, and now his son, Martin, lived there. It was winter, and the cabin's only heat was a wood stove in the living room. Gisela and I slept on a small cot in a closed-off section of the porch. We covered ourselves with multiple blankets to keep warm.

I was always the first to get up in the morning, let the cat out, then load the stove with wood so there would be some warmth when the others got up. It was the same cat that Christine had brought with her from Lebanon and it stayed with us at the cabin where it could roam freely and was thought to be safe. When the cat didn't return to the cabin one night, I searched and found it lying at the side of the road, killed by a car. The children were heartbroken over their loss and the fond memories it represented.

Martin was also unemployed and the lack of money inspired us to seek food from the wild. Martin took his shotgun and we went to the woods searching for game. Instead of game, we spied a small tree that would do as a Christmas tree but we didn't have an axe with us. So, with several gunshots, the small tree was toppled. It reminded us of the "Charlie Brown" Christmas tree: spindly, but fitting.

Just before Christmas, I eavesdropped on a conversation between Duane and Christine. They were discussing what they would like for Christmas, and then they agreed not to ask for anything since mommy and daddy couldn't afford it. For the few gifts they did receive, they showed genuine appreciation. To further assist, the children became entrepreneurs. Duane took a paper route and Christine did baby-sitting to earn spending money. With Gisela's limited income, we finally managed to secure a small two-bedroom apartment and borrowed what furniture we could from relatives. The girls occupied one bedroom, Duane slept on the living room sofa while Gisela and I slept on a mattress on the floor in the other bedroom.

We were soon able to purchase an old station wagon. The $250 car wasn't much to look at, but it was transportation. When I first started driving this car, I shielded my face so people wouldn't recognize me. I felt embarrassed and ashamed to be in this predicament. Although my pride was injured, my determination was strengthened.

I formulated plans to go to the Middle East, but first I would need financing. Within the next six months, I was able to interest a few investors in a project to promote business to the Middle East, and we formed a trading company. The initial problems with my partners involved strategy. Some of the investors had their own ideas about the course the company should take but had little to offer in the way of practical help. I knew that an ample amount of time would be needed to develop a market for products and that more money would be required than was invested. However, the investors were anxious to commence business and urged me to make an exploratory trip to the Middle East. The purpose of this trip was to learn what goods or services were needed, and at the same time determine what American goods were marketable in that region. The stockholders were delighted with the prospects and envisioned getting "rich quick." They felt a big contract would solve all our financial requirements. I felt that the best prospects were with smaller repetitive accounts; however, since we were desperate for immediate funds, I agreed to pursue the large projects. I reasoned that it was their money, and the possibilities did exist for landing a large project by being in the right place at the right time. Not to go empty handed, some local companies were contacted whose products appeared to have merit in the Middle East market. With a small portfolio of products, I was ready for my trip.

*****

Osama Anabtawi, a Palestinian whose family fled their home in Nablus with the exodus of many other Palestinians when Israel expanded its territorial boundaries, had settled in Jordan to begin a new life. His father became a professor at the University of Jordan and a Member of Parliament. Osama completed his secondary education in Amman, the capital city of Jordan, and through the generosity of His Majesty, King Hussein, he became a Jordanian citizen.

During the 1967 War with Israel and its Arab neighbors, Osama's family moved once again and had settled in Beirut, Lebanon. From there, Osama went to the United States to continue his education and earned a degree in engineering. He married an American girl, was employed by a large engineering firm in Chicago and became an American citizen. His employer then sent him to Beirut to head up their offices there. Gisela and I met Osama and his wife in Beirut and became good friends.

With the outbreak of war in Lebanon, Osama's company moved their offices to Amman, Jordan. On a visit to Jordan while I was still working in Lebanon, Osama introduced me to a former schoolmate of his, Mohammad Madi. Mr. Madi had married King Hussein's cousin, Princess Zein. Mohammad offered his assistance to me and expressed his willingness to help with business in Jordan. A one-year visa for businessmen was the norm, however, Mohammad obtained a four-year visa for me and it was still valid.

Hotel accommodations were difficult to obtain anywhere within the Middle East and reservations were required well in advance of any planned trip, unless one had connections. I made my air reservations one week prior to my intended departure for Jordan and asked the travel agency to secure reservations for me at the Jordan Intercontinental Hotel. After several unsuccessful attempts to receive confirmation, I was forced to extend my departure date. The main office of the Intercontinental Hotel in New York was contacted for assistance. They also failed to receive acknowledgment to their requests and even sent a hand telegram to the hotel. That too, failed.

I decided to call my distinguished friend, Mohammad Madi, and ask his assistance. I gave him my date of arrival and asked him to arrange accommodations for me at the Jordan Intercontinental Hotel. Without waiting for confirmation, I departed as scheduled with a connecting flight in Frankfurt en route to Amman.

Arriving in Amman the following afternoon, I quickly cleared customs with my visa issued in Amman, and took a taxi to the hotel.

"My name is Abe March," I said to the receptionist.

"Do you have a reservation, sir?"

"I certainly hope so. Would you please check?"

The receptionist went through his ledger, then looked at me and said, "You are Abraham March?"

"That's me."

"Ah, yes. We have your reservation, sir. Welcome to Jordan."

He handed me the registration card and snapped his fingers for the bellboy.

"Here is your key, sir. Your room is ready for you. If there is anything you need, please call me. I will make sure everything is to your satisfaction."

He spoke briefly to the bellboy in Arabic, and then said; "He will show you to your room."

The bellboy bowed courteously and I followed him to the elevator.

I was pleased at the courtesy extended to me. A large basket of fruit sat on the dressing table. Next to it was a plate of assorted cheese and a bottle of wine. A small envelope with my name on it lay alongside which read, "With the compliments of the Management. We hope you have a pleasant stay."

I unpacked and was preparing to take a shower when there was a knock on the door. I wrapped a towel around my waist and opened the door. There stood a young man smiling and bowing.

"Is there anything I can get you sir? Do you need anything?"

"No, everything's fine," I replied. "If I need something, I'll call you. Thanks, anyway."

I was puzzled. I didn't remember receiving this type of service when I was here before. I'll have to mention it to Mohammad and pass along my compliments about the service, I thought.

I completed my shower, and then called Mohammad.

"Ah, so you have arrived. Welcome to Jordan!" He said.

"Thank you. It's good to be here again," I replied.

"I apologize that I couldn't meet you at the airport but I had guests and couldn't leave them. I trust you had a pleasant flight."

"Yes, everything went well. I am curious about one thing, however. How did you manage to get me my reservations? I was unable on my own to get reservations here. The service is great!"

"The hotel was fully booked, so I had to arrange it another way. You are registered as a guest of His Majesty. I had His Majesty's office call the hotel to make your reservation. They always find room when His Majesty's office calls. You are expected to pay for the room, of course," he laughed.

"Of course. I really appreciate your help. Perhaps I can see you tomorrow?"

"Yes, anytime. Rest tonight and we shall talk tomorrow."

Since it was still early in the evening, I opened the bottle of wine and ate some of the cheese while I took in the view of the city from my balcony.

Amman, as it is called today, is the capital city of the Hashemite Kingdom of Jordan. The Greeks and Romans once called it

Philadelphia over 2,000 years ago. It is located on the seven Jebels (hills) with its expanded population and industrial development spread out into the countryside.

The Jordan Intercontinental Hotel, located directly across the street from the U.S. Embassy, was well equipped to conduct business. Banking facilities, boutiques, travel services and other shops lined the arcade with parking facilities in the center. From the hotel, I could see a picturesque view of the city with its mosques and buildings clinging to the sides of the hills, and new construction appeared everywhere.

Many Lebanese and other foreign firms had moved to Jordan to escape the war in Lebanon and establish alternate headquarters. There was much activity and traffic-jams were now commonplace. Living accommodations were at a premium and inflation had risen sharply and continued its upward spiral. It was an ideal location for corporate headquarters with easy access to other Middle Eastern countries, provided one could afford to live there.

The Jordanians were especially courteous and sincere in their efforts to make one feel welcome. They love and respect their King who has provided them with the climate for economic stability and the free enterprise spirit common to western democratic societies.

My meeting the next day with Mohammad Madi went well. He discussed the industrial growth in Jordan and the kinds of materials that were sought. An engineer himself, he was engaged in housing projects. More affordable housing was of interest to him and we discussed the possibilities of pre-fab housing. That was of interest for Jordan but had its drawbacks for other Middle Eastern countries. The extreme heat of the desert made any wooden structure a matchbox. Wood was scarce and imported primarily for the interior decor of the home. While we discussed these matters, Prince Ali stopped by to see Mohammad and I was introduced. The Prince was also interested in moneymaking projects and suggested I see him when I passed through Jordan again. He also told me I could call on him if I had difficulty in finding future accommodations.

I concluded my business with Mohammad and asked his assistance in gaining a visa to visit Saudi Arabia. Normally, one cannot travel to

Saudi Arabia unless you have a sponsor. A sponsor is someone native to Saudi Arabia and who invites you to visit there. A sponsor or agent is also required in most every Middle East country to conduct business. On my previous trip to Saudi Arabia, Amin Issa Jouma was my sponsor and had arranged for my visa. Now I wished to go there but was unable to reach Mr. Jouma by telephone.

Mr. Madi called the Saudi Arabian Ambassador and arranged for me to meet him to obtain a visa to his country. I carried with me a note from Mr. Madi that I presented to the Ambassador, and my visa was promptly granted.

I used the hotel travel agency to make my flight arrangements but they were unable to secure hotel reservations for me in Alkhobar or in Dammam. I wanted to call Mr. Jouma in Alkhobar at his place of work but was told that I would need to wait two days for the call to go through. Calling within the Middle East was difficult due to the limitation of telephone lines whereas calls to the USA and Europe were immediate. I didn't wish to waste two days waiting, so I decided to take a chance and make the trip anyway.

I checked out of the Jordan hotel and placed my attaché case near the door and asked the receptionist to keep an eye on it while I ran an errand. The receptionist said, "Mr. March, you are in Jordan!"

It's easy to forget that each country in the Middle East is different and must be measured separately. A common mistake by first time visitors to the Middle East is to think that all Arabic countries are the same as the one they visited. The differences among Arab countries are as great as among most English-speaking countries that share a common language.

Chapter 2
Dammam, Saudi Arabia
Spring 1977

The Jordan airport was crowded with late night passengers bound for Far East destinations. I checked my bag, paid the airport tax, cleared customs and passed the security check before entering the waiting lounge. The Jordanian army augmented airport security giving passengers an added measure of safety.

Compared to western standards, the lounge was dirty. The superficial cleaning by the janitors did not eliminate dirt embedded with age. Passengers strolled around the waiting area their arms loaded with gifts and other merchandise unattainable in their own country. Their checked baggage bulged at the seams and some heavy steamer trunks required two people to handle.

A loud speaker announced my flight number and the scramble to the departure gate began. I didn't need to join the rush since my ticket was first class and my seat reserved. Economy class did not grant seat assignments, so there was always a scramble to get a good seat if indeed one had a seat at all. Overbooking of flights was common and the possession of one's seat was secured by occupying it.

I settled into my seat and accepted the drink handed me. Drinks aboard the aircraft would be the last alcoholic beverages I would have for awhile, since alcohol was prohibited in Saudi Arabia. My ETA in Dhahran was shortly after midnight, so I relaxed as I sipped my drink and tried to keep my mind off problems I might encounter without confirmed hotel reservations. I attempted sleep but sleep would not come. The several hours of flight passed quickly, but as always, just before landing I became drowsy and dozed off.

The announcement to fasten seat belts in preparation for landing aroused me. As the plane began its descent, I could see fire lights from oil wells illuminating the desert and I was reminded of the oil shortage back home due to the oil embargo. On my return trip to Jordan I planned to meet with Prince Ali to seek his assistance in acquiring oil for an American client. Obtaining oil outside official channels required special contacts and of course, special financial gratuities. I did not yet have high-placed contacts in Saudi Arabia and must therefore rely on sources outside the country.

Dammam, located at the eastern end of Saudia Arabia is the principal port of Saudia Arabia in the Gulf. Dammam, Al Khobar and Dhahran are the three closely linked cities in the region. ARAMCO, the headquarters for the Arab American Oil Company, is located at the former Dhahran Air Base. The new international airport for the region being designated as Dhahran.

Upon landing, the plane's engines churned-up clouds of sand dust as we rolled along the runway. From my window I studied the grandeur of the Dhahran airport complex. Somehow it seemed out of place here in the desert but reflected the wealth of this oil-rich country.

I collected my baggage, cleared customs and made my way to the exit. It would have been much simpler if I had been able to contact Mr. Jouma. He surely would have picked me up. If it wasn't so late at night, perhaps I could have found my way to Mr. Jouma's house. However, I didn't have his street address, only a P.O. Box number, and to find his house would have been difficult even in daylight.

The taxis were all occupied. As I waited for more to arrive, a Saudi, his soiled white robe flapping in the breeze, his head wrapped with a Koufieh that covered his nose and mouth with only the eyes visible, approached me.

"Taxi?" He inquired.

"Yes. Nam!" I replied, looking around for the cab.

The Saudi took my bag and I followed him. The night breeze fanned the desert heat and the blowing sand particles stung my face. The Saudi threw my bag on the back of a Datsun Pick-up truck.

"Is this a taxi?" I asked.

"Taxi," he replied, motioning for me to get in.

I climbed in. At least it was transportation, I thought. No use trying to keep clean now as I attempted to brush the sand dust from the black upholstered seat.

The Saudi gave a twist of his hand and said, "Wayn?"

"Algosaibi Hotel," I ordered. I knew this hotel was near where Mr. Jouma lived.

The taxi's radio blared with the wail of Arabic music. I shielded my face from the sand dust blowing around in the cab. It was too hot to close the window and the warm breeze felt good. As we proceeded toward Alkhobar, I observed the buildings silhouetted against the skyline and the sand dunes looming like mountains in the moonlit sky. Near scattered flat-roofed huts, a herd of camels dotted the desert grazing on the sparse foliage. As we drew near the city of Alkhobar, I began to recognize some landmarks. The street we were driving on suddenly widened into a boulevard lined with newly planted palm trees. This street had been under construction two years before and was still being worked on. Three Arabs stood by the road and held out their hands as we approached. The driver stopped the cab and conversed with them briefly, then motioned them onto the back of the cab. I kept a watchful eye on my baggage as we continued toward town. It was difficult not to worry about things like that after living in Beirut. However, here in Saudi Arabia, theft is rare. The severity of punishment deters crime. A thief may have his right hand cut-off for his first offense, his left hand or an ear on the second offense; feet may be next and depending on the crime, decapitation. The only thing apt to be stolen here, I figured, was the seat of my pants from a shrewd business deal. For that, I would have only myself to blame. I was looking forward to a good shower and a comfortable bed.

Before reaching the hotel, the cab stopped and the riders jumped off. A short distance farther, the cab turned into the driveway of the

Algosaibi Hotel. I glanced at my watch and noted that it was already after 1:00 AM.

The lobby was deserted except for two porters who were stretched out on a chair and sofa and a night clerk shuffling through some papers. I walked to the desk and placed my attaché case on top.

"My name is March, Abe March," I said.

"Do you have a reservation, sir?"

"I certainly hope so. You don't think I'd come all this way without one, do you?"

The clerk looked through his reservation ledger, then said, "I find no reservation for you here, sir."

"That's impossible," I replied, attempting to look astonished. "You must have a room for me."

Once again the clerk went through his book; then he checked the telex reservation bookings. "I'm sorry sir, but you have no reservations and the hotel is full."

"What am I going to do? Is there another hotel nearby where I might find a room?"

"I think they are full, also. Who did you come to see in Saudi Arabia? Perhaps we can call them and see who made your reservation."

I explained that my friend had no home telephone and that I did not know his street address; that reservations were to have been made by the travel agency.

"Come back to my office and I'll try to find a room for you."

"I'd really appreciate it," I said. "By the way, how much is the fare for the taxi from the airport to here?"

"Fifteen to twenty riyals."

"Thanks. Could you exchange some dollars for riyals?"

"Surely. How much do you want exchanged?"

"Fifty dollars should do for tonight," I replied.

"You will need more than that if you intend to pay for a room."

"Yes, of course, but I will change more money tomorrow at a bank, unless I am required to pay for the room in advance."

"No, that is not required."

I counted the money and went outside to the waiting driver. I handed him twenty riyals, and not wishing any argument, turned away. The driver followed me demanding thirty riyals. I called for the bellman and explained the situation. The bellman noticed that the man was not an official taxi driver and spoke harshly to him. He then said, "It's all right, he won't bother you. Twenty riyals is OK."

After several telephone calls, a hotel room was located in Dammam, situated on the other side of the Dhahran Airport. They wanted agreement on price.

"How much is it?"

"Eighty riyals," replied the clerk.

"Do I have a choice?" I asked.

"No, I don't think so. If you want this room tonight, that's what you'll have to pay."

I was exhausted and it was nearly 2:00 AM. "OK, I'll take it. Please confirm it for me," I said.

A taxi was summoned and the fare agreed upon before leaving. I didn't want any hassle with the driver and wanted to be sure I had enough riyals to pay. The hotel was on the other side of the airport, approximately twenty miles distant. Considering the price, I was looking forward to a good room.

Disappointment and helplessness seized me as the taxi stopped in front of the building. The only resemblance to a hotel was the small sign, which read, "Hotel." For one night, I thought, I could put up with anything. Besides, the inside may be quite nice.

Payment in advance was not requested; however, the desk clerk kept my passport—a common practice. It would be returned when I checked-out and paid my bill. There was never any question of skipping out, for without a passport, you couldn't leave the country.

I opened the door to my room and stared in disbelief. Two small cots, a beat-up dresser and a small nightstand constituted the furniture. A noisy window air conditioner humming between filthy drapes was not my idea of a comfortable place to sleep. The thin carpeting was so soiled that it was impossible to determine the original color.

I placed my bags on the floor and inspected the first cot. Small black curly hair particles lay between the sheets. I didn't examine the other cot deciding instead to sleep on top of the sheets. But first, I would take a refreshing shower.

I peered into the bathroom and determined I would not have my shower after all. The shower pipe was broken off at the stem and standing against the wall. The commode looked and smelled like a sewer while the washbasin, which must have been white at one time, was nearly black with grime and dirt. Feeling much cleaner than my surroundings, I lay down to sleep.

The heat would have been unbearable without the air conditioner, but the loud humming and vibrating noise prevented much sleep. Before long, the sunrays lit up the room and I got up. I took a hand bath using the end of a towel, dressed and went downstairs for breakfast, but it was too early. I would have to wait until 7:00 AM.

The restaurant swarmed with flies. Small wooden tables with plastic tablecloths sat on bare cement floors. I needed something in my stomach, so I brushed off the seat and sat down. I settled for some Arabic bread and tea, eating slowly so the time would pass and I could call Mr. Jouma at his office. Finally I reached him.

"Hello Issa, this is Abe March."

"Hello, how are you? Where are you calling from?"

"I'm in Dammam at a hotel."

"Why are you there? Why didn't you come to my house?"

I explained what had happened and that I didn't wish to impose on him.

"I'm coming to get you. You will stay at my house."

I would have preferred my privacy, but under the circumstances and not to offend him, I graciously accepted.

When Issa arrived, he kissed me several times on both cheeks signifying the warmest of greetings.

"How is the family? Why didn't you bring them with you? How is your son?" asked Issa.

"My family is fine. My son sends his kind regards. He still talks about the trip he made with you to Jordan."

"It was my pleasure. Come, where's your bag?"

"Let me first check out. My bag is sitting by the cashier."

Issa was insisting on paying the hotel bill and I was refusing.

"But they have overcharged you. You are paying too much for this hotel," he argued, and I couldn't disagree with him about that.

Refusing an Arab friend's hospitality was virtually impossible. I explained my predicament of the night before, and then agreed to let Issa pay for me and he got a reduced rate.

Issa was accustomed to the heat and had no air conditioning in his car. For me, it was very hot and already over 100 degrees Fahrenheit. The air blowing through the windows seemed only to fan the heat. Disabled cars, literally abandoned when they broke down, were seen along the roadside. According to Issa, getting mechanical repairs was difficult and it was simpler to buy another car than to repair the old one.

When I stepped out of the car in front of Issa's house, my feet sank into the soft sand. Although the street was paved, it was nearly covered with sand that also blanketed the sidewalks.

Issa carried my luggage and I followed him to the entrance of the building. The cement steps were badly cracked, some with large gaping holes. A rat scurried away as we approached and Issa stomped his feet on the steps to frighten others away as we climbed the stairs.

The door was opened by one of Issa's daughters who smiled shyly and stood aside as we entered. Issa's wife came forward to greet me, saying, "Ahlan wa sahlan (Welcome, twice welcome)."

I acknowledged the warm welcome, and was invited to remove my shoes and wash my feet. I did so and it felt good. I was then provided with sandals and a cool drink of water.

The house was well furnished. Expensive oriental carpets covered the floors and the latest model color television was positioned in one corner of the room against cracked walls, evidence of the shoddy workmanship of foreign contract laborers.

It was August and the heat of the desert was extreme. It was also Ramadan, the Moslem time of fasting. During Ramadan, no food is consumed during daylight. They even refrain from smoking and drinking water. At sundown however, a large feast is prepared. I was a foreign guest and that made for an exception, at least that's what Issa told me.

As we sat and talked, the pleasant aroma of food filled the air. Issa's young son crawled around the room getting into everything to the amusement of Issa. After having three daughters, he was very proud when a boy was born. A boy brought honor to his house. It was the son who would head the household and take on the responsibility for the family when Issa was gone.

The table was set with only three plates for the males. Dishes heaped with food were placed on the table, and when everything was ready, Issa, his son and I, sat down to eat. Issa took his place at the head of the table while I sat to his right and his son to his left. The women stayed in the background, watching, and bringing more food as we ate.

I ate heartily and before I could finish the food on my plate, it was once again filled with rice, mutton and savory vegetables. Finally, after insisting convincingly that I could eat no more, the plates were taken away and new ones placed on the table. Bowls of fresh fruit were brought containing bananas, apples, oranges, grapes, and other fruits imported from Lebanon and Jordan.

After the meal, Issa and I left the table and sat on the sofa where coffee was served to us in tiny cups. We sipped the Arabic coffee and smoked while the women went to the table to eat what remained of the food.

While inside the house, women in Saudi Arabia are uncovered and wear western-style clothing. But when they go outside, they wear a veil to cover their face and a black outer garment reaching their feet. It always struck me as odd that women wear black, which attracts heat, while men wear white, which reflects heat. The Saudi women lead very restricted public lives. They are forbidden to drive a car, take a taxi alone, or even leave the country unless escorted by a male member of the family. However, the influx of foreigners to Saudi Arabia showed signs of softening these hard rules. Women have entered the teaching profession but are limited to teaching members of the female sex. Along with travel to European capitals, the Saudis are beginning to adopt western habits which will most certainly influence change in Saudi Arabia, although gradually.

I went with Issa to his place of work at the Dr. Fakry Hospital in

Alkhobar. Between his duties as Radiologist, we discussed business. I went to a water fountain to get a drink. As I took my first swallow, I noticed the stares of the patients in the hallway and at once realized my error. However, Issa told me it was OK for me to drink. I was not a Moslem and therefore the rules of Ramadan didn't apply to me. My sensitivity to their customs however, made me more cognizant of my future actions. I was curious about the salty taste of the water. Issa explained that it was from the desalination plants that converted seawater to drinking water. There was always a certain amount of salt remaining in the water, and it had its own natural therapeutic benefit and salt tablets were less important.

Issa wanted me to meet his friend who lived in the house above him.

"He's Palestinian," said Issa.

"That's all right," I replied. "If he's a friend of yours, I'd like to meet him."

Immediately upon entering the home of Hassan I felt some tension when Issa introduced me as his American friend, but Hassan was polite and hospitable. As our conversation progressed, the subject turned to politics. Hassan looked directly at me and said, "I'm with the PLO in Lebanon."

Since I showed no reaction to this statement, he continued.

"You see, Mr. March, according to our custom, even when an enemy is among us, he has protection. We give him food and lodging. When he leaves the protection of our camp or home, he is once again the enemy."

"Do you consider me an enemy," I asked.

My direct question made Hassan uncomfortable, but after a brief moment he said, "Your government supports Israel and Israel is our enemy. Since you support Israel, that makes you an enemy of the Palestinians."

"I take exception to that," I said. "You make me your enemy because of some statement by my President or some action by my government. That does not mean I believe or think exactly like my government. One of the wonderful things about being American is that we can believe, say and think what we want. I don't happen to think my government's actions are entirely proper concerning the Palestinians. I believe you have a just cause and hope that a solution is found that will bring peace and provide a homeland for the Palestinians. I've lived in Beirut for a couple of years and have come to understand more about the situation."

Hassan's eyes lit up and he said, "Many more Americans should come to the Middle East. More tourists should come, then they can go back home and tell people what they saw."

"I'm not so sure tourists are the answer. Unfortunately, the tourist only tells the bad that he sees. He doesn't talk about the good things but rather compares his way of life to yours and the bizarre things he sees which will make for interesting conversation. That's unfortunate," I said.

"What do you think can make things better?" asked Hassan.

"That's a difficult question. It will take more time; it requires more truth and understanding between people and their culture. It requires more communication between common people. International business is one way that has helped but that's a slow process. Just remember one thing, Hassan. You'll find the Americans very understanding once they have the facts and they are a very sympathetic people. Unfortunately, they only know what they hear in the news. As you know, there is seldom any good news. The only news that is printed concerns the bad and that's what sells."

"You like whiskey?" asked Hassan.

"Yes, but you don't have it in Saudi Arabia."

Hassan smiled and went to his cupboard and brought a bottle of whiskey that was three-fourths empty. He smilingly poured a small amount in three glasses.

"We have ways to get it," he said. "We drink in friendship. You are welcome in my home anytime."

We talked more about differences in culture and the attitudes of people. After I left Hassan's house, I thought about our conversation and reflected on how political decisions affect the citizens of every country. I remembered the incident in Canada when my son was beaten by his schoolmates because he was American. To realize that people are not treated as individuals but on the politics of their country is sad.

If citizens the world over could get to know one another, they would find that the average citizen is much the same as they are: full of anxiety, struggling to survive, wanting to make a decent life but caught up in politics that influence their attitudes and behavior. I further contemplated the scenario: if leaders in today's world were required to lead their armies into battle as was done in early times, I wondered how many wars would have been prevented.

I spent the week meeting other Arab businessmen and discussing their product and service needs. We also visited the ARAMCO complex. It reminded me of an American military base complete with all facilities and housing area. Sprinklers watered the grass on the front lawns of homes, which was an uncommon sight once outside the compound of this desert region.

One man I met was interested in creating a new business. He had the cleaning contract for the ARAMCO oil company and his cleaning crews cleaned the ARAMCO offices. He wanted to get involved in other pursuits. I mentioned briefly the aborted plans I had for building a cosmetic factory in Iran but that it was no longer a possibility. He immediately wanted to know how much money was required. He said the cosmetic factory could be built in Saudi Arabia.

"As a Saudi, I can get whatever money I want from the government." With amusement he said, "They will give me forty years to repay. In forty years, I'm dead. I never repay."

I told him I would think about the possibility. Money was an important factor but so was the expertise to operate and manage the business. A business plan would be required which considered production. Most of the labor force in Saudi Arabia was imported labor and many of the workers were illiterate. With no women in the work force and the unwillingness of the Saudi's to perform manual labor, a cosmetic factory was not likely at this time.

Having concluded my business meetings in Alkhobar and Dammam, I arranged for air transportation to Riyadh, the capital city of Saudi Arabia, however hotel reservations in Riyadh could not be confirmed.

Chapter 3
Riyadh, Saudi Arabia
Spring 1977

    Located in the central region of the desert, Riyadh is the capital city of the Kingdom of Saudi Arabia. The name Riyadh stems from the Arabic word meaning a place of gardens and trees and is a more fertile area in the heartland of Arabia. Is extremely hot but without the humidity common to the coastal areas of Arabia. From the air, it looked like a sprawling oasis and was a welcome sight after seemingly endless miles of sand.

    I walked down the steps of the aircraft and the blast of heat hit me like a furnace, then an immediate chill from the extreme change in temperature as I entered the air-conditioned terminal building of the King Khalid International Airport. I collected my baggage and without asking the fare, took a taxi to the Riyadh Intercontinental Hotel. I would ask the receptionist at the hotel to pay the taxi for me to avoid haggling over price.

    Modern street lamps lined the wide boulevard leading to town. New building construction with western-style architecture was evident everywhere. The slow building process of concrete construction was still used and appropriate for the desert heat. These new structures were not only changing the appearance of the desert city but also signified the change it was bringing to its inhabitants.

    The splendor of the new Riyadh Intercontinental Hotel blended with the changing character of the city. I hoped there would be a room for me so I could relax; enjoy the pool and some western-style luxury.

    Immaculate small shops enveloped the huge hotel lobby. The large lounge area that was arranged with separate sitting areas, especially suited for private business discussions, was situated by a western-style coffee shop. Western businessmen paraded through the lobby easily distinguished by their business suits while other patrons were engaged in serious conversations in this comfortable atmosphere.

I went through my routine of the distressed traveler, but to no avail. No, they had not received my reservation. Yes, they would try to find me another first class hotel since my reservations must have been misplaced, and they would do everything to assist.

A room was found for me at the Elkereji Hotel and a taxi was summoned to take me there. As the taxi wound its way through the heavy traffic, I wondered if I would be faced with the same lodging I had found in Dammam. Through the open window of the taxi, the wail of the mosque could be heard signaling prayer time. The taxi stopped and the driver took a small rolled-up carpet from the front seat and got out of the cab. He walked to the median strip separating the highway and spread his carpet on the sand. He knelt, then raised his hands over his head and leaned forward touching his head to the ground repeatedly in his prayer ritual. I could see others doing the same. In approximately ten minutes, the driver folded his carpet, returned to the cab and resumed driving.

I was pleasantly surprised to discover that the Elkereji Hotel was new. The lobby was expensively furnished, Arabic-style, with many oriental carpets placed around the floors and others decorating the walls. Although the price at the Elkereji was higher than the Intercontinental, I was grateful to have a room. Though sparsely furnished, my room had new furniture but noted how it was covered with fine sand-dust. The bedding felt sandy but it was new and had not been slept in. Shoddy workmanship was evident here also. The walls had blotches of cement and mortar on them that had not been removed since construction. The bathroom was equipped with new modern fixtures but they too were speckled with paint, and mortar fragments were splattered on the wall tiles, bathtub and floor. It appeared as though I was the first to occupy the room, and only lacked the vigilance of a cleaning crew.

I undressed and scrubbed the bathroom with a towel then shook the sheets and wiped the dust from the chairs. It wasn't the Intercontinental, but it was a palace compared to the room I had in Dammam.

The telephone system was not equipped for direct dial, and not being a western hotel, the staff spoke little English. I tried unsuccessfully to place a call to the USA, and then inquired about the use of a telex.

"I'm sorry, sir, telex not working. New hotel. Maybe tomorrow she work."

I went into the lounge and listened to a conversation between an American construction worker and his friend, complaining about the hotel. They had been moved from the Saudia Hotel to the Elkereji. Their company was paying more here, but they were receiving less in the way of services and comfort. I joined the conversation and inquired about the Saudia Hotel. They said the food was good; each room had a TV, that there was a swimming pool and each night a movie was shown for the entertainment of the guests. Total room and board was less expensive than the flat room rate at the Elkereji. Upon learning this, I went to the telephone and placed a call to the Saudia Hotel.

"This is Abe March. I want to make a reservation for a single room."

"Yes, Mr. March. When would you like the room?"

"Tomorrow," I replied.

"What company are you representing?"

I thought for a moment. I was representing various companies so I chose one at random and said, "Schenck Corporation."

"Mr. Albert Schenck?"

The way the clerk asked the question meant it was either very good or very bad. Since I already had a room, I took the chance and said, "Yes."

"Just a moment, Mr. March."

I waited, and soon the clerk came back on the line and said, "For how long would you like the room?"

"One week only," I replied.

"It will be all right, sir, starting tomorrow. How is Mr. Schenck?"

"The last time I saw him he was well. It's kind of you to ask."

"Not at all. We will see you tomorrow then."

I wasn't sure who this Albert Schenck was, but obviously someone important to them. The Schenck I knew was not named Albert and had never been to Saudi Arabia.

I checked out of the Elkereji the following morning and went to the Saudia Hotel. It was exactly as the men had described, complete with everything, less expensive and the food was good. I could now concentrate on business. I was careful to avoid talking with the reservations clerk fearful that he might wish to know more about the health of Mr. Schenck.

The hotel's communication facilities all functioned and I was able to make my phone calls and send telexes. Local business discussions could be conducted only in the mornings. From noon to 5:00 PM most business offices were closed. That was the time to relax, take a nap or swim in the pool during the intense heat of the afternoon. I could resume business after 5:00 PM.

I arranged my first appointment and had the receptionist write down the address in Arabic. I went to the street and flagged down the first taxi driving by. I handed the slip of paper to the driver and got into the car. The driver looked at the paper and drove on. After a short distance, he stopped the car. He pointed to the paper and gave a twist of his wrist. I realized at once he couldn't read, so I instructed him to drive on. Reaching an intersection, I noticed an Arab in western dress and asked the driver to stop.

"Excuse me, but do you speak English?" I asked.

"I speak English."

"Good. Perhaps you can help me. The address where I wish to go is written on this paper but I'm afraid the driver doesn't read."

The man conversed with the driver, translating the address while the driver repeatedly nodded his head saying, "Nam, nam, nam," in understanding. I expressed my thanks to the man who replied, "Not at all. Welcome to Saudi Arabia!"

I made various calls on business merchants and executives. Appointments were difficult to arrange without connections. One simply had to go to the place of business and wait. Upon entering the office and naming the person I wished to see, I presented my business card. I was then directed into the office, introduced to six or seven other visitors, and invited to take a seat. Refreshments were offered while the businessman continued talking with each visitor in turn, always changing the language to suit the caller. I was always impressed with the Arab businessmen's knowledge of languages and regretted that I had not concentrated on other languages when I was in school. However, emphasis was not placed on learning other languages. English was considered to be the universal business language, so why bother with another, was the attitude.

My thoughts were interrupted when the businessman said, "What do you have, Mr. March?"

I felt uncomfortable stating my business in front of others but there was no choice. I began by explaining the various products I represented and handed brochures to the businessman. Before I could complete a presentation, there always seemed to be an interruption. Another person would enter, or the telephone would ring. The businessman would then resume discussions with others, then return to me. During the interval, I would mentally prepare my next approach, and when it was my turn, briefly summarize what had been stated earlier before continuing. The interruptions may have been beneficial to the businessman giving him time to consider what was being presented before a response was necessary. Perhaps it was a clever way of "thinking it over." What impressed me most was his ability to remember the various conversations and respond intelligently to each.

Except for oil, Saudi Arabia has little to sell. The Saudis are buyers and most everything they have is imported. Having the luxury of money to spend, salesmen from all over the world come to Saudi Arabia in hopes of landing the big sale. The Saudis are in no hurry to buy. Their lack of immediate response or eagerness to buy frustrates most western salesmen and their impatience often results in unprofitable or unsuccessful trips. Because of this impatience, western salesmen will too readily reduce their prices while the Saudis remain silent and non-committal. Often the salesman will depart before getting a response. The Saudi's patience gets them the best price and often "baksheesh" is customary to land the deal.

Water is their most precious commodity. The price of bottled water costs more than gas. Much of the available water is brackish and when used in mixing concrete, the evidence can be seen in traces of salt in the hardened mortar.

A solution was sought to purify the brackish water. Although there were desalination plants by the seacoast that converted salt water to a more palatable and usable form, it was a costly process. More efficient ways to solve their water problem were sought and I recorded this in my notes.

I concluded my business that day with requests for price quotations. I would have to telex the companies in the USA for an official price quotation so I departed. It was dark and the evening traffic was heavy. The taxi driver kept looking at me and spoke to me in Arabic. I understood little of what he was saying and became confused. I thought the driver asked me if I was married and I said, yes. Then he pointed to me and to himself with a suggestive gesture and said, "Zigi, zigi?" This was a new term to me and I replied, "Maa fihim," (I don't understand). The driver repeated, "Zigi, zigi," again pointing to himself; and me then he placed his hand on my leg. Now I understood.

"La, la! Saudia Hotel—Ya'allah!" I said, making it clear I was only interested in getting to the hotel promptly.

The lack of contact between young men and women in Saudi Arabia along with the restrictive rules and conditions placed on them for marriage fosters homosexuality. Those with financial means travel to Egypt or Beirut for their sexual pleasures.

With no bars or nightclubs for entertainment, the hotel cinema was crowded. At the conclusion of the movie, a tall glass of fruit juice topped off the evening. With little else to do, getting acquainted with other businessmen passed the time and was a source for new contacts.

I concluded my business in Riyadh and intended to go to Jeddah but it was impossible to get hotel accommodations. I was strongly advised not to go there without them. Instead, I decided to go to Abu Dhabi in the United Arab Emirates where I had contacts. It was necessary to have my tickets changed and flight reservations made. I had to present my ticket to Alia, the Jordanian airline for a ticket endorsement to Saudi Airlines, since it was the only airline flying from Riyadh to Abu Dhabi. I endured long lines and the process required a full day to change my ticket.

I was instructed to be at the airport two hours before departure if I expected to get on the flight. Although my ticket was marked "OK," it meant little unless I had a boarding pass, and they were issued on a first-come basis. First class had been fully booked so I was given economy fare, one-way to Abu Dhabi. I was told to purchase my ticket out of Abu Dhabi to Jordan when I arrived in Abu Dhabi.

I arrived at the Riyadh airport early and waited in line for more than an hour before reaching the ticket counter. Office boys and other messengers carrying tickets for their guests went to the front of the line and pushed their tickets under the nose of the ticket agent. They were recognized and issued boarding passes while the people in line waited, pushing their bags inch by inch forward, to prevent others breaking in on them. I pushed along with the others.

I finally got my boarding pass, checked my luggage, cleared customs and security, always waiting in long lines at each clearance checkpoint until I reached the departure lounge. Fifteen minutes before departure, a two-hour delay was announced.

Chapter 4
Abu Dhabi—United Arab Emirates
Late Spring/Summer 1977

In the U.A.E., one could obtain a four-day visa at the airport. I had been to Dubai twice before but this was to be my first trip to Abu Dhabi. I was unable to reach my business contact by telephone or telex from Riyadh but felt the opportunity to visit Abu Dhabi warranted the chance while I was in the area.

The plane touched down at 1:30 AM. I hurried to the customs booth ahead of the other passengers and presented my passport to the officer to secure my visa.

"Your ticket," demanded the officer.

I handed it to him and the officer examined it.

"You have no ticket leaving Abu Dhabi?" He inquired.

"I will buy it here before I leave," I said.

"Wait over there," said the officer. I stepped out of line and moved to the side.

After the officer processed the other passengers, he motioned for me to return to the booth.

"You cannot enter Abu Dhabi without a return ticket. You have money for a ticket?"

"Yes, of course. I will buy one here before I leave."

"There are no ticket offices open at this hour and they are on the outside. You cannot go outside without a visa. I cannot give you a visa without a return ticket."

"So what am I to do? I was told I could get a visa and the tickets I need here at the airport. How can I get a ticket if I am not permitted to go outside?"

The officer thought for a moment, and then called another officer over to his booth. They talked together, and then asked, "You have money for a ticket?"

"Yes, I told you I have the money."

"Go with this man," he said, pointing to his left. "He will get your ticket."

I followed the man to another counter. He explained that many people come to the U.A.E., and then decide to stay, claiming they have no money to leave. Therefore, they do not allow anyone to enter the country unless he has a return ticket out.

I assured him that it had been a mistake on my part and that I appreciated anything he could do to help me. I gave the correct amount of money and some extra, and the officer left the customs area. After a long wait, I went to the other officer and asked the whereabouts of his colleague.

"He will be here soon. It's prayer time."

When the man returned, he wrote a ticket for a flight leaving Abu Dhabi four days later.

"You will have to confirm your reservation. I only write the ticket to get your visa but cannot confirm your seat. There is no one working at this hour."

I took my ticket and visa, collected my baggage and was ushered through baggage inspection. I carried my own luggage to the exit and walked to the front of the taxi stand.

"Taxi?" inquired a short peculiar looking little man whose head was wrapped with a scarf resembling a turban.

I nodded and handed my luggage to him, climbed into the cab and said, "Hilton Hotel."

The driver responded, "Abu Dhabi?"

Where else I thought, nodding my head affirmatively.

The car started with a jerk throwing me back in my seat. Grasping the steering wheel with both hands, the little driver peered over the steering wheel and began turning it from side to side with quick jerky movements causing the taxi to lurch back and forth on the straight road. At the first intersection, he braked hard throwing me forward, then back again when he stepped on the gas. Holding onto the door handle to keep from being thrown about, I watched his actions with amusement, surmising that he just learned to drive.

Upon entering the outskirts of Abu Dhabi, the taxi came to an abrupt stop. I looked quickly to both sides of the street but didn't see a hotel.

The driver turned in his seat, looked at me and said, "Wayn Heel-tone o'tel?"

I took a closer look at the driver. His beard jutted out from his small face and the street lamp reflected his sharp features and dark skin. He was definitely a Yemeni, I thought, probably brought into Abu Dhabi as a laborer who turned taxi driver without knowing the city.

"How should I know where the Hilton Hotel is? This is my first time in Abu Dhabi. You're the taxi driver. Surely you know where the Hilton is!"

The driver's face showed bewilderment. He didn't understand a word I was saying, so I motioned for him to drive on. Ever so often, the driver would stop the car, point at a large building and say, "Heel-tone?"

"La," I would reply, and then be thrown back in my seat again when he stepped on the gas.

I looked at every tall building hoping to see a sign, which would read, "Hilton Hotel." It was supposed to be one of the tallest and most modern hotels in Abu Dhabi. Surely everyone here knew where it was located—except my driver, I thought. The streets were empty except for an occasional car. I glanced at my watch and noted the time to be just after 3:00 AM. I spied someone walking along the sidewalk and signaled the driver to stop. I motioned for the man to come to the car.

"Do you speak Englizi?" I asked.

There was no response.

"Hilton Hotel. Heel-tone, O'tel," I repeated.

Immediately the man's eyes flashed with a sign of recognition. He spoke rapidly, giving directions to the driver.

"Shoukran," I said, as the driver placed the car in gear. The car leaped forward with definite purpose, throwing me hard against the back seat. We traveled quite a way along the sea and I began to wonder if we might be going in the wrong direction until I spied a large building in the distance. There was no illuminated sign but as we drew nearer, it gave the appearance of a hotel-type structure.

When we pulled-up alongside the building, the driver turned around in his seat, pointed to the building and announced triumphantly, "Heel-tone!"

The doorman picked up the suitcase and I asked him what the normal fare was from the airport to the hotel. While the doorman waited, I handed the money to the driver. The driver held the money in his open hand looking first at the money and then at me. I explained the difficulty in reaching the hotel to the doorman and said I didn't feel I should pay extra for the incompetence of the driver. The doorman agreed and talked to the driver as I walked into the hotel.

There was no reservation. No, they could not be mistaken. Yes, the hotel was full. No, they didn't know of any other hotel that might have room.

I leaned over the counter. "Please," I said. "You must have a room, any room. I've traveled far and I'm very tired. It's not possible for me to call my business contact here at this hour of the morning. Couldn't you please find something?"

The clerk went through his ledger and said, "There is a suite that was reserved for today but they did not show up. You can stay there for tonight only. You must check out the first thing in the morning."

I thanked him and was presented with two keys. "Why do I need two keys?" I asked. "I only need one room."

"It is a suite and there are two rooms. You are paying for the suite, sir, and it is yours to use."

I was escorted to the suite and after tipping the bellboy, wandered around the suite. It was complete with living room, dining room, kitchen and bar. The adjoining door led to the bedroom. Too bad, I thought, I won't get to enjoy it.

With only three hours sleep, the ringing of the telephone awakened me.

"What time will you be checking out sir?"

"It's only 7:00 AM! According to the sign on the door, check-out time is 12:00 noon."

"You must check out this morning, sir. The suite is reserved."

It was useless to sleep any longer, so I got up. After showering, I went for breakfast. I would have to wait until offices opened before I could call my business contact. Meanwhile, I familiarized myself with the city looking at maps, studying the classified section of the telephone directory and examining brochures about the area.

At approximately 10:00 AM, I made contact with my business party and arranged an appointment. I further explained my dilemma in finding accommodations. They offered to send a driver who could take me around the city to find a room.

I spent quite a long time looking for accommodations, but every hotel had the same story, no room.

"I will pay extra," I pleaded.

"I'm sorry, sir, we have no room."

As a last resort, the driver took me some distance out of the city where he felt we might find a room, but again nothing.

"You must have a room for me," I pleaded. The man smiled and said, "I can give you my life, but I cannot give you a room. We have none."

I directed the driver to take me to the office. After introductions and a cup of tea, I expressed my concern about finding lodging for the night.

"Don't worry, Mr. March. We will make arrangements for you. Perhaps you can stay with one of our British employees who live in a house we provide. We will first discuss business and then arrange for your stay."

The following day was Friday, the Moslem Sabbath. No one worked, so I accompanied my new British friends to their club and spent the day at the beach.

Abu Dhabi was booming with construction stretching out into the desert. A new port was also underway to increase their capacity to export more oil. Dome-shaped Arab-style architecture with arched entrances surrounded by pillars was more prevalent than in Riyadh.

What was lacking, I thought, were sidewalks and greenery. The dusty streets and mounds of sand surrounding the buildings somehow gave the appearance of a nuclear winter. With new desalination plants, water for irrigation would soon transform parts of the desert into areas for plant growth.

Cars parked wherever and however they wanted, most always blocking the entrance to buildings. There was no perception for organization and litter was everywhere. Money could buy expensive materials but could not buy the discipline to maintain it. With their continued industrial pursuits, however, a middle class will one day emerge and effect cultural change.

Discussing this transition with my British friends, they told me of an incident about a Bedouin, accustomed to living in his desert tent, who was provided with a modern apartment. The Bedouin had moved his family into his new home but built a fire in the middle of the living room floor for his wife to cook, oblivious to the modern stove and appliances of a fully equipped kitchen. The Bedouin didn't know how to use these items and was satisfied to continue in his old ways.

The rapid transition from poor to rich leaves a wide cultural gap and brings with it much uncertainty and suspicion of the modern ways, still clinging to the old. With no history of a middle class, the transition in bridging this gap will be slow. It can only occur when industries other than oil become more prevalent and when the work force no longer relies solely on imported labor.

My business discussions held promise. As traders and entrepreneurs, they were interested in new products and quotations were requested.

*****

Returning to Amman, Jordan, was like returning to an oasis after enduring the intense heat of the desert, the restrictive nightlife and the difficulties with language. The evenings in Amman were cool and comfortable. Trees lined the streets, green grass glimmered under water sprinklers and the women, beautiful women, mingled openly with men.

Prince Ali was out of the country, so I had to postpone my discussions with him until my next trip. I therefore met with Mr. Wasif Taher, the proprietor of a trading company to explore the possibility of a business cooperation. After several meetings, I learned that Mr. Taher was formerly the interpreter to Colonel Muhmmar Qaddafi of Libya. Mr. Taher asked me many questions about my contacts and then inquired if it were possible to get airplanes.

"What kind of planes?" I asked. "Do you mean small private aircraft or commercial?"

"No, I mean military jets."

"Why would you ask me that? If Jordan needs planes they can make their own arrangements directly with Washington," I said.

"Suppose it was not for Jordan and someone wanted military planes. Do you know anyone who could arrange it?" he asked.

"Who wants the planes?"

"For the moment, I'd rather not say. I'd like to know if you have the connections."

"Perhaps, but let me make some inquiries," I said.

I called my friend Mr. Schmidt in Munich. I asked if he had connections to get military aircraft. Mr. Schmidt said, "Sure. Who wants them?"

"I don't have all the details yet. I'll contact you on my way back to the States. I'll be coming via Frankfurt and we can get together then."

"I take it these planes are not to go through official channels."

"That's my impression," I said.

"No problem. Get me the details," said Mr. Schmidt.

When I met Mr. Schmidt in Frankfurt, I informed him that a request had been made to acquire military aircraft for Libya. "I don't know what the problem is," I said, "but they are interested in purchasing twenty to twenty-five fighter jets."

"You don't know the problem? Col. Qaddafi is stirring up problems for everyone, and he's the last person the U.S. will sell to. But that's no problem for us; the Shah can get anything he wants from Washington. It can be arranged for the planes to go to Iran. From there they will have to be torn down and crated for shipment, piece-meal, to Libya. They certainly couldn't be flown. Too many problems crossing international boundaries and too many people involved. But for enough money, anything can be arranged. Let me make some inquiries and I'll be able to give you a more definite response. Are they particular about the type of aircraft?"

"I'm sure he wants the latest he can get."

"Yes, you can be sure of that. However, I believe Qaddafi will take anything he can lay his hands on. He'll have to pay through the nose, though."

"From what I understand, money is no problem," I said.

"Good. Let me get back to you."

"What's happening in Iran now? Did anyone pursue the construction of a cosmetic factory?"

"No, it's still on hold. If we conclude this deal with the planes, money won't be a problem for either of us."

"What have you been up to? Are you still working with the Shah?"

"Yes, when he needs me. I've already helped him transfer large sums of money out of Iran and he wants to move more out. He's looking for investments outside the country, and that keeps me busy."

The next communiqué I had with Mr. Schmidt came while I was in the States.

"Abe, the birds we spoke about?"

"Yes?"

"It definitely can be arranged. I went to Washington and to California to see the right people to get the approval for purchase. I'll go to Iran next, but I must first be assured that this is serious."

"It is serious. I was assured of that before I left Jordan. However I'm not so sure that I wish to be involved in this. Since I came home, I've heard nothing but bad about the Colonel and this could put me in a very precarious position. I might even be in trouble with my government if I were involved."

"Abe! We can get five million profit per bird. We'll split it between us. Of course, we'll have to grease a lot of wheels but there will be plenty left over if we're talking twenty birds."

"Let me put you in direct contact with Mr. Taher. He can give you the particulars and you can arrange what you want with him. I know the money sounds good, but I'm nervous about it."

"Don't worry about a thing. I'll handle it from here on," he said.

I heard nothing for another month, then Mr. Schmidt called me.

"It looks like the deal is dead regarding the birds."

"What happened?" I asked.

"I met with Q's (Qaddafi's) representative in London on neutral ground. He said the money wasn't the issue. Q didn't want to pay for something and then discover an important part was missing and it wouldn't operate. We, on the other hand, didn't want to purchase or ship unless we were sure of payment. In this type of business, no one trusts anybody, if you know what I mean. Who does one scream to if something goes wrong? Under the circumstances, we are unable to find a solution to this deadlock, so it appears the deal's off."

"Personally, I'm glad. I really don't know what I'd have done if I had that kind of money staring me in the face."

"If you want the big bucks, you must also take big risks," said Mr. Schmidt.

I realized that truth, but in this case, the risks were too great.

Chapter 5
Big Projects—Kuwait
Summer 1977

Kuwait, the richest oil producing country in the Middle East at that time, also headquartered large investment groups. When it became known that I traveled to the Middle East and had contacts in that region, our stockholders were approached by numerous entrepreneurs that had projects requiring large sums of money. Foreign capital was sought for projects considered too risky by local money people.

A plan to build a Heritage Park in Gettysburg, Pennsylvania, required fifteen million dollars to develop. The project director, having exhausted local resources, wanted the money and was not concerned about the source.

Another project of greater magnitude concerned the sale of leasing rights to the largest fields of anthracite coal in central Pennsylvania, located in Northumberland County. According to U.S. Geological survey reports, there was estimated to be twenty billion tons of coal within a twenty-four square mile area. With the price of oil increasing due to the oil embargo, alternative fuel sources were being studied by private industry and many were once again looking to coal. The promotion of this project expected to earn a quick profit by selling the leasing rights to this rich deposit of anthracite. The asking price for the lease was one hundred million dollars. Don Warner, one of my associates, flew with me in his private plane to the offices of the alleged leaseholder for this large coal deposit, and we were led to believe that they did in fact have the rights to the leases. After our discussions, an agreement was signed whereby a five percent commission was to be paid our company if we were successful in finding a buyer.

We also learned of an inventor near Philadelphia, Pennsylvania, who claimed to have invented a mobile desalination unit more efficient than existing desalination technology. Due to the excellent possibilities for marketing this technology in the Middle East, Don Warner and I went to see the inventor. The inventor went into his storage room and brought out dusty mechanical drawings describing the unit. He claimed to have built a model and tested it some years before but since there had been no interest in its development at that time, he dismantled the model and sold off the parts. He claimed the unit could be built again and would fit on the back of a flatbed tractor-trailer. It was self-contained and even generated its own electricity. We were impressed. I felt that it would be ideal for the desert regions of the Middle East so we hired an engineering consultant knowledgeable in desalination technology. The consultant had previously worked for Westinghouse in researching new methods of desalination and was intrigued by what we told him. He met with the inventor, and after signing a non-disclosure agreement, learned more about the inventor's technology. The consultant's report to us was positive: we hired a patent attorney to see if the process was patentable, and it appeared to be so. Since the inventor lacked the finances to build another model, we attempted to negotiate terms with him in order to raise the funds required to build a new model to confirm his test results, and to market it. After many frustrating meetings, we finally gave up. The inventor refused to give up sufficient equity interest in his invention that would allow us to raise the funds and market the unit. To my knowledge, the inventor still owns one hundred percent of nothing, and the drawings are collecting more dust.

Another entrepreneur sought oil. They had elaborate plans to refine the oil in Haiti and they only lacked the supply source. Due to the oil embargo against the USA, oil was only available outside official OPEC channels. Within Saudi Arabia, an allotment of oil was available to various Sheiks and Princes who acquired these rights when oil was discovered on their land, or because their status as a member of the royal family permitted them to dispose of their allotment as they saw fit. Obtaining a supply of oil was a project I wanted to discuss with Prince Ali of Jordan.

Without thoroughly checking the validity of the various projects coupled with the anxiety of my partners to land the big sale, I hurriedly arranged another trip to the Middle East. I stopped in Munich to see Mr. Schmidt to see if he could generate interest for these investment projects with German businessmen, and then continued on to Amman, Jordan. I solicited the help of Mohammad Madi in contacting people with the resources to invest in projects of this magnitude.

The acquisition of oil was discussed with Prince Ali who graciously received me in his home. The Prince was optimistic that utilizing his contacts within the Arab region he could secure the supply source. We naturally discussed a commission arrangement for himself and I was to meet with him again at a later date.

I visited Mr. Madi who recommended I see Al-Kazemi in Kuwait. Mr. Al-Kazemi was associated with an investment group who had unlimited financial resources. Mr. Madi wrote a letter of introduction that I carried with me.

I wanted to stay at the Hilton Hotel, which I deemed a proper setting for the business I was to discuss. As expected, the hotel was full. Idi Amin, the flamboyant leader of Uganda, was visiting the government of Kuwait to seek financial aid and was occupying three floors of the hotel with his entourage. As I inquired about accommodations elsewhere, a commotion in the lobby drew my attention to soldiers entering through the front door. The Ugandan soldiers motioned for everyone to rise; then they stood at attention, holding their rifles in front of them as the door opened and Idi Amin made his entrance. His immense frame and stature commanded attention. He sauntered, taking wide slow steps as he made his way across the lobby to the elevators. As he walked, he turned from side to side, waved at the people and flashed his large white teeth with a big smile. Entering the elevator, he once again turned to the people in the lobby and gave a wave of his hand before the doors closed on him. His guards remained positioned by the elevator doors and accompanied anyone who entered the elevator to insure no uninvited guest would enter the floor areas assigned to Idi Amin.

I found a room for the night in another hotel then returned to the Hilton the following day where I secured a room. I then met with several prospective investors from the Kuwait Investment Group who showed an interest in the coal project. They wanted more information substantiating the claim of coal reserves and the validity of the leasing rights. They showed no interest in the Heritage Park project since it appeared the amount was too small for their tastes.

The most interesting problem I found in Kuwait was their lack of an adequate source of fresh water. I was told with much amusement, that whenever they would dig for water, they would get oil.

In the month that followed, Mr. Schmidt found interested investors in the coal project that actually traveled to the States and flew by helicopter over the Northumberland coal region. Their investigation revealed that the leasing rights were not valid and they stopped further pursuit. My visit to Kuwait had been futile.

* * * * *

I was requested by a Middle Eastern client to find a building contractor for the construction of a hospital. I contacted Davis International in Ohio to see if they could handle the project. Mr. Davis had worked with me on a quotation for a cold storage facility, however for this project, he suggested I contact a Mr. Photiades in Nicosia, Cyprus, who had experience in the Middle East region and who was reported to be a very powerful and influential businessman. Mr. Photiades arranged for my accommodations at the Cyprus Hilton Hotel where we met. After preliminary discussions, he took me to dinner at an exclusive restaurant frequented by the elite of Cyprus. A beautiful young lady accompanied us and I assumed she was his girlfriend. Mr. Photiades ordered the meal and when the food arrived, I wasn't sure how I was to eat what appeared to be very small chickens or squabs. Noticing my perplexity, Mr. Photiades grabbed the object and took a bite that included the soft bones. He said that this was the way to eat it, so I followed his lead. When I finished, I asked him what kind of foul it was, since it tasted so good. He informed me that it was just a bird that the locals shoot but they are considered delicacies. One eats the entire bird including the entrails. Great! I thought. The bird had been tasty, but I was thankful that I didn't know beforehand that the stuffing was natural.

During the meal, Mr. Photiades talked about Cyprus and business in general. The young lady sitting across from me kept looking at me and smiling suggestively. I did my best to divert my attention from her and avoid any impression of flirtation. Mr. Photiades continued talking, recollecting the visit to Cyprus by Dr. Henry Kissinger, then the Secretary of State. Dr. Kissinger visited Cyprus in an effort to resolve the dispute between the Turks and the Greeks. Archbishop Makarios and Mr. Photiades were part of the Greek delegation to these talks concerning the dispute of the island's ownership. According to Mr. Photiades, in making a point to Dr. Kissinger, the Archbishop said that there were principles involved that must be considered. Dr. Kissinger allegedly responded that principles were not important. Mr. Photiades remarked that principles concerning their rights were a key issue. He did not feel that Kissinger's attitude could help them in solving their problems.

After dinner we returned to the hotel. We said goodbye and arranged to meet the following morning. Mr. Photiades left the hotel but the girl remained. She told me she was also staying at the hotel. I was surprised and also confused about her relationship with Mr. Photiades. I certainly didn't wish to jeopardize my business with him over some girl. I told the girl that I was retiring for the evening and wished her a good night. I went to the elevator and she followed me. It was coincidental, I thought, that her room was on the same floor as mine. Then I discovered that her room was next to mine. When I opened the door to my room, she asked if she could come in. She wondered if my room was the same as hers. Fearing that Mr. Photiades might show up unexpectedly, made me quite nervous. I politely excused myself and bid her a final good night. My naiveté concerning her role was later explained to me after I left Cyprus. Mr. Photiades had engaged this girl for my pleasure. I spent some time wondering if I should include that episode when I told my wife about my trip. I eventually decided to do so. Gisela laughed.

Chapter 6
Palestinian Raid—Amman, Jordan
November 1976

My first appointment in Amman was delayed for a day, so I decided to visit Petra, a three-hour drive south of Amman. Enroute to this ancient city, I listened attentively as the taxi driver pointed out historical areas with Biblical significance along the 'Kings Highway.'

The Nabataean city of Petra is over 2500 years old. It was an ancient center of multi-national business. Petra ("The Rocks") had been a large city in its time, entirely enclosed in a valley except for two tiny and all but inaccessible paths and one rugged but accessible path called a 'Siq.' The Nabataens were Arabs of Bedouin stock who found their way—probably fighting their way, into the valley through the narrow, nearly one-and-a-half mile long, eight-foot wide Siq. Here they built a permanent city and used it as a base to offer protection for caravans passing outside their stronghold, collecting protection fees, serving as warehousemen and running caravans of their own to many lands.

I hired out a horse and proceeded down the narrow Siq. The Siq, a crevice in the solid rock, provided a silent world of perpetual twilight. It is so deep and long that sounds and light hardly penetrate. After a twenty-minute ride, I spied the Treasury almost peeking around a corner in the rock walls. I looked in admiration at this nearly perfectly preserved structure carved out of rock. Twelve high columns, several arches and a half dozen indentations that hold statues much larger than a man, adorn this high cave building. Details carved into the stone would be difficult to duplicate by modern-day sculptors. Farther into the valley, there are numerous other cave-like dwellings hewn out of the cliffs. Stone-paved streets that were neatly fitted together over 2,000 years ago still remain.

The trip to Petra was exciting; however, my adventure on horseback had its side effects and I experienced sore aching muscles the next morning.

After breakfast, I went over my notes and prepared for my 9:15 AM appointment with Osama Anabtawi. It was only a short distance to his office, so I decided to walk. It was 9:05 AM when I passed through the lobby and left the hotel. As I walked through the parking lot in front of the hotel, I passed a man carrying what appeared to be a heavy suitcase. I left the parking lot and turned the corner of the street leading to Osama's office when I heard gunshots. I was startled but continued walking. People leaned out of windows trying to ascertain the source of the gunfire as it echoed around the buildings.

Reaching Osama's office, I asked if he knew what the shooting was about.

"We don't know but it seems to be coming from the second circle, near the Jordan Hotel. Didn't you see anything?"

"No, I heard shots, but I didn't see anything," I said. "I hope the war from Lebanon isn't coming to Jordan."

"Come, we'll go to the roof of the building next door. From there we'll be able to see what's going on," said Osama.

We climbed the six flights of stairs and went onto the flat roof.

"My God!" I shouted. "The hotel is under attack!"

Within minutes, helicopters were hovering around and over the hotel. Machine guns were firing but it was not possible to see the ground area in front of the hotel. Osama was troubled.

"We'd better go down and see what we can find out. Our kids are in school and it might be better to bring them home—just in case," he said.

Osama's secretary was on the telephone. She was told that there had been an attack on the American Embassy and that the gunmen had run across the street into the hotel and were being pursued by the army.

Reminiscences of the Palestinian uprising in Jordan in 1970 ("Black September"—as a result of which King Hussein had driven the PLO out of Jordan) made them fearful that this outbreak of shooting could lead to serious fighting.

Several cars were dispatched to the school for the children. Osama called his wife and told her to go immediately to the store and stock up on food—just in case.

It was now 6:00 AM in the United States. Gisela always watched 'The Today Show' each morning at 7:00 AM. I knew she would be hearing about the attack on the hotel. I tried to place a call to her but the long distance lines were all busy.

The 'Today' program started with a news bulletin. As nearly as Gisela recalls, it went as follows:

"In the early morning hours, Palestinian commandos belonging to the rejection front, attacked the Intercontinental Hotel in Amman, Jordan. Most of the guests at the hotel are western businessmen and are being held hostage. The Jordanian army arrived at the hotel within minutes and have surrounded the hotel attempting to free the hostages. As of this moment, the hostages have not been freed. At least one person is known dead…"

Gisela ran to the telephone and placed a call to the hotel in Amman. The operator tried the call but there was no answer.

"Honey, there are troubles over there this morning," the operator informed my wife. "I don't think we'll get through."

"I know that! My husband is in the hotel! While you have the line open, could you try another number for me?"

"Honey, get all the numbers together you want and we'll try one after the other until we find somebody."

"Do you think we should try the Embassy?" asked Gisela.

"Honey, they will be swamped with calls. It's better to try someone else you know there."

Gisela placed her first call to Mohammad Madi where I was to have an appointment later that morning. The phone rang and was answered immediately.

"Hello."

"Hello, this is Gisela March."

"Hello, How are you?"

"Could you please tell me if Abe is at the hotel?"

At that moment, the line went dead. The operator came back on the line and said, "Somehow, we have been disconnected. Do you have another number?"

Gisela gave the number for Osama Anabtawi's home. The telephone rang and one of the children answered.

"Do you want to speak with the children?" asked the operator.

"Yes, let me speak with anyone there."

"Hello, hello…"

Another voice came on the line.

"This is Gisela."

"Oh, Hi. This is Kathy. How are…"

"Can you tell me if my husband is at the hotel?"

"No, he isn't. Osama called a little while ago and said that Abe was with him at his office. Your husband tried to get a message to you but could not call out."

"I'm so relieved. I was so worried. Please, if you talk to him, tell him I love him."

"I will, Gisela. Don't worry, we'll take good care of him."

I had waited at Osama's office. We continued to speculate on what was happening at the hotel and I was concerned about my personal belongings, having seen black smoke pouring out of windows near my room.

"I'm going to the hotel," I said.

"I'm going with you," replied Osama. "I think we'd better walk. They may not permit any cars in the area."

I walked fast with Osama trying to keep up with me. The streets were crowded with military personnel and armored vehicles positioned at all access routes to the hotel. Traffic was detoured and curious onlookers kept away. I flashed my American passport and was permitted to proceed and Osama followed.

The area in front of the hotel showed the scars of battle. Broken glass littered the sidewalks; several cars had been blown up and were still smoking. The face of the hotel was blackened by smoke and marred by bullet holes. An ambulance was parked by the entrance with its lights flashing and a body was being carried to it.

"You can't go in there," said the soldier.

"But I'm a guest at the hotel."

"May I see your I.D.?"

I showed my passport and the soldier said, "Wait here. They are searching each room to be sure there are no more gunmen inside. As soon as the search is completed, you will be permitted inside. You can then check your room to see if anything is damaged or missing. Give a complete report to us and the government will compensate you for any loss."

"What happened here?" I inquired of the soldier.

"Four gunmen tried to take over the hotel and hold hostages, but we got all of them as far as we know."

"Have you any idea why they did it?"

"We're not sure, but we will find out soon. Three of the gunmen are dead, but we were able to take one alive. He's seriously wounded but should recover. He will then be interrogated."

"Then it had nothing to do with the Embassy?"

"No," said the soldier.

Only guests were permitted inside, so Osama returned to his office and I entered the lobby. A pool of blood lay by the reception counter. Bullet marks defaced the walls, chairs were overturned and strewn about, the large drapes covering floor to ceiling windows now flapped in the breeze through holes in the glass. It was a mess.

While standing with other hotel guests in the lobby, an army officer instructed us to go to our rooms and check for damaged or missing items and to use the stairway since the elevators were out of order.

We were careful to avoid stepping on the blood that was smeared over the steps where bodies had been dragged out. The sixth floor had burned when an explosive grenade was thrown through the window by the army in an effort to dislodge the gunmen.

I entered the seventh floor. The smell of smoke was strong and soot covered the walls and floor. Bullet marks were on the walls, and at the end of the corridor, the windows were riddled with bullet holes. A large bloodstain lay directly in front of the door to my room. I entered the room and looked around. There was no evidence of any damage or that anything had been disturbed, so I wandered through the corridors looking into rooms whose doors had been pried open. Glass was scattered over beds and furniture from broken windows and mirrors.

I went to the top floor. The doors to the Royal Suite were open with people inside. This once beautiful suite was in shambles. The windows looked like sieves and the walls were peppered with bullet marks.

"Come one in, Abe. Join the party."

"What party?" I asked. I recognized two of the men I had met in the lounge the night before.

"Our survival party."

"Were you here when all this happened?" I asked.

"Yes, and we're trying to forget. Have a drink and join us."

"Thanks, but it looks like you drank everything in the Mini Bar."

"Do you have anything in your room? If you do, bring it up. There won't be any service in the hotel tonight and we should scrounge up everything we can."

I returned with my arms loaded with the contents of my Mini Bar. At that moment, several army officers entered the suite and were invited to join us in a drink. They politely refused but sat for a while and explained what had taken place. The spokesman for the group said that four gunmen had driven into the parking lot in front of the hotel around 9:00 AM, and that one of the men was carrying a large suitcase. I interrupted to say that I had seen the man and passed him as I was leaving the hotel.

"You're lucky you were not a few minutes late," said the officer. He went on to say that the man carrying the suitcase was about to enter the hotel when he was challenged by the security guard and asked for his identity papers. The gunman dropped the suitcase, opened it and pulled a gun on the guard. The suitcase was full of guns and grenades. Then, three other gunmen came running into the hotel and began rounding up guests in the lobby as hostages. An army contingent was just across the street and as soon as the first shots were fired, they came running to the hotel.

One month before, the army had gone through a training exercise for such an eventuality and they were prepared. The idea was to panic the gunmen and not give them time to gather hostages (as had happened in Damascus at an hotel there, where over twenty people were killed). The soldiers rushed the gunmen, and drove them upstairs. Meanwhile, helicopters dropped men onto the roof. Much of the damage to the hotel from the outside came from the troops who kept firing in an effort to panic the gunmen and not give them a chance to gather hostages. They killed three of them. They had wanted to capture them alive but from what they could learn, this particular group was a splinter group of the PLO operating out of Iraq who refuse to be taken alive. They had been fortunate to capture the fourth as he attempted to kill himself and they hoped to learn more when he recovered. In addition to the gunmen killed, the receptionist was also killed when the gunmen first entered the hotel. A waiter was killed and several guests were wounded.

Alex Eftyvoulos of the Associated Press had been in Amman and was en route to Beirut when he learned of the raid on the Jordan hotel. He was directed by his agency to return to Amman. He arrived at 11:30 PM looking for a story. He approached me in the lobby and asked if I was at the hotel when the trouble started.

"If you're looking for a story," I said. "Go to the Royal Suite. The gentlemen there have experienced the attack."

Alex thanked me and asked me to join him. I learned more of what happened as they told Alex their story.

One of the men had been in the corridor when the shooting started and ran into the rooftop restaurant and jumped behind the bar. A waiter had been severely wounded in the stomach. He took off his shirt and used it to apply a bandage, attempting to push the waiter's intestines back in place. They gave much praise to the 'Red Berets' of the Jordanian army for their efficiency and deportment. Other guests had crawled into the kitchen area of the Royal suite and sat there while bullets hit the wall dividing the room. They expected at any moment for the gunmen to enter and kill them. They talked of how they felt at that moment, thinking they had only a short time to live.

The next day saw a massive clean-up operation. King Hussein

himself visited the hotel, expressed his regrets and apologized for any inconvenience and assured everyone that he would provide reimbursement for any damages. It was little wonder why the people of Jordan loved their King. He has the common touch.

A day later, it was announced that the Beirut airport was open and the first flight into Beirut was scheduled by Alia airlines. I was anxious to go. It would be my first trip back to Beirut and if the troubles had subsided, perhaps I could salvage some goods and have an opportunity to recover some of my losses.

I tried to book reservations on the flight but was informed that the flight was overbooked with several hundred passengers on the waiting list, mostly Lebanese. I decided to find another way and engaged the services of a taxi to take me to Damascus. From there I could secure further transportation to Beirut.

En route to Damascus we passed Jerash. It is said to be the most beautifully preserved and restored Graeco-Roman provincial city in the world. The city as it stands now, is principally Roman and was chiefly built in the first and second centuries A.D. Some of the finer features are the large elliptical colonnaded Forum, the larger of two theaters, which could seat 5,000 spectators, the Triumphal Arch to the Emperor Hadrian, the street of columns whose paving stones still show the chariot wheel-marks, and the impressive Temple of Artemis. Inscriptions among the ruins attribute the city's founding to Alexander the Great. I remembered visiting Jerash with my wife who had accompanied me on one of my trips to Jordan. On that trip, Gisela met Princess Zein. The Princess had taken Gisela to see the Royal Stables. After telling the Princess about our daughter Christine's love for horses, the Princess presented Gisela with a halter from one of the horses to take to Christine as a gift. Christine still treasures it.

Continuing from Jerash, the road wound around mountains with picturesque views of valleys and hillside villages. It wasn't long before we reached the Syrian border where we waited in a long line for clearance through customs.

After an hour's wait, I obtained a transient visa and entered Syria. The road to Damascus changed into a straight highway heavily traveled with trucks. Beehive villages, which looked like a collection of black igloos, were scattered along the highway. Other igloo type structures were built from the black rocks taken from the fields. The range of mountains to the left, the Golan Heights, marked the dividing line between Syria and Israeli occupied territory.

Damascus, Syria, the oldest continuously inhabited city in the world, was very crowded at midday. The roar of trucks and traffic congestion on the narrow streets mingled with the clamoring sound of street peddlers broadcasting their wares. It was hot. The exhaust fumes from the many vehicles and the odors of open markets filled the air and fanned my face through the open car window. Damascus had that special inexplicable smell that reminded me of Beirut.

The taxi drove to a service plaza in the center of town. The service plaza was thronged with would-be passengers waiting their turn for transportation for all routes from Damascus. There were two lines of taxis for Beirut. Passengers were loaded according to their destinations within the city of Beirut. The Christian sector was serviced by one line while the other line carried passengers to the Moslem sector.

My home was in the Moslem sector, near the American University of Beirut where most of the foreigners had lived. The Commodore Hotel where I wanted to stay was also in this sector. With the aid of the taxi driver to expedite my passage, and with a small gratuity for his service, I obtained a seat in a car along with three other passengers: two Syrians and one Lebanese Palestinian. The fare was established before departure but not requested in advance.

There was little conversation en route. At the Syrian-Lebanese border, the driver took my passport and transient visa to the Customs House on my behalf while the other passengers went into the Customs building to present their own documents. The Palestinian was the first to return to the car. We chatted while waiting for the other passengers. Behind us a new customs house was under construction. The female laborers, carrying buckets of water on their heads, would hand the water to the men mixing concrete. The girls wore long dresses and had their heads fully covered. Other Syrian laborers were enjoying themselves making remarks as the girls walked by, vying for attention.

The taxi driver and the two Syrian passengers came toward the car in a heated argument. The driver was insisting on his money and the Syrians were refusing to pay. They did not have the proper papers to leave Syria and were refused entry into Lebanon. They would have to return to Damascus. They wanted their luggage but the taxi driver refused to give it to them unless they paid their fare. The argument continued and a crowd gathered. They then presented their case to the crowd who listened without comment. The Syrians claimed they should not have to pay since they had engaged transportation to Beirut and now could not go there. The driver insisted on his fare since he could have taken other passengers and was already halfway to Beirut. Finally, a compromise was reached whereby the Syrians paid half the fare in return for their luggage.

Chapter 7
First American Back
November 1976

Entering Lebanon for the first time in over a year was exhilarating. Roadside stands selling fruit and vegetables were familiar sights and as we continued on our way, vendors shouted bargain prices of black market alcohol and cigarettes. The mountains of Lebanon loomed ahead and at its summit, Beirut would come into view. I didn't know what to expect in Beirut but my apprehension was placated by the excitement and anticipation of seeing some of my friends again.

Potholes made our travel slow and the road winding up the mountain was narrow and dangerous. The Syrian army used this road to transport tanks and artillery that were being used to supervise the cease-fire in Beirut. When we reached the summit and began our descent, the beautiful sight in the distance brought back fond memories of this once peaceful city and the pleasures it had afforded my family and me.

What a wonderful place it had been to live before the troubles started. The hustle and bustle of the city, the optimism of its citizens; the making of friends and their warm hospitality. The numerous opportunities to conduct business with the attitude that it could be done, was without precedent. The complexity of the city with its mixed population of Moslem, Christian, Jew, Arab, French, German, Dutch, Armenian, American and others, lived and worked together. It was not only politics that was destroying this country but it was now the age-old cause of war—religion. Peoples of the world choosing sides, ignoring the rights or wrongs but siding with those whose religious preferences resembled their own. I found it difficult to imagine that this "one God," to whom they prayed, could hear their prayers and grant each his desire to destroy the other.

Evidence of the many battles fought outside Beirut appeared everywhere. Each village we passed was littered with debris. Tanks and other military vehicles were strategically positioned while on every corner sand bunkers were manned with machine guns. Burned-out vehicles had been simply shoved off the highway by bulldozers. Craters from heavy artillery shells had to be navigated making our progress slow.

The full impact of the destruction was yet unknown to many. It would take years to rebuild but there could be no reclamation of lives lost to this senseless killing. Tensions remained high and any shot fired, could erupt into another battle.

It was dusk when the taxi reached the Commodore Hotel. I paid the driver and was greeted by the doorman.

"You have come back!"

"Yes, it's good to be home," I said.

I entered the lobby and was immediately recognized by the assistant manager.

"Ahlan, ahlan, Mr. March. You are back!"

"Shoukran. Yes, I'm back," I replied as I embraced him.

"You are here to stay?"

"I came to see what, if anything, remains of my house and to decide if and when I can return."

"You are welcome here anytime."

"Thanks. I appreciate that. Do you have a room for me?"

"Surely, What room would you like?"

I was given a corner room on the same floor assigned to the news media. ABC, BBC, CBS, NBC and other letters of the alphabet were posted on room doors. The media was using the Commodore as their base headquarters. The familiar sound of Telex machines could be heard as reporters transmitted their stories to news offices around the world.

I freshened up and went to the lobby. The bar was full of newsmen engaged in friendly conversation about local events and I had only to listen to be brought up-to-date on the present situation. It was an advantage to hear the news first hand, which often differed from what their editors actually published.

At first the newsmen assumed I represented another news media. When they learned that I was there as an independent businessman, I was besieged for interviews, and I obliged them. I was the first known American businessman to return to Beirut.

I became good friends with a free-lance reporter, John Stoneborough, from London. John was interested in a story, but he was also good company and we talked until it was time to retire for the night.

A demarcation line separated the city between the predominantly Christian Rightists and the Moslem Leftists. Few people passed over this 'green line,' as it was called, during the day, even though it was controlled by the Syrian army. At night, no one of opposing factions dared to cross the line. Street lamps were not working in most places and others had been shot out making it unsafe to be on the streets.

I telephoned my former distributor and friend, Albert Tabet, who lived in the Christian stronghold of Hasmeyeh. Albert was delighted to hear from me and wanted to see me.

"Perhaps you can come to the hotel tomorrow," I said.

"No, I cannot pass the green line. It is too dangerous. No one from this side goes into the Hamra district. Why don't you come to my house tomorrow? You are a foreigner and there will be no trouble for you."

I promised to see him but I first wanted to see my house the next day. I placed a call to a former secretary, Sarah. She was happy to hear my voice and was surprised that I was in Lebanon.

"You must come see us," she said.

"I will, but you can also come to the hotel. It's only a few blocks from your house."

"Mr. March, I have not been out of my house for nearly a year. I'm afraid to go into the streets!"

"Well, tomorrow I'll get you out of the house. I'm going to my house first thing in the morning and afterward, I'll come by."

"Oh, Mr. March, you must not go there alone. It is occupied by some people and you cannot go there. It could be trouble for you. My aunt lives next door to your house and she says they have taken many of your things out. Tomorrow I think they plan to move all the furniture."

"Then I must get there before they move it," I said.

"If you must go, my brother has a car and will go with you. First you must pass by the Syrian commandant and get a paper, which permits you to enter your house. In case there is trouble, you will be protected."

I arose early and John Stoneborough joined me for breakfast. I mentioned that I was going to my house after breakfast and had heard that it was occupied. John asked to go along, "Perhaps I can get a story," he said.

Sarah, and her brother Mohammad, arrived at the hotel with the car. Sarah was well dressed and excited about her adventure into the streets. I introduced them to John and then we drove to 'Bain Militaire;' the former military club now being used as a command post for the Syrian occupation forces. I was introduced to the commandant while Sarah explained what we wanted. The commandant listened intently. Whacking the swagger stick he was carrying against the desk, he stood to his feet.

"If anyone causes you trouble, I'll whack their heads off," he said, and once again struck the desk with his stick. Sarah did not need to translate that. We left immediately and drove to the house only a few blocks away.

The former concierge had long since departed. He was Christian and had fled when the fighting intensified. Another man and his family now occupied the concierge room. The new concierge didn't stop us when we walked up the one flight of stairs to my door. I tried my key in the door but the lock had been changed. I then knocked several times but there was no answer. The concierge came up the stairs to inquire what we wanted. I told Sarah to tell him that this is my house and I want inside. Sarah translated this and the concierge said, "There is no one home now. You cannot go in there. People live there."

"There's something I don't understand," I said. "Why is it proper for someone to move into my house and take it over when I'm not here, but improper for me to enter my own house when the present occupants are not here?"

This was translated and the concierge just shrugged his shoulders and went back down the steps. I was about to kick in the door but stopped short as someone yelled from below that the tenants were coming.

A woman with three small children came up the steps. She looked puzzled. Sarah explained to her that I wanted into my house. She immediately opened the door and we all went inside. While the chattering between Sarah and the woman continued, I walked through the house followed closely by John and Mohammad.

The kitchen was a filthy mess. Grease and dirt covered the stove, the sink, the kitchen table; everywhere I looked was filth. I was glad Gisela could not see this. The refrigerator was used as storage; apparently they thought it didn't work. I had unplugged it when I left and no one thought to see if it was plugged in. I looked into the cupboards for our good china, but it was gone. I yanked open every door and could not recognize any of the items as my own. Some of my furniture stood in the living room but was badly soiled. I went into the hallway and tried the door to my bedroom. It was locked.

"Tell the woman to give me the key to my bedroom!" I yelled.

Sarah relayed this request to the woman as I waited.

"Mr. March, she doesn't have the key to these two bedrooms or for the closets. The lady says other people were here first. The people found a larger place, so they allowed her to stay here but told her she could use only the one bedroom. They locked the other bedrooms and took the keys. She doesn't know what they have stored in there."

I thought for a moment. Perhaps they moved my things into these rooms and were being kept safe for me. It's also possible that this poor woman and children have no other place to live. I expressed my thoughts to John and he agreed. It was better not to kick in the doors until I learned more. I suddenly felt sympathy for this woman and her children.

"Who are the people who let you stay here?" I asked.

The woman explained who they were and Sarah noted the address.

The woman said the people were coming tomorrow to move out the remaining items of furniture in the living room.

This made no sense to me. If my possessions were being protected behind those doors, why would they be taking out my furniture? I thought I had better locate these people and talk with them before taking any action.

John could not accompany us, so we dropped him off at the hotel. Then we drove to an area on the other side of Raouche called Ramlet El Baide. New luxury apartment complexes built here had rented for $40,000 a year. It was at one of these buildings where we stopped. Mohammad remained in the car while Sarah and I went into the building. There was no electricity, so we walked the stairs with the aid of a candle that Sarah retrieved from her purse.

I rapped on the door and it was opened immediately. There were at least fifteen people in the large living area sitting on once beautiful furniture. Sarah made the introductions and we were invited to sit. From what I could determine, these people were all part of one family: aunts, uncles and children of their immediate family.

At first, the people were very pleasant and offered cigarettes and coffee, which we both declined. Sarah explained whom I was and that I wanted to move back into my house. At this point, the tone of the conversation changed. The older woman began talking loudly to Sarah. I understood enough to pick-up words to get the gist of the conversation, which Sarah later explained in more detail.

"You are a Moslem," the woman said. "Why do you help this foreigner?"

"I was his secretary and I am only trying to help him. All he wants is his house back."

At this, one of the sons stood up, and shaking his finger at Sarah said, "The Arabs are rich. We don't need the foreigner. The foreigner must go home."

The older woman then went into an act of crying. Wailing, she said, "My husband was killed. We have nowhere to go. It's only right we take what we can get. The rich have much money; now we will be rich."

Sarah stopped her cold. "You say you are a Moslem. Why don't you act like one? You know that what happens to you is the will of Allah. If your husband died, it was the will of Allah."

The crying suddenly stopped. Sarah was defying her own people to stick up for me and I was proud of her. I understood the meaning of the statement, " Once you have an Arab as a friend, he is always your friend."

The woman spoke. "We go tomorrow and take our things out of the house. Don't let him take any of our things."

Sarah said, "He won't take your things; he only wants what is his. What's locked in those bedrooms?"

"The things in the bedrooms belong to us. He cannot go in there."

Sarah stood and said, "We go now. Tomorrow we will be there with a paper from the army and you will have to leave his house."

We left the apartment and made our way down the stairs.

"Tomorrow we must have that paper from the commandant before we go to the house," said Sarah. "Without it, there could be trouble. They may have guns stored in the bedrooms."

"What happened to my things then, if the bedrooms are full of theirs?" I asked.

"My aunt said she saw people take many of your things out."

"They can't get away with this. We know who took them, and tomorrow we'll confront them with it," I said.

The streets were completely dark now and deserted. Mohammad kept his eyes on the road as we traveled along the sea. We reached the hotel and agreed to meet at 9:00 AM the following morning. I went straight to the bar. John was there and asked me to join him.

"How did it go, Abe?"

"Well, we located the people, but I'm not so sure we are going to get much cooperation from them. I believe I should have broken into those bedrooms today. They claim to have their own things stored there. I don't know where my things are."

"What things are you referring to?"

"My television, stereo, china, oriental carpets,—everything! I'm wondering if they've also taken our clothes."

"Here, have a drink," said John, continuing to pump for more information. When the hour grew late, we said good night and agreed to meet for breakfast.

"Are you coming with me today?" I asked John as we sat down to breakfast.

"No, I'm going to the south of Lebanon. I've been trying to get an interview with the medical officer who was in charge at Tel al-Zataar. Early this morning, I got a call that the interview was arranged for today. This will be a very important discussion to learn more of what happened during the bombardment of Tel al-Zataar and get their side of the story."

"You'll tell me about it when you get back?" I asked.

"If you give me your story," replied John.

"It's a deal," I said and we shook hands on it. I was very curious about the events surrounding the battle at Tel al-Zataar. I only knew what had been reported in the news and those stories were all suspect to me now. Most western media pitted Christians against Moslems and the general attitude favored the Christians without regard to any possible wrongdoing on their part.

Sarah and Mohammad arrived promptly at nine. They had already been to the Syrian commandant and obtained an official order for the occupants to vacate my house.

A small flatbed truck parked outside was already half-loaded when we arrived. Sarah and I hurried inside while Mohammad parked the car.

The house was littered with boxes. Some were full and others were being filled in haste. I went into my bedroom and it was already bare. The closets, which once held my good clothes, were empty except for a few old shirts lying on the bottom. Important papers that I had placed in a footlocker were scattered around the room and the locker was gone. A jewelry box remained in Gisela's closet but it was empty. All her beautiful clothes were gone along with the irreplaceable mementoes of her deceased mother. I went into my son's bedroom where the people were busy packing. I had stored some products in this room and they were nowhere in sight.

"Where are all my things?" I asked, while Sarah translated.

"We don't know. They were gone when we came here," replied the woman. The men, who appeared to be her sons, were filling the boxes.

The woman asked, "Is this yours?" She held up a carton of razor blades.

"No," I said.

Item after item was held up before they placed them into boxes but not before they asked the question, "Is this yours?"

I became exasperated. "Wait a moment!" I shouted. "Why do you ask me if it is mine? The question is, is it yours?"

They were obviously perturbed by this and began throwing things into boxes without asking the question any longer. I was at a loss to know what to do. All my things were gone, and these people were packing things that obviously didn't belong to them either. As one of the men bent over to lift a carton, I noticed his belt.

"That's my belt you're wearing. Take it off!" I shouted.

"No, this is not your belt. We got it in London."

Taking the man completely by surprise, I walked over to him, yanked the belt open and pulled it off his waist. I knew it was my belt, one that I had brought with me from the States.

"Look here!" I said, pointing to the inscription on the belt. "Made in U.S.A."

Sarah translated to be sure it was understood.

"Now tell me you don't know where my other things are. I wouldn't be surprised to find everything at your other house."

Sarah didn't translate this. Instead, she spoke directly to me, saying, "I think you better go to the Syrian commandant and tell him what happened. You must not do anything to them or they'll kill you. You have caught them in a lie, and this will make them want to get back at you." Sarah and I had moved into the hallway as we spoke.

"But they're lying. Why shouldn't I hurt their pride? They're thieves!" I said.

Sarah took me by the arm and led me farther from the room.

"You must not talk like that here," she said. "We better go to the commandant." I reluctantly agreed.

We left the house and drove the short distance to the Syrian commandant's headquarters. We were ushered into the commandant's office immediately. Mohammad, as usual, remained in the car. He wouldn't leave it for fear it would be stolen.

The commandant rose from his chair as we entered his office. Sarah started talking at once, explaining the problem and requesting assistance. The commandant face flushed and he yelled out an order. Two soldiers came running into his office and stood at attention. He barked some orders, and then turned to me while Sarah translated.

"These men will go with you to help get your things back. If there is trouble, they know what to do."

The two soldiers climbed into the back seat of the car with their weapons and Sarah brought them up to date on the events. When we reached the house, everyone had gone. We walked through the rooms with the soldiers opening and closing closet doors as they exclaimed repeatedly in Arabic, "They took everything. There's nothing left."

Sarah gave them directions to the house we had visited the night before. The soldiers departed saying that they would talk with the commandant before going to the house in Ramlet El Baide.

(I was later to learn that Lebanese soldiers were laying claim to deserted houses, taking what they wanted and then placing their friends or other displaced people in these homes. Some bartered for the houses, and the soldiers were making money on the barter as well as on the sale of the contents.)

"Is there somewhere you would like to go?" Mohammad inquired.

"Not today," I said, "but if you're available tomorrow, I'd like to look around the city."

"As you wish, Mr. March. When do you want to go?"

"When you get up in the morning, call me at the hotel and we can decide when to meet," I said.

They dropped me off at the hotel and I went to my room. I wanted to wait for John but also wanted to contact my former managing director, Joseph Akoury, who was staying with his sister in Ashrafeyeh. Sarah gave me his telephone number and explained that Joseph had gone to the mountains when the troubles started but had now moved in with his sister and her husband when the cease-fire was announced. Joseph was surprised that I was in Beirut and wanted to see me.

"Can you come to Hamra?" I asked.

"It is difficult, but I will try. I will have to return home before dark."

"I understand. Perhaps you would prefer to wait until tomorrow and join us. We are going to drive around Beirut and see the war damage."

Joseph agreed to meet me at the hotel in the morning.

John had returned from his trip to south Lebanon and asked me to come to his room. He asked about my day and took notes.

"Do you think they will recover your things?" He asked.

"No, I don't. I believe the things they took have already been disposed of—probably out of the country. They wouldn't keep them now anyway since we know who they are. Now, tell me about your interview."

"You already know what happened at the Palestinian refugee camp, Tel al-Zaatar."

"I know what I read in the press, but tell me what you learned," I asked.

John explained how Tel al-Zaatar was constantly bombarded until it was completely destroyed. It had been in all the newspapers. The Christian Phalangists did not let up their shelling despite the Red Cross and other outside pressures. They permitted no one in—not even to get the wounded except near the end, when it was too late for many of the wounded and sympathy was turning in favor of the Palestinians. John said that he met the doctor who was in charge during the siege. The doctor explained how he operated on hundreds of wounded but eventually ran out of medical supplies. They had no food, no drinking water; even when the doctor could have saved some, the people died of dehydration and infected wounds. Many tried to escape and were shot down. Others attempted to find food and water but never returned.

"What was it like at the interview? How do they feel now?" I asked.

"I talked to a six-year-old girl. I asked her where her daddy was. She said he had gone to the mountains. The doctor told me that her father was dead. The girl was told this story to avert further shock. The doctor told me that this little girl had saved her brother's life by dragging him into the shelter after his leg had been nearly blown off. The kid died later—no medication."

"What's their attitude now?" I asked.

"You can imagine they want revenge. What the Israelis failed to do themselves, they accomplished by supporting the Lebanese Phalangists at Tel al-Zaatar. They have made martyrs out of these people. Large posters describing Tel al-Zaatar cover the walls of the room I was in. The children are being indoctrinated never to forget it. The doctor told me that they would never stop fighting until they have their homeland back. I believe they mean it!"

"Are you saying, Tel al-Zataar was a massacre?"

"Absolutely!" John exclaimed. "They intended to kill every Palestinian there. Even after the Palestinians had no power to resist, they continued shelling the place and shot anyone in sight. They wanted no survivors."

"We're going to Tel al-Zataar, tomorrow," I said. "Want to come along?"

"You bet. When are you leaving?"

"First thing in the morning. Mohammad will drive us. I also have a Christian friend who will join us. This way, we have Moslem and Christian in the same car, including the press. We should have no trouble."

The following day, Joseph Akoury joined us at the Commodore and we set off. The destruction in the old business section of Beirut was total. Rubble was everywhere and bulldozers were clearing the streets to permit the passage of cars. Pillars of some of the buildings had been literally chipped away by the constant pelting of bullets and eventually crumbled. Walls that remained standing were full of holes. The ancient arcade where chariots had once paraded through the streets was in ruins. It was sad to see the destruction of these historical sites that had endured centuries.

We drove by the port of Beirut and it too was in shambles. Overturned, burned-out buses blocked the street and another route had to be taken to Tel al-Zaatar. It was quiet and eerie as we cautiously drove along the streets.

Tel al-Zataar appeared like a ghost town nearly leveled to the ground. Thick concrete building walls were held together by strands of reinforced steel rods.

"Joseph, have you any idea what happened here?" I asked.

He nodded his head, yes.

"What can you tell us about it?"

"There are some things it's best not to say," he replied.

"Joseph, we're friends. You can tell us."

He shifted uncomfortably in his seat, and then said, "As you can see, there was much fighting here."

"That's rather obvious. What we'd like to know is why? Why did they want to destroy this place? Why didn't they let the wounded and the women and children leave?"

Joseph shook his head. "I don't really understand it. But you see, the soldiers, well, they were given drugs to make them brave. They fought bravely and fiercely. They did many things that they would not normally do."

"Like what?" asked John.

"Well, the Phalangists were told that one of their buddies had been placed between two cars, tied-up and then pulled apart. They wanted revenge. So they dragged people into the streets and then ran over them with trucks. The Phalange supporters were standing on the side watching and applauding. This made them do more things."

"Like what, for example?" John persisted.

"They cut their things off."

"You mean they were dismembered?"

"I guess that's what you call it," Joseph replied.

"What kind of people did they do these things to? Were they soldiers?"

"Anyone they found."

"You mean even women?" I asked.

Joseph lowered his head, and then nodded. No one said anything for a few moments. I finally broke the silence and asked him how he knew this.

"My friend was here. He saw it."

"What friend?" asked John.

"I cannot tell you this. If anyone found out who told this, they would kill him."

"If who found out?" asked John.

"In this situation, he would be in danger from both sides, and I really don't want to say anymore about it."

"You want to see more? Would you like to go to some other areas?" asked Mohammad.

"I've seen enough," I said. " Let's go back to the hotel."

In talking with various newsmen, I learned of their frustration in writing stories to their respective agencies about what they witnessed, but their stories were never published. It would take some years before the media would have the courage to talk about atrocities committed by those friendly to the U.S.

Chapter 8
Aftermath of War
November 1976

The friendly atmosphere at the hotel suddenly changed. The newsmen were no longer as cordial toward me, and John was also aloof.

"What's wrong John?" I asked. "You've been avoiding me lately."

"Why didn't you tell me you're with the CIA?" he asked.

"The CIA! Are you serious?"

"Of course I'm serious. The word around the hotel is that you're with the CIA. Why else would you be here?"

"John, you've got to be kidding. The CIA?" I laughed.

John regarded me carefully and then said, "You've really gotten around in the Middle East. You lived in a number of other countries as well, haven't you?"

"Yes, we have moved a lot for business reasons but I also believe the family has benefited by it. We feel the exposure to different cultures has been good for the children. I was promoted and transferred a number of times by the company I worked for but came to Lebanon on my own."

"Does the Agency move you frequently?" John asked.

"What Agency? Dammit, John, are you trying to trip me up or something? I told you I'm not with the CIA or any other Agency. I'm simply a businessman who is crazy enough to be here with some small hope that I can salvage some of my personal possessions. My business is gone but perhaps I can generate other business to help recover some of my losses. Lebanon is going to need everything imaginable in the way of supplies to rebuild this country. I may be able to help find some things they need and profit by it. It seems to me, if I lost it here, I might just as well get it back here. The early bird catches the worm, you know."

"O.K., Abe. I'll take your word for it. Let's have a drink."

A pool of independent taxis catered to the guests of the Commodore Hotel and was taking advantage of the media with high prices. They lined the street in front of the hotel in late-modeled cars, each displaying 'The Press' signs in Arabic and English. Word spread among the guests to avoid using them whenever possible. The drivers spoke English and they crossed the Green Line without difficulty; however, the price gouging was no longer acceptable.

I made arrangements to go to Albert Tabet's house in Furn El Shebak for lunch. I was to be introduced to a Catholic priest who wished to discuss some business. As I left the hotel, I was immediately assailed by the taxi drivers.

"Taxi, taxi!" they shouted.

"How much to Furn El Shebak?" I inquired.

"One way or round trip?"

"One way," I replied.

"This means I must come back alone. There are troubles, sir. It is not easy for me to go into that area. If I come back alone, it could be dangerous."

"Look," I said. "Do you want to take me or not?"

"Yes, of course."

"Then how much is the fare?"

"Thirty pounds."

"Thirty pounds! That's ridiculous. You think I just came to Lebanon? I lived here. I could go to Furn El Shebak for five pounds."

"There's trouble now, sir."

"I know there's trouble. Will your life be spared if I pay you more money? I'm not paying thirty pounds."

"Twenty-five pounds, sir?"

"I'll give you fifteen and no more. Do you want to take me or not?"

The driver walked to his car and opened the door. "O.K., fifteen pounds," he said.

Crossing the Green Line was no problem. The Syrian guard stopped the car and the driver pointed to the sign in his window and said, "Kalafi." The soldier looked at me and I flashed my passport. I also carried a small camera with me and looked like the press. The soldier waved us on.

Kissing me on both cheeks, Albert Tabet received me warmly. I shook hands with his wife, and then on impulse, kissed his beautiful daughter who blushed with delight. Shortly thereafter, the Reverend Father arrived and introductions were made. Mr. Tabet explained to me that the Reverend Father did not speak English very well and that he would translate.

The Priest claimed to have many projects that the church wished to undertake in the area of Jounieh. Jounieh had its own Port area and the plan was for it to become the new capital for the Phalangists in the north if they succeeded in partitioning Lebanon. It now seemed that Lebanon would not easily be partitioned, but they wanted to build the area of Jounieh into a major business center anyway. It appeared that the troubles would soon be over and they wanted to do it quickly before the rebuilding of Beirut got underway. They wished to establish their own unofficial capital in Jounieh and draw much of the business out of Beirut.

"The church has much land in Jounieh," said the Priest. "We want your ideas on what can be built on this land. We think small shops, offices, or even a hotel or hospital could be built there."

"Let's look at the area where you have land and perhaps we can discuss some ideas together. Can we go there?" I asked.

"Today?"

"Yes, why not? Do you have a car?" I asked.

"We can arrange transportation," replied Albert.

We sat down to eat. Lunch was the big meal of the day and the table was heaped with delicious Arabic fare. Tabouli, made from finely chopped parsley, tomatoes and grain, was my favorite salad and I helped myself to a large portion. The Reverend Father preferred to drink arak and insisted that I have some also. A small amount of water was added to the drink and it changed from a clear liquid to a milky color. The arak tasted much like the native drink of Greece, ouzo. The meal was topped-off with a variety of fruits, and then we moved into the living room for our coffee.

Albert leaned close to me and said, "The Reverend Father would like you to sign a paper in case you get any of these projects, so he will get his commission."

It surprised me that a priest would take a commission on the side for work done for the church.

"I'm not sure I understand," I said. "What kind of commission protection does he want? Aren't these projects for himself?"

"No, he will introduce you to the patriarch and other church officials. It is their projects, but the Reverend Father wants a signed paper to be sure he gets a commission for introducing you to them."

"What about your commission?"

"I'll take mine from the Reverend Father."

"O.K.," I said. "You prepare the paper and I'll sign it."

Within a few minutes, Albert had produced a portable typewriter and was typing up a commission agreement. The Reverend Father, Joseph Masri, smiled and talked with me. He did understand English well and his alleged difficulty speaking the language provided him with an excuse not to request the commission agreement himself.

After lunch, we went to see the patriarch before continuing to Jounieh. The Patriarch, Monseigneur Bacha, Archeveque Greque Catholique de Beyroute, Patriaical Syrien Catholique d'Antioche, (his official title), together with Mr. Selim Hajj, sat with us and discussed the possibilities of development in the Jounieh area.

After the discussion, Albert Tabet, the Reverend Joseph Masri and I, departed for Jounieh. We passed through an area where a Palestinian school once stood but was now flattened to the ground. The priest pointed to the destruction of the school, and with a gleam in his eyes and a wide grin said, "We did good here, no?"

"What do you mean?" I asked.

"The school. Look how we smashed it. The whole school is to the ground," said the priest while rubbing his hands together in delight. "They will never use this school again."

I made no comment but wondered how this man, a priest, could talk this way. From what I observed, the term "Christian" seemed simply a title.

The car turned onto the road along the seashore heading north. To my left, I noticed a large open area where a refugee camp had simply vanished.

"Where is the camp?" I asked.

Father Masri spoke first. "We wiped it out. See, there is nothing left. Much gold was found here."

"Where is the gold now?" I asked.

The priest smiled and said, "The church has it. The church is very rich now. We have much gold and money from the war."

We continued farther north, and then turned off the highway to a monastery situated directly at the highest point on top of the hill. Here I met some other priests who were part of the development project. The monks who maintained the vineyards surrounding the monastery served me wine. It was cold inside the monastery and the wine was helpful.

Upon entering Jounieh, I observed a city untouched by war. It was difficult to imagine that only twelve miles south, heavy fighting had occurred. The town was bustling with activity and new signs on storefronts used names that once lined the streets of Hamra in Beirut.

After spending several hours driving around Jounieh and discussing the possibilities of new developments, we returned to Albert Tabet's house. I wanted to get back to the hotel and asked if the driver would take me.

"We are sorry, Mr. March, but our driver cannot cross the Green Line. He is a soldier for the Phalangists and if they found him on the other side, they would kill him. We will try to get a taxi for you."

Several calls were made until a taxi was found who would take me back to the Commodore Hotel. The price was high but with no other choice, I paid it.

When I arrived at the hotel there was a message from Joseph

Akoury. I returned his call. Joseph wanted me to come to Ashrafeyeh to talk with a friend of his who claimed to have important business to discuss. The man wouldn't cross the Green Line so I agreed to meet him in Ashrafeyeh.

There was at least another hour of daylight, so I called Mohammad and asked him if he would drive me to Ashrafeyeh, and he agreed. Mohammad arrived at the hotel in a different car explaining that he had car trouble and that his uncle would drive me. Mohammad's uncle wasn't too keen about crossing the Green Line but had been convinced that there would be no problem with me in the car, and he had consented to drive.

The main road was blocked near Bescharra Al-Khoury Street. A Syrian soldier stopped us, checked the car and its occupants, and then directed us to an alternate route. When we turned into the street where Joseph lived, Joseph was standing on the sidewalk waiting for us. He got into the car and directed us to the address where he had arranged the appointment.

As we prepared to get out of the car, Joseph turned to me and said, "Mr. March. My friend wants to talk privately with you. It would not be good for these men to come with us. They are Moslem."

I was embarrassed but knew he was right. Joseph, a Christian, was a good friend with Sarah and Mohammad, and it was he who had introduced them to me. His remark concerned the businessman we were to meet. Joseph discussed the matter briefly with Mohammad and his uncle, telling them that we would be only a short while and that it might be better if they wait in the car.

I followed Joseph into the building and up three flights of stairs to an apartment. After introductions, coffee and cigarettes were offered before entering into discussions.

An hour passed and we were still talking. I told the man that we had people waiting for us in the car and couldn't keep them waiting much longer. Joseph agreed, but the man wished to discuss another point. Another forty-five minutes elapsed before we departed. When we stepped into the street, the car was gone. We walked back and forth looking at both street corners but there was no sign of the car.

"What could have happened to them?" I asked.

"Perhaps they decided not to wait and returned to Hamra," said Joseph.

"How will I get back to the hotel?"

"I don't know. Let me call Sarah and see if they returned."

Joseph called but they had not returned.

"You think something could have happened to them here?" I asked.

Joseph shrugged his shoulders. "I don't think so, I hope not."

We waited a half hour and I asked Joseph to call Sarah again.

"Yes, they just arrived," said Sarah.

"Why didn't they wait for Mr. March?" asked Joseph.

"After you left them waiting in the car, several men noticed them sitting there and told them to leave the area. My brother and uncle were afraid if they stayed something might happen to them. They don't want to go back there now. It's already ten o'clock and it's very dangerous to try it," said Sarah.

Joseph agreed with Sarah and relayed this information to me.

"How do you suggest I get back to the hotel?"

"I don't know," Joseph replied. "You are welcome to stay at my sister's house."

"Thank you, but I really need to get back to the hotel. I'm expecting a call from my wife. Is there somewhere I can find a taxi?"

"Not at this hour. Perhaps you might find one by the Green Line, near the security buildings."

"You mean, where the security buildings used to be?"

"Yes, of course, but there are Syrian troops there. If you walked across the line, perhaps you could get a taxi on the other side."

We walked through the deserted streets in the direction of the Green Line. Occasionally a ray of light shone through windows casting shadows on doorways and parked cars. We soon reached the end of the housing area. The long stretch of road ahead was in complete darkness extending between rows of warehouses.

"This road will lead you directly to the security area by the Green Line," said Joseph.

I knew Joseph didn't intend to go any farther and couldn't blame him. He would have to return the same way alone.

"The only thing that bothers me," I said, "is what I will encounter when I reach the end of this street. They will surely challenge me in Arabic. If I don't respond properly, they may start shooting. Why don't you tell me what I should say if someone challenges me."

"O.K. I'll walk halfway with you and give you a chance to practice."

We walked along stepping carefully to avoid any objects that might be lying on the road. The darkness was total. The only sounds we heard were our own footsteps and our voices rebounding from the walls on both sides of the street. We were nearing the halfway point, when suddenly from our rear, a car's headlights broke the darkness. We stood motionless as the car slowly approached. This is no time to act suspiciously, I thought. I moved into the middle of the street and held up my hand. The car stopped. I walked to the driver's side of the car.

"Do you speak English?" I asked the driver.

"Yes," he replied.

What relief! I didn't realize how hard my heart was pounding until then.

"I need a ride to Hamra and can't find a taxi," I said.

"You are with the Press?"

"Yes," I lied.

"Get in. I will take you."

I said goodbye to Joseph and asked him to call me in one hour at the hotel. Joseph promised he would.

"I'm with UPI. My name is Nasir Tabet."

"Glad to know you. I'm Abe March, free-lance. I really appreciate this lift. I didn't know how I was going to get back to the hotel."

"My pleasure. Anything to help a colleague."

The street was longer than I had realized. As we approached the Green Line, two soldiers stepped in front of the car signaling for us to stop. Nasir spoke rapidly to them in Arabic, flashed his Press Card and showed his identity card. The soldiers shone their flashlights into my face and looked into the back seat. Satisfied that everything was in order, they waved us on. Reaching the other side of the Green Line, we were once again stopped. This time, the soldiers ordered Nasir to open the trunk of his car. I produced my passport, and after careful scrutiny, we were permitted to pass.

Soon after I arrived at the hotel, Joseph called and asked me if I had arrived safely.

"Yes, we had no problem," I said.

"I was worried for you. Fifteen minutes after you left, I heard shooting by the green Line. I'm glad you're O.K."

"Thanks Joseph. So am I."

* * * * *

There was a feeling of camaraderie at the hotel. The bar was full of newsmen telling stories and making jokes. Each night, a feature film was shown, compliments of the news bureau. It was not all fun, however. Conversations became serious about developments within the country. From what I could glean from the various news reporters and my own knowledge of the area, I knew the troubles were far from over. My visit to Lebanon was premature and it was not the time to think of returning with my family. The discussions I had about the prospects for business were being placed on hold. Before any investment would be made, the businessmen wanted to wait until they were sure things had settled down more. The main cease-fire was holding, but skirmishes still continued in and around the city.

An ABC news crew took me with them to Jounieh. They wanted a story about the sudden growth of Jounieh and the views from a western businessman about the prospects for development and stability. As the cameras rolled, I discussed those possibilities but my outlook called for greater stability within the country before real development could take place. Without the banking institutions and the trade that made Lebanon attractive for investment, the economy would continue to suffer. It was up to the government to solve its problems and once again create the climate for business. This outlook was grim.

Prior to my departure from Lebanon, I went for a walk along the sea. The clear blue sky matched the sea on the horizon with no visible separation. Fishing boats bobbed up and down along the coast in quest of their daily catch. A few swimmers splashed about in the surf with their tanned bodies glistening in the sun. A light breeze blew in from the sea causing the palm trees to sway in rhythm. I could almost hear the music and see the belly dancers, as this magic spell possessed me. What would happen to the Lebanon I had come to love? What events in the Middle East were in the offing that would change the very character and lives of the city and its people? What political influence would cause the fighting to end? Would the root of the problem be resolved or would there be politically expedient measures adopted? Should one be silent and look the other way or have the courage to speak out against injustice?

What can I do? I wondered. I must continue my own struggle to make a living.

Postscript: 2006—Germany

Personal—I am now retired and live in a small town in South West Germany's wine region. I am a member of the Men's choir; I help out with the wine harvest, and enjoy hiking. My wife Gisela enjoys gardening, sings in the Church Choir and is an avid reader.

My three children all received their Bachelor's degree from Penn State University. My youngest daughter Caroline further received her Master's degree from Duke University. She is married, has two children and lives in Virginia. My daughter Christine is married and lives in Germany. Duane received his Masters Degree from UNC at Chapel Hill and his Doctorate degree in ancient history from Berkeley. He is still single and lives in Germany.

End Notes

I started writing about my experience in 1976 when the events were fresh in my mind. The writing continued over a period of several years. The original purpose of this writing was to have a personal record of these events for my family. And, being out of work at that time, it helped to provide diversion from my plight. I was encouraged to seek publication earlier, but I felt that the sensitivity of some aspects of this work could be counter-productive for my career. When I retired, my daughter Caroline encouraged me to seek publication.

Printed in the United States
56910LVS00004B/295-306